NEGARA

NEGARA

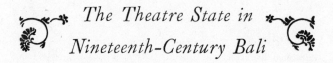

The Theatre State in
Nineteenth-Century Bali

CLIFFORD GEERTZ

PRINCETON UNIVERSITY PRESS

Copyright © 1980 by Princeton University Press
Published by Princeton University Press, Princeton, New Jersey
In the United Kingdom:
Princeton University Press, Guildford, Surrey

All Rights Reserved
Library of Congress Cataloging in Publication Data will be
found on the last printed page of this book

This book has been composed in Linotype Baskerville

Clothbound editions of Princeton University Press books
are printed on acid-free paper, and binding materials are
chosen for strength and durability

Printed in the United States of America by
Princeton University Press,
Princeton, New Jersey

ISBN 0-691-05316-2
ISBN 0-691-00778-0 (pbk.)

For Lauriston Tardy,
George R. Geiger,
and Talcott Parsons,

teachers

CONTENTS

ILLUSTRATIONS

Maps

Figures

Color Plate

PREFACE

This study is intended to reach several audiences, and, in the hope that it might in fact do so, it has been constructed so that it may be read in several ways.

In particular, the notes have been set off from the text much more sharply than is common in monographic works; are keyed to it only very loosely by page and line rather than through numbered super-scripts; and take a rather expansive form, many of them being general commentaries on subjects raised in the text, fairly extensive critical reviews of the literature bearing on one point or another, or even mini-essays on matters somewhat tangential to the central narrative. As a result, the text has been written so that someone—scholar, student, or general reader—interested in traditional states, political theory, anthropological analysis, or whatever, but not especially concerned with the ins and outs of Indonesian studies, can read it with little or no reference to the notes. The argument is all there in the text, together with the essential empirical material supporting it, uncluttered by asides, references, or in-group qualifications. On the other hand, someone—Indologist, Southeast Asianist, Balinese specialist—interested in a circumstantial view of the basis upon which the argument has been built or in the further development of specific technical points will find the notes of critical importance, particularly since the subject of the traditional Balinese state has never been integrally treated before—indeed hardly treated at all as such—and since the materials relevant to it are so widely scattered and of such varying type and uneven quality. Most readers will position themselves somewhere along this continuum between the generalist and the specialist, and the somewhat unusual arrangement of narrative and commentary has been designed to make it easy for them to attend to as much or as little of the scholarly apparatus as their purposes would seem to dictate.

A work as long in the making as this one produces a large number of debts. My main Balinese informants are cited in the notes and my gratitude to them is immeasurable. Of those who have read the manuscript, I must thank specifically Hildred Geertz, who also helped gather the material, James Boon, Shelly Errington, F. K. Lehman, and Peter Carey, though they are but representative of the many who have helped me and assume no special liability by being named. Mrs. Amy Jackson provided unusually extensive secretarial assistance, for which I am most grateful. I should also like to thank

Mr. William Hively of Princeton University Press for his editorial assistance and counsel.

Finally, this work has been assisted at various points by the Rockefeller Foundation, the Committee for the Comparative Study of New Nations of the University of Chicago, and the Institute for Advanced Study, Princeton.

Princeton
August 1979

NEGARA

INTRODUCTION

Bali and Historical Method

> To ask questions you see no prospect of answering is
> the fundamental sin in science, like giving orders
> which you do not think will be obeyed in politics, or
> praying for what you do not think God will give in
> religion.
>
> *R. G. Collingwood*

When one looks panoramically at Indonesia today it seems to form
a dateless synopsis of its own past, as when the artifacts from different levels of a long-occupied archaeological site, scattered along a table, summarize at a glance thousands of years of human history. All
the cultural streams that, over the course of some three millennia,
have flowed, one after the other, into the archipelago—from India,
from China, from the Middle East, from Europe—find their contemporary representation somewhere: in Hindu Bali; in the China-
towns of Jakarta, Semarang, or Surabaya; in the Muslim strongholds
of Aceh, Makassar, or the Padang Highlands; in the Calvinized regions of Minahassa and Ambon, or the Catholicized ones of Flores
and Timor. The range of social structures is equally wide, equally
recapitulative: the Malayo-Polynesian tribal systems of interior
Borneo or the Celebes; the traditional peasant villages of Bali, west
Java, and parts of Sumatra and the Celebes; the "post-traditional"
rural proletarian villages of the central and east Java river plains;
the market-minded fishing and smuggling villages of the Borneo
and Celebes coasts; the faded provincial capitals and small towns of
interior Java and the Outer Islands; and the huge, dislocated, half-
modernized metropolises of Jakarta, Medan, Surabaya, and Makassar. The range of economic forms, of systems of stratification, or of
kinship organization is as great: shifting cultivators in Borneo, caste
in Bali, matriliny in West Sumatra. Yet, in this whole vast array of
cultural and social patterns, one of the most important institutions
(perhaps *the* most important) in shaping the basic character of
Indonesian civilization is, for all intents and purposes, absent,
vanished with a completeness that, in a perverse way, attests its

3

historical centrality—the *negara,* the classical state of precolonial Indonesia.

Negara (nagara, nagari, negeri), a Sanskrit loanword originally meaning "town," is used in Indonesian languages to mean, more or less simultaneously and interchangeably, "palace," "capital," "state," "realm," and again "town." It is, in its broadest sense, the word for (classical) civilization, for the world of the traditional city, the high culture that city supported, and the system of superordinate political authority centered there. Its opposite is *desa*—also a Sanskrit loanword—meaning, with a similar flexibility of reference, "countryside," "region," "village," "place," and sometimes even "dependency" or "governed area." In its broadest sense *desa* is the word for the world, so variously organized in different parts of the archipelago, of the rural settlement, of the peasant, the tenant, the political subject, the "people." Between these two poles, *negara* and *desa,* each defined in contrast to the other, the classical polity developed and, within the general context of a transplanted Indic cosmology, took its distinctive, not to say peculiar, form.

— 2 —

How many negaras there have been in Indonesia is completely beyond record, but that the number runs well into the hundreds is certain, into the thousands likely. From the time of the earliest Sanskrit inscriptions in the first half of the fifth century onward, kingdoms of various dimensions and durability rose, intrigued, fought, and fell in a steady, broadening stream. The more illustrious names—Mataram, Shailendra, Shrivijaya, Melayu, Singasari, Kediri, Majapahit, and, after the Islamic conversion, Demak, Bantam, Aceh, Makassar and neo-Mataram—are but the more prominent participants in a continuous process of state formation and dissolution that only Dutch domination finally brought to an end (in some parts of the archipelago, only in the present century). The political development of precolonial Indonesia does not consist of a relentless unfoldment of a monolithic "Oriental despotism," but of an expanding cloud of localized, fragile, loosely interrelated petty principalities.

A tracing of that development—a fundamental task for anyone who is concerned to understand the pattern of politics not only of the Indic phase of Indonesian civilization, but of the Islamic, colonial, and republican phases that succeeded it—is beset, however, with a profusion of difficulties, a good many of them artificially manufactured. Not only are the data scattered, equivocal, and all too often poorly presented; but the mode of interpreting them, a matter largely in the hands of philologists, has been, with a few outstanding exceptions, sociologically unrealistic in the extreme. Analogies, usually to classical, feudal, or even modern Europe, fabricated chronicles, unprovable in principle, and a priori speculations about the nature of "Indonesian thought" have led to a picture of the Indic period which, though not without its elements of plausibility, perhaps even of truth, has about it that unmistakable air of fantasy systematized which derives from attempting to know what one has no way of knowing.

Most scholars of Indic Indonesia have sought to write the sort of history for which they have not had, and in all likelihood never will have, the material and have neglected to write precisely that sort for which they have, or at least might obtain, the material. The history of a great civilization can be depicted as a series of major events—wars, reigns, and revolutions—which, whether or not they shape it, at least mark major changes in its course. Or it can be depicted as a succession not of dates, places, and prominent persons, but of general phases of sociocultural development. An emphasis on the first sort of historiography tends to present history as a series of bounded periods, more or less distinct units of time characterized by some special significance of their own: they represent The Rise of the Shailendras, The Displacement of Javanese Civilization Eastward, or The Fall of Majapahit. The second approach, however, presents historical change as a relatively continuous social and cultural process, a process which shows few if any sharp breaks, but rather displays a slow but patterned alteration in which, though developmental phases may be discerned when the entire course of the process is viewed as a whole, it is nearly always very difficult, if not impossible, to put one's finger exactly on the point at which things stopped being what they were and became instead something else. This view of change, or process, stresses not so much the annalistic chronicle of what people did, but rather the formal, or structural, patterns of cumulative activity. The period approach distributes clusters of concrete events along a time continuum in which the major distinction is earlier or later; the developmental approach distributes forms of organization and patterns of culture along a time continuum in which the major distinction is prerequisite and outcome. Time is a crucial element in both. In the first it is the thread along which specific happenings are strung; in the second it is a medium through which certain abstract processes move.

Both sorts of historiography are of course valid, and when both are possible they complement one another. The flow of particular events, chronicled in its full detail, gives substance to the schematic outline of structural change; and the constructed phases of developmental history—themselves frames for historical perception, not segments of historical reality—give intelligible form to the recorded flux of actual occurrences. But when, as in Indic Indonesia, the bulk of the occurrences are simply not recoverable, no matter how industriously one reads between the lines of myths and inscriptions or intuits parallels with distant artifacts, an attempt to reconstruct particular deeds leads at best to endless (because undecidable) controversies about hypothetical matters of fact and at worst to the fabrication of a connected "story" about classical times which, though it looks like history, is really retrospective crystal gazing. "Krom's Hindu-Javanese history," C. C. Berg has remarked, "is a story about kings and their achievements in which we find scattered remarks about elements of culture. I for one would prefer a history of culture and elements of civilization in which the reader would find scattered remarks about kings." It is just this sort of history which the documents, inscriptions, and texts of the classical period, interpreted in terms of ecological, ethnographic, and sociological processes, permit us to write; but, apart from a few fragmentary, abortive efforts such as those of B. K. Schrieke and J. C. van Leur, it remains unwritten.

— 3 —

The writing of this latter sort of history depends most critically upon the possibility of constructing an appropriate model of socio-cultural process, one both conceptually precise and empirically based, which can then be used to interpret the inevitably scattered and ambiguous fragments from the archaeological past. There are a number of ways of doing this. One can draw upon what is known about comparable, but more thoroughly studied, developmental sequences elsewhere—in the case at hand, those of pre-Columbian America or the ancient Near East, for example. Or one can formulate, on the basis of a far-ranging historical sociology, ideal-typical paradigms that isolate the central features of the relevant class of phenomena—the approach made famous, of course, by Max Weber. Or one can describe and analyze in some detail the structure and functioning of a current (or recent) system that one has some reason to believe bears at least a familial resemblance to those one seeks to reconstruct, illuminating the more remote by the light of the less.

I shall use all of these complementary approaches, hoping to correct the weaknesses of one with the strengths of another. But I shall put the third, the ethnographic, at the center of my analysis, both because I think it the most immediately relevant in the present instance and because, as I am a social anthropologist rather than an archaeologist or historian, it is the one over which I have most control and with respect to which I am most likely to have something novel to contribute.

Specifically, I will construct, both out of my own fieldwork and out of the literature, a circumstantial picture of state organization in nineteenth-century Bali and then attempt to draw from that picture a set of broad but substantive guidelines for the ordering of pre- and protohistorical material in Indonesia (and, beyond it, Indic Southeast Asia) generally.

The apparent relevance of Bali, the last refuge of "Hindu" culture in the archipelago, for an understanding of the Indic period in Indonesia, and especially of its center, Java, has often been remarked. But it has as often been misconceived. To make clear in just what ways recent Bali can be made to shed light on Indonesia's distant past (and, equally important, in what ways it cannot) it is first essential to clear away a number of widespread methodological fallacies. This is such treacherous terrain that one must take each step with obsessive deliberation, proceeding, as the Javanese simile has it, like a caterpillar creeping over water.

The first such fallacy to be exploded is the notion, perhaps first popularized by Thomas Raffles, that modern Bali is a "museum" in which the culture of precolonial inner Indonesia has been preserved intact. There is no reason to believe that Bali, for all its isolation from the mainstream of Indonesian development after the rest of the archipelago was Islamized (an isolation which has itself sometimes been overemphasized), did not change for 350 years after the destruction of Majapahit (ca. 1520). Thus, any attempt to see fourteenth- and fifteenth-century Java as but a more elaborate nineteenth-century Bali is dubious in the extreme. Whatever usefulness a study of Bali has for Indonesian history, the study cannot be based on the assumption that, by strange good fortune, the island has been spared a history.

Second, it must be recognized that the evidence for the existence of any particular social practice or cultural form, or any specific custom, belief, or institution in Java (or other parts of Indic Southeast Asia), must rest ultimately not on Balinese evidence, but on Javanese, or Cambodian, or whichever. The fact that the Balinese have endogamous patrilineages, irrigation societies, and a developed witch-cult is in itself no proof that similar customs existed in early Java. All that such facts can be used for is to suggest possibilities for which Javanese (or Cambodian, Thai, Burmese, etc.) evidence can then be sought. They are useful for deriving hypotheses, but useless as support for such hypotheses once derived. This is perhaps an elementary point. But it has been ignored more often, and with more pernicious results, than any other methodological maxim in anthropological reconstruction, not only in Indonesia but generally.

And third, even when the historical mutation of Balinese culture is taken into full account and the illogicality of proving theories about Java by evidence from Bali is recognized, it is also necessary to realize that even in the fourteenth century (not to speak of the tenth or seventh) Indonesia was, socially, culturally, and especially ecologically, far from uniform: Majapahit "conquest" and all, Bali still differed from eastern Java, and much more from the Indicized regions of the archipelago as a whole. Thus, even if one is satisfied that a particular Balinese pattern—say, a heavy emphasis on prestige stratification—was present elsewhere in Indic Indonesia, one cannot assume it took precisely the same external form. The scale of the Balinese states crowded into the narrow southern piedmont, for example, was almost certainly always smaller than those of somewhat more spacious Java, with obvious effects on their organization. Further, the island's natural orientation toward the south and the treacherous Indian Ocean rather than toward the north and the tranquil Java Sea caused it to be almost wholly marginal to the elaborate international trade economy which played so crucial a role in the Indic-period economy generally. The superb drainage pattern in Bali, and its climate—perhaps the most ideal for traditional *sawah* cultivation in all of Indonesia—made irrigation both less technically problematic and less seasonally uncertain than almost everywhere in Java. And so on. Not only must Balinese data be corrected for time, but also for place, before they can be used as general guidelines for the interpretation of Indic civilization in Indonesia and beyond.

— 4 —

How, then, is the ethnography of recent Bali useful at all for such interpretation? In the first place, although Balinese life did change significantly between the fourteenth and nineteenth centuries, the change was to a very great extent endogenous. In particular, two

8

revolutionary events that elsewhere radically transformed the social and cultural order, Islamization and intense Dutch domination, did not occur in Bali. Thus, though the island's history is no less dynamic than that of the other Indicized regions of the archipelago, it is far more orthogenetic and a good deal more measured. Bali in the latter half of the nineteenth century may not have been a mere replica of Bali in the middle of the fourteenth, but it was at least fully continuous with it, a reasonably regular development out of it. As a result, much that had been erased or altered beyond recognition in Java or the coastal regions of Sumatra remained in Bali. No cultural fossil, this tight little island was nonetheless, like Tibet or Yemen, culturally quite conservative.

Second, by renouncing any intent to write an annalistic account of the classical period, we are relieved of the major incentive to generate historical fables. If we do not attempt to use ethnographic material to reconstruct a connected sequence of particular occurrences, a story of kings and their achievements, then the temptation to answer unanswerable questions is powerfully lessened. Whether Kertanagara was a common drunk or an intoxicated saint, whether the Shailendras were a Javanese dynasty ruling Sumatra or a Sumatran dynasty ruling Java, or whether Airlangga's division of his realm actually occurred or not (all perduring controversies in the annalistic literature on the Indic period) are not the sort of issues to which an analysis of political organization in Bali has any pertinence. What it does have pertinence to is an understanding of the characteristic form of the Indicized state in Indonesia, the intrinsic structure of the classic polity.

This is true because, no matter what alterations the Balinese state had suffered by 1906, no matter how special its environmental setting or divergent its cultural context, it was still but one example of a system of government once very much more widespread. On the basis of the Balinese material, one can construct, therefore, a model of the negara as a distinct variety of political order, a model which can then be used generally to extend our understanding of the developmental history of Indic Indonesia (Cambodia, Thailand, Burma).

Such a model is itself abstract. Although it is constructed out of empirical data, it is applied experimentally, not deductively, to the interpretation of other empirical data. It is thus a conceptual entity, not an historical one. On the one hand, it is a simplified, necessarily unfaithful, theoretically tendentious representation of a relatively well-known sociocultural institution: the nineteenth-century Balinese state. On the other, it is a guide, a sort of sociological blueprint, for the construction of representations, not necessarily or even probably identical to it in structure, of a whole set of relatively less well-known but presumptively similar institutions: the classical Southeast Asian Indic states of the fifth to fifteenth centuries.

CHAPTER 1

Political Definition: The Sources
of Order

The Myth of the Exemplary Center

In 1891 what was to be the last of the dozen or so kings of Mengwi, an inland Balinese palatinate some fifteen kilometers north of the present capital, Den Pasar (see map 1), found his capital besieged by his two most familiar enemies, Tabanan and Badung, allied at last against him. His army routed, his nobles all fled or fallen, and Badung troops headed by a small but, against defenders armed with only lances and daggers, terribly proficient company of mercenary Bugis riflemen waiting at the edge of town, he was an end-game chess king left without pawns or pieces. Old, sick, unable to walk, he commanded his servants to carry him on the royal litter from the palace toward the invaders. The Bugis gunners, who had been expecting such an appearance, shot his bearers and he rolled helplessly on the ground. The Badung troops (largely low-caste Sudras) moved to take him, but he refused capture and they were obliged, out of due respect, to kill him. The seven principal kingdoms of the south Bali heartland—Tabanan, Badung, Gianyar, Klungkung, Karengasem, Bangli, and Mengwi—were thus reduced to six.

But the victors' glory was only momentarily enjoyed. In 1906, the Dutch army appeared, for reasons of its own, at Sanur on the south coast and fought its way into Badung, where the king, his wives, his children, and his entourage marched in a splendid mass suicide into the direct fire of its guns. Within the week, the king and crown prince of Tabanan had been captured, but they managed to destroy themselves, the one by poison, the other by knife, their first evening in Dutch custody. Two years later, in 1908, this strange ritual was repeated in the most illustrious state of all, Klungkung, the nominal "capital" of traditional Bali; the king and court again paraded, half entranced, half dazed with opium, out of the palace into the reluctant fire of the by now thoroughly bewildered Dutch troops. It was

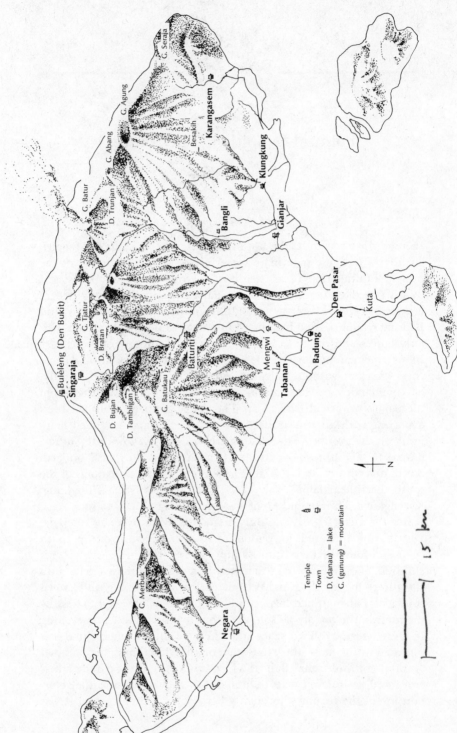

Map 1. Bali

Temple
Town
D. (danau) = lake
G. (gunung) = mountain

N

15 km

G. Seraja

G. Agung

Karangasem

Besakih

G. Abang

Klungkung

G. Batur

D. Trunjan

Bangli

Gianjar

Den Pasar

Kuta

Buléléng (Den Bukit)

Singaraja

C. Tjatur

D. Bratan

Baturiti

Mengwi

D. Bujan

D. Tamblingan

G. Batukau

Tabanan

Badung

G. Merbuk

Negara

quite literally the death of the old order. It expired as it had lived: absorbed in a pageant.

— 2 —

The expressive nature of the Balinese state was apparent through the whole of its known history, for it was always pointed not toward tyranny, whose systematic concentration of power it was incompetent to effect, and not even very methodically toward government, which it pursued indifferently and hesitantly, but rather toward spectacle, toward ceremony, toward the public dramatization of the ruling obsessions of Balinese culture: social inequality and status pride. It was a theatre state in which the kings and princes were the impresarios, the priests the directors, and the peasants the supporting cast, stage crew, and audience. The stupendous cremations, tooth filings, temple dedications, pilgrimages, and blood sacrifices, mobilizing hundreds and even thousands of people and great quantities of wealth, were not means to political ends: they were the ends themselves, they were what the state was for. Court ceremonialism was the driving force of court politics; and mass ritual was not a device to shore up the state, but rather the state, even in its final gasp, was a device for the enactment of mass ritual. Power served pomp, not pomp power.

Behind this, to us, strangely reversed relationship between the substance and the trappings of rule lies a general conception of the nature and basis of sovereignty that, merely for simplicity, we may call the doctrine of the exemplary center. This is the theory that the court-and-capital is at once a microcosm of the supernatural order— "an image of . . . the universe on a smaller scale"—and the material embodiment of political order. It is not just the nucleus, the engine, or the pivot of the state, it *is* the state. The equation of the seat of rule with the dominion of rule, which the negara concept expresses, is more than an accidental metaphor; it is a statement of a controlling political idea—namely, that by the mere act of providing a model, a paragon, a faultless image of civilized existence, the court shapes the world around it into at least a rough approximation of its own excellence. The ritual life of the court, and in fact the life of the court generally, is thus paradigmatic, not merely reflective, of social order. What it is reflective of, the priests declare, is supernatural order, "the timeless Indian world of the gods" upon which men should, in strict proportion to their status, seek to pattern their lives.

13

The crucial task of legitimation—the reconciliation of this political metaphysic with the existing distribution of power in nineteenth-century Bali—was effected by means of myth; characteristically enough, a colonizing myth. In 1343 the armies of the great east-Javanese kingdom of Majapahit are supposed to have defeated, near Pèjèng, those of "the king of Bali," a supernatural monster with the head of a pig. In this surpassing event the Balinese see the source of virtually their entire civilization, even of themselves, as, with but a handful of exceptions, they regard themselves as descendants of the Javanese invaders, not the ur-Balinese defenders. Like the myth of The Founding Fathers in the United States, or of The Revolution in Russia, the myth of The Majapahit Conquest became the origin tale by means of which actual relations of command and obedience were explained and justified. " 'In the beginning was Madjapahit'; what lies before it is a chaos of demons and villains about which the Balinese knows practically nothing."

What comes after, however, he knows only too precisely, if not always too systematically. Following the conquest, Gajah Mada, the famous prime minister of Majapahit, asked for spiritual assistance from a Javanese Brahmana priest in pacifying his chaotic, because now rulerless, neighbor island—Bali. This priest had four semi-divine grandchildren (his son had married an angel). The first, Gajah Mada appointed king of Blambangan, a petty state at the easternmost tip of Java; the second, he set to rule in Pasuruan, a harbor kingdom on the northeast coast of Java; the third (a woman), he married to the king of Sumbawa. The fourth, Ida Dalam Ketut Kresna Kepakisan, he dispatched to govern Bali. In 1352 this manu-factured king, accompanied by an entourage of high Javanese nobles, set up his court and palace—his negara—at Samprangan, a few kilometers from where the Balinese ruler with the pig's head had met his fate. With the aid of both his inborn charismatic force and of various sacred objects carried as heirlooms from Majapahit, Kepakisan soon brought order out of anarchy. In 1380, the tale continues, dissension broke out within the ruling group when Kepa-kisan's heir proved to be insane (he married his sister to a horse) and had to be deposed in favor of a younger brother, who was only dissolute. The court was removed for spiritual reasons to Gèlgèl, immediately south of Klungkung, and what the Balinese consider to have been their greatest period inaugurated. Toward the turn of the seventeenth century, a more serious rebellion is said to have dissolved the unity of the ruling class altogether, shattering the realm into fragments. The main court moved the mile or so to

Klungkung, where history found it, and the other major courts of recent times—Badung, Karengasem, Tabanan, and so on—spread out over the countryside, setting themselves up in substantial independence of it, but continuing nevertheless to formally acknowledge its spiritual superiority.

Whatever elements of historicity this legend may have (aside from a few rounded dates, schematic events, and stock personages, it probably has very few), it expresses, in the concrete images of a just-so story, the Balinese view of their political development. In Balinese eyes, the foundation of a Javanese court first at Samprangan and then at Gèlgèl (where, it is held, the palace was designed to mirror in exact detail the palace of that most exemplary of exemplary centers, Majapahit itself) created not just a center of power—that had existed before—but a standard of civilization. The Majapahit conquest was (and is) considered the great watershed of Balinese history because it cut off the ancient Bali of animal barbarism from the renascent Bali of aesthetic elegance and liturgical splendor. The transfer of the capital was the transfer of a civilization; as, later, the dispersion of the capital was the dispersion of the civilization. Despite the fact that they are both, in a sense, colonial myths, since they begin with settlement from more cultured foreign shores, the Balinese conception of their political development does not, like the American, present a picture of the forging of unity out of an original diversity, but the dissolution of an original unity into a growing diversity; not a relentless progress toward the good society, but a gradual fading from view of a classic model of perfection.

— 3 —

This fading is conceived to have taken place both over space and through time. During the Gèlgèl period (ca. 1400-1700), the various rulers of the regions of Bali (Badung, Tabanan, Blahbatuh, Karengasem, Bangli, Kapal, and so on), supposed descendants of one or another member of the entourage of nobles who accompanied the immigrant king, are said to have lived in secondary palaces surrounding, in appropriate arrangement, that of the paramount king, the direct descendant of Kepakisan himself. Bali was thus (in theory, but almost certainly not in fact) ruled from a single capital, whose internal organization was an expression not only in spatial, but also in ceremonial, stratificatory, and administrative terms, of the general structure of the realm. When the revolt, led by the lord of Karengasem, occurred, the paramount king fled inland to what is now

Bangli; the various lords (who, except for the lord of Karengasem, remained loyal) retreated to their several regions. After the revolt was crushed, the king (or rather his successor) returned, as noted, not to the spiritually discredited Gèlgèl, but to a fresh start in Klungkung, the once adjacent lords remaining, however, in their bailiwicks. And, in time, the same process—segmentation and spatial separation, coupled with continued formal deference to the parent line—is considered to have taken place, not necessarily by violence, in each of these regions and subregions as well, yielding the scores of courts—large, small, minuscule, and infinitesimal—which dot the known historical landscape.

The final, that is, nineteenth-century, result was an acrobat's pyramid of "kingdoms" of varying degrees of substantial autonomy and effective power. The main lords of Bali held the paramount lord upon their shoulders and stood in turn upon the shoulders of the lords whose status derived from their own, as theirs did from his, and so on down the line. The whole structure was based, however, primarily on ceremony and prestige, and it became, as we shall see, the more fragile and tenuous in actual political dominance and subordination the higher up the pyramid one went; so the other simile that suggests itself is of an intricate house of cards, built up rank on rank to a most tremulous peak. The exemplary center among exemplary centers was still Klungkung, the direct heir of Samprangan and Gèlgèl, and through them of Majapahit. But its orienting image of order was refracted through a series of lesser centers, modeled on it as it had been on Majapahit, an image dimming, naturally, as it diffused through this progressively coarser medium.

Not only did it dim as it spread "horizontally" over the landscape; but also, as a result of an intrinsic process of cultural corrosion we may call the sinking status pattern, as it spun out "vertically" across the generations.

The sinking status pattern rests on the notion that mankind has descended from the gods, not only genealogically but also in having lower intrinsic worth. It has declined at differing rates in different lines, through various worldly events and social happenings, into mere humanity, producing thereby the present, extraordinarily complex system of prestige ranking. Because of its Indic trappings, this system is usually called a caste system, but in Bali it is more accurately referred to as a title or title-group system. It gives, at least in theory, an ascribed, unequivocal, and, so far as the individual is concerned, unchangeable status in an honorific hierarchy to every person (or, more precisely, every family) in Bali. Each person's standing, indexed by his or her title, is a reflex of the mythical history of that person's paternal line as it has steadily sunk from its divine ancestral origin to its present, less august estate. The qualitative difference in prestige between various lines (i.e., different titles) is a result of their different rates of decline; they have not all sunk to the same level. Unlike one's caste in India, present rank is not an outcome of one's own actions in previous incarnations, but of the mere accidents of a wayward history.

So far as the Balinese royal line is concerned, the expression of this pattern is both manifest and quite consciously apprehended.

The line begins, as all human lines begin, with a god, whose title is therefore Batara. It then descends through various semi-divine figures, who bear the title Mpu, to the father of the first Javanese king of Bali, a Brahmana priest with the title Dangiang. The king himself, Kresna Kepakisan, no longer remained a Brahmana after his passage to Bali, however, but was lowered a notch to Satria status, his title becoming as a result not Dangiang but Dalem, a title that all the Gèlgèl kings who followed him bore as well. But whereas the first six of these kings ascended at their deaths directly to the world of the gods without leaving a corpse behind— a process known as *moksa*, "dis-incarnation," "liberation"—the seventh, and the one during whose reign the civil war that spelled Gèlgèl's downfall broke out, died an ordinary, mundane death. Further, he was the last king to be called Dalem. His successor, the founder of Klungkung, was called Déwa Agung, a still lower title by which all the Klungkung kings were subsequently known.

Similarly for the regional, "secondary" kings. As they were descendants not of the (originally) Brahmana Kepakisan but of the Javanese Satrias in his entourage (who had also dropped a notch in transit), they started out lower to begin with and also subsequently sank, in varying degrees and for various reasons, including their initial "mistake" of leaving Gèlgèl to set up negaras of their own. The tertiary breakoffs, who in turn left the palaces of the regional kings to found new ones nearby, bore even lower titles. And so on, down to the lowest levels of the gentry. Thus the general picture, if we leave aside for a moment the not always completely consistent or uniformly perceived ethnographic details, is one of an overall decline in status and spiritual power, not only of peripheral lines as they move away from the core of the ruling class, but also of the core itself as the peripheral lines move away from it. Through the course of its development the exemplary force of the once unitary

17

Balinese state weakened at its heart as it thinned at its edges. Or so, at least, the Balinese think.

— 4 —

Yet this was not felt to be an inevitable deterioration, a predestined decline from a golden age. True, a few sophisticated intellectuals invoked, in a desultory sort of way, the Indic Mahayuga or "aeons" system and viewed the present as a Kaliyuga, the last and worst of the four great ages before the inception of a new cycle; but this seems never to have been a particularly important conception generally. For most Balinese the decline was the way history had happened to happen, not the way it had had to happen. Consequently, the efforts of men, especially of their spiritual and political leaders, ought to be directed neither toward reversing history (which as events are incorrigible is impossible), nor celebrating it (which as it amounted to a series of retreats from an ideal would be pointless), but rather toward nullifying it—toward reexpressing directly, immediately, and with the greatest possible force and vividness the cultural paradigm by which the men of Gèlgèl and Majapahit had, in their time, guided their lives. As Gregory Bateson has pointed out, the Balinese view of the past is not really historical, in the proper sense of the term, at all. For all their explanatory mythmaking, the Balinese search the past not so much for the causes of the present as for the standard by which to judge it; that is, for the unchanging pattern upon which the present ought properly to be modeled, but which through accident, ignorance, indiscipline, or neglect it so often fails to follow.

It was this almost aesthetic correction of the present to conform to a vision of what the past had once been that the lords were trying to effect with their great ceremonial tableaux. From the most petty to the most high they were continually striving to establish, each at his own level, a more truly exemplary center, an authentic negara, which, if it could not match or even approach Gèlgèl in brilliance (and few of the more ambitious hoped even for that), could at least seek to imitate it and so recreate, to some degree, the radiant image of civilization that the classic state had embodied and the postclassic degeneration had obscured.

In these terms, nineteenth-century Balinese politics can be seen as stretched taut between two opposing forces: the centripetal one of exemplary state ritual and the centrifugal one of state structure. On the one hand there was the unifying effect of mass ceremonial

18

under the leadership of this or that lord. On the other there was the intrinsically dispersive, segmental character of the polity considered as a concrete social institution or, if you will, as a power system composed as it was of dozens of independent, semi-independent, and quarter-independent rulers.

The first, the cultural ℯlement, came, as we have seen, from the top down and the center outward. The second, the power element, grew, as we shall see, from the bottom up and the periphery inward. As a result, the broader the scope to which exemplary leadership aspired, the more fragile the political structure supporting it, for the more it was forced to rest on alliance, intrigue, cajolery, and bluff. The lords, pulled on by the cultural ideal of the consummately expressive state, strove constantly to extend their ability to mobilize men and materiel so as to hold larger and more splendid ceremonies and build larger and more splendid temples and palaces in which to hold them. In so doing, however, they were working directly against the grain of a form of political organization whose natural tendency, especially under intensified pressures for unification, was toward progressive fragmentation. But, against the grain or not, they struggled with this paradox of cultural megalomania and organizational pluralism to the very end, and not always without some degree of temporary success. Had not the modern world at length caught up with them, they would no doubt be struggling with it still.

Geography and the Balance of Power

Whether you regard the landscape of south Bali as all piedmont or all littoral depends on whether you stand on the volcano slopes and look toward the sea or stand on the beach and look toward the slopes. If you stand halfway in between you can, from most points, look both ways and see the cones towering five to ten thousand feet straight up into the clouds immediately above and the pitch-black strand arcing gently, like the sooted rim of a giant kettle, immediately below.

The scene, a cascade of rice terraces and palm-covered natural shelves, is Lilliputian in scale: intimate, comfortably enfolding. From the large crater lake in Mount Batur to Gianyar, the approximate center of the region, some 3,000 feet below, is only about twenty-five miles (see map 1). From the highest line of intensive wet-rice agriculture (±2,000 feet) to the shore is only fifteen to twenty miles in the west (Tabanan), twenty to twenty-five in the center (Den Pasar), and ten to fifteen in the east (Klungkung). Crossways, from Tabanan through Den Pasar, Gianyar, and Klungkung to Karengasem, it is, by the winding and dipping Dutch-built highroad, about sixty miles; by crow-fly, about thirty-five. Into this compact area, about 1,350 square miles in all, are today (1971) crowded about eighty percent of Bali's 2,100,000 people, upwards of 15,000 per square mile. There is little reason to believe that their pattern of concentration, though of course not the level of population, was significantly different in the nineteenth century or, for that matter, for most of Bali's history. If ever there was a forcing house for the growth of a singular civilization, this snug little amphitheater was it; and if what was produced turned out to be a rather special orchid, perhaps we should not be altogether surprised.

Not only is the entire region of bandbox dimensions; it is further partitioned by a series of very deeply cut river gorges, which, splaying out from the mountains toward the sea, divide the entire southern drainage into a set of small, somewhat pie-shaped slices. And since the settlements are strung along the slices, on the narrow spurs between the gorges, east-west (or crosswise) communications are a great deal more difficult than north-south, lengthwise ones. Even today, a man living on one such spur will usually find it easier, especially if he is transporting something (as is almost always the case), to walk down to the highroad, travel a mile or two either east or west, and then climb up a nearby spur than to proceed directly across the terrain. (By automobile, bicycle, or horsecart he has no choice but to do this.)

In the nineteenth century, when the highroad did not exist, such crosswise movement, though far from impossible, was even more arduous. In the Bangli of 1876, for example, to travel the eight miles to Klungkung it was necessary to pass over no less than seven deep, unbridged ravines; it was easier to export goods through Bulèlèng, some seventy miles over the mountains to the north, than through Karengasem, about twenty miles directly east. Farther south, near the shore, the terrain is less rugged, leveling out to a narrow (though even there not altogether flat) plain. But still, a lord setting out to visit a neighbor often found it simpler to journey to the beach, pilot a fishing boat along the coast to the appropriate landing, and then move inward again, rather than to proceed immediately overland. So far as state organization is concerned, the effect of this sort of landscape was to set up a very intricate and unhomogeneous field of geopolitical forces whose action was anything but integrative.

To simplify the picture rather drastically, there was a constant lengthwise struggle between lords located higher up toward the mountains and those located lower down toward the sea for the control of any particular set of spurs, and a crosswise one among the more successful participants in these local contests competing for preeminence within the drainage as a whole. But to recomplicate it immediately, the two sorts of processes, the one primary, small-scale, and continuous, the other secondary, large-scale, and sporadic, took place not only concurrently but also in terms of one another. The "international" politics of between-region combat were directly superimposed upon, even fused with, the "domestic" politics of within-region rivalry; they were acted out not among a set of en-capsulated states, miniature *imperia*, but rather through an un-broken network of alliance and opposition spreading out irregularly over the entire landscape. Politics differed in scale from the base of the system to its apex, but not in nature. Even marginal political readjustments could have extensive implications, and any significant change in the islandwide balance of power was reflected almost instantaneously in the most parochial contexts.

The primacy, in a sociological sense, of the lengthwise (smaller-scale) power struggle over the crosswise one had several implications for the character of Balinese politics. First, and most obviously, it meant that, insofar as they were territorial units at all, the orienta-tion of the realms of south Bali was always north and south rather than east and west, giving them a long, generally rather narrow, striplike shape. Second, it meant that altitude, that is, position along the slope, was the most significant geographical factor in shaping the lords' notions of appropriate policy. And third, it meant that the center of political gravity of each of the regions tended to come to rest at about the point where the hills began to level out into the plains.

Politics, in this up-down dimension, consisted of an unremitting effort on the part of the lords situated farther down toward the coast to control (domesticate is perhaps a better word) those situated farther up toward the mountains, and the equally unremitting efforts of those farther up toward the mountains to remain effec-tively independent and to undercut the power of those directly below them. The short-run interest of the upland lords was thus always in fragmentation, at least of the region generally; that of the lowland ones in integration. Or, put another way, the concern with regional unity and its obverse—local or subregional independence—varied with height above sea level. With one possible exception, all the really powerful courts of nineteenth-century Bali were the southernmost along their particular spurs or set of spurs; and, aside from Badung (which somewhat to its disadvantage was farther out into the lowlands proper), all lay almost precisely on the 350-foot line, just above the place where something which can reasonably be called a plain begins.

The outcome was thus a set of tilted oblongs set parallel to one another, each fluctuating almost constantly between a state of reasonably clear-cut but, as we shall see, extremely complex political integration when the lowland lords had the situation in hand, to some degree, and a state of no less complex near-anarchy when, at least as often, they did not. The greater power of the lowland lords did not rest on any markedly greater control of agricultural surpluses. Though there were more terraces and more people per square mile in the plains, the hill terraces were much better watered and more productive. There was always a poor correlation, at best, between the wealth of a region and the power of its paramount lord; and the nature of political organization, as we shall also see, acted to separate "ownership" of land from "ownership" of men, so that the correlation of wealth and power was commonly not any better within realms than it was across them. Rather, it was their crucial location in the communications network which, for the most part, gave the lowland lords their edge in what was inevitably a very fluid situation.

Given the topography, the rim of the plain was the strategic point for controlling east-west traffic. The advantage of the lords along the Tabanan-Gianyar-Klungkung arc was that they could establish and maintain crosswise ties as well as lengthwise ones and, through diplomacy or war, bring the two dimensions into some sort of fragile and usually temporary union. The higher up the slope a court was, the greater its crosswise isolation; the lower down, the more developed its crosswise contacts. On its most general level, Balinese politics was more a matter of geometry—solid geometry—than it was of arithmetic.

In their struggle to maintain independence (or partial independence: it is not possible to locate a genuine hegemony anywhere in this entire system), the upland lords had a few weapons of their own. First, they were more strategically located with respect to the irrigation system and could upset, or threaten to upset, the water supply of those downslope from them. Second, located in more rugged country, the upland lords had a natural advantage when it came to resisting military pressure; and in fact, at the highest altitudes, a few usually dry-farming peasant communities existed beyond the effective reach of any lords at all. And third, the most important, a major lord of a neighboring realm was usually only too glad to give aid and comfort to any upland rebellion that weakened a lowland rival. The balance within any one realm was thus always a most delicate one, tipping now toward the lowland capital and integration, now away from it and toward fragmentation. Like everything else about Balinese state organization, this was all a relative matter; and most of the time at least something minimally definable as a centered kingdom was discernible in each of the regions. But as a polity it was never more than an unsteady alliance, a temporary arrangement which about as many people were scheming to disrupt as were working to maintain.

If the lengthwise struggle moved toward and away from the margin of the plains, the crosswise one moved along that margin. Here the political center of gravity, that for all south Bali, tended to migrate toward the midpoint of the Tabanan to Karengasem arc (i.e., in and around Gianyar-Klungkung), and the same oscillation between fragmentation and integration occurred as the political process flowed in toward this focal zone and then ebbed again away from it.

In this dimension, the level of integration never reached very significant heights, at least during the nineteenth century. A serious bid for islandwide supremacy immediately stimulated a powerful countermovement among other lowland princes, and the political problems faced by a would-be unifier were infinitely more complex than they were for one whose ambitions remained regional. The princes located nearer the center were always interested in extending control, in this case interregional control, whereas those located to the east and west were more concerned with maintaining independence. The degree to which one or the other tendency prevailed at any particular time was a reflex of the degree to which the various regional princes had been able to secure a firm grip upon their own areas. When the more central principalities were stronger there was a move toward the multiplication of crosswise relationships; when the more peripheral ones were stronger there was a move toward the reduction of such relationships. But if intraregionally the balance was at least slightly tipped in favor of the unifiers, interregionally it was tipped, and more than slightly, against them.

— 3 —

In short, a bird's-eye view of classical Bali's political organization does not reveal a neat set of hierarchically organized independent states, sharply demarcated from one another and engaged in "foreign relations" across well-drawn frontiers. Still less does it reveal any overall domination by a "single-centered apparatus state" under an absolute despot, "hydraulic" or otherwise. What it reveals is an extended field of highly dissimilar political ties, thickening into nodes of varying size and strength at strategic points on the landscape and then thinning out again to connect, in a marvelously convolute way, virtually everything with everything else. Though there were border strips between some of these regional principalities, sometimes deliberately left unoccupied but more often thoroughly infiltrated with spies and agents provocateurs from all directions, frontiers were "not clearly defined lines but zones of mutual interest," not "the precise MacMahon lines of modern political geography" insulating one "country" from another, but transition areas, political ecotones through which neighboring power systems "interpenetrated in a dynamic manner."

At each point in this diverse and mobile field, the struggle was more for men—for their deference, their support, and their personal loyalty—than it was for land. Political power inhered less in property than in people; was a matter of the accumulation of prestige, not of territory. The disagreements between the various princedoms, as recorded in edicts, treaties, and legends, or as remembered by informants, were virtually never concerned with border problems, but with delicate questions of mutual status, of appropriate politesse (the instant cause of one important war was an impolitely addressed letter about an insignificant matter), and of rights to mobilize particular bodies of men, even particular men, for state ritual and, what was really the same thing, for warfare.

V. E. Korn relates an anecdote concerning south Celebes, where political arrangements approximated those of Bali, which makes this point with the grave irony of traditional wit. The Dutch, who wanted, for the usual administrative reasons, to get the boundary between two petty princedoms straight once and for all, called in the princes concerned and asked them where indeed the borders lay. Both agreed that the border of princedom A lay at the farthest point from which a man could still see the swamps, and the border of princedom B lay at the farthest point from which a man could still see the sea. Had they, then, never fought over the land between, from which one could see neither swamp nor sea? "Mijnheer," one of the old princes replied, "we had much better reasons to fight with one another than these shabby hills."

CHAPTER 2

Political Anatomy: The Internal

Organization

of the Ruling Class

Descent Groups and Sinking Status

The intricacy of the balance of power in traditional south Bali was matched by that of the institutions upon which it rested. The most elemental of these was the radical, ascriptive distinction between gentry and peasantry: between those whose titles gave them an intrinsic claim to supravillage authority and those, some ninety percent of the population, whose titles carried no such claim. The former, called collectively the *triwangsa* ("three peoples"), consisted of the three upper "castes" (i.e., varnas): Brahmana, Satria, and Wesia. The latter consisted of the fourth, or Sudra, "caste." From the former, also referred to as *wong jero*, or (roughly) "insiders," came the leaders of Bali. From the latter, *wong jaba*, or "outsiders," came the followers.

Yet, as usual, the reality of the situation was much more irregular than this simplistic summary suggests. In the first place, not all those with triwangsa titles, even very high ones, actually played significant political roles at any particular time. A sharp distinction was made between those triwangsa who "owned power" (i.e., had control of the actual instruments of rule) and those who did not; and whereas the former received deference and obedience from the Sudras, the latter received deference alone. The natural growth of population tended to increase the number of individuals with an ascriptive claim to power but no actual access to it, and well before the nineteenth century the effective ruling class must have formed but a minority within the gentry as a whole. Nevertheless, to be a triwangsa, a wong jero, meant one was at least a potential rajah; and every upper-caste man, no matter how politically insignificant, worked to find some place in the state from which he could, by in-

26

trigue, flattery, useful service, or just plain luck, achieve the authority for which his patrician heritage rendered him theoretically
eligible.

Yet even this picture is not quite complete. Although Sudras
could not become lords, princes, or kings in the proper sense—
could not, given their inborn disabilities, be truly exemplary figures
—they could, and in a number of cases did, play central roles in
supravillage politics. At the other extreme, Brahmanas, though
eligible for the most prestigious status (aside from kingship) in all
Balinese culture, that of Sivaite priest (*padanda*), were, with a few
carefully limited exceptions, systematically debarred from access to
the concrete agencies of command.

In Weberian terms, Sudras could achieve the power necessary for
the establishment of effective authority, but inevitably lacked the
trappings of moral qualification which are also necessary for such an
establishment; whereas Brahmanas had the qualifications in full
degree, were in fact the purest embodiments of cultural excellence,
but could not achieve the requisite power. Only the Satrias and
Wesias were possessed of the one and could acquire the other so as
to attain genuine authority, substantial legitimacy, and become the
pivot upon which the entire system—priests, commoners, and less
successful gentry—turned.

— 2 —

The second, and undoubtedly the most consequential, institution
upon which state organization rested was an unusual, perhaps even
unique, variety of kinship system. All members of the upper castes
were gathered into agnatic descent groups of various strengths and
sizes, which one might call lineages except that they were structurally quite different from the lineage as it has commonly been
described in modern anthropological literature.

In the first place, these groups were not exogamous, but preferentially endogamous, the most preferred marriage of all being with
a patri-parallel cousin (that is, for a male ego, his father's brother's
daughter). Second, the formation of new groups from old ones did
not come about by the splitting of old ones. It came about by the
appearance of new ones within the old ones. This process, more
accurately called differentiation than segmentation, left the old
groups intact and unaltered, in an overall sense, by the changes
taking place within them. And third, these differentiated subparts
of the greater whole were explicitly ranked by the order of their

27

birth. That is, their rank shifted with time and with the creation of newly differentiated groups: older subgroups sank in relative status as new ones appeared. The result was a hierarchical, very flexible, but yet quite systematic descent-group structure upon which the actual distribution of political authority could rest. The title system conferred legitimacy; the kinship system gave it concrete social form.

The basic unit of this system—the quasi lineage the Balinese most commonly call a *dadia*—consists of all those individuals who are conceived to be agnatic descendants of a common ancestor (in the case of the gentry, descendants of one or another of the more illustrious Majapahit immigrants). Whether small, as in the case of triwangsas without power, or very large, as in the case of politically potent lines, each dadia is a completely self-contained corporate entity. Dadias are never grouped into any larger units on either a descent, a territorial, or a "caste" basis. And though, as we shall see, they are highly differentiated internally, they are in a fundamental sense unfissionable: they never (in theory, anyway) break apart into independent segments.

In any given region, subregion, or locality, and for that matter over Bali as a whole, it was such dadias that competed for power and, power secured, entered ritual claims to legitimate authority. Whether they consisted of twenty people or two hundred, they were, at one and the same time, both irreducible and uncompoundable units of state organization. They could expand and contract, wax and wane, conquer and collapse; but they could neither split nor, except in uncertain alliance, combine. The bias of the dadia system was thus toward political particularism. The very factors which made the group strong—endogamy, indivisibility, capacity for internal development—made its wider-ranging integration in a descent framework difficult to the point of impossible and partitioned the Balinese polity into a set of rivalrous factions of varying size, strength, and structural complexity.

Internally, the dadia was much less simply patterned, and whatever political authority the group as a whole was able to achieve was unevenly distributed within it in a manner both intricate and precise. The more powerful a dadia became, the more differentiated its internal structure became. The more differentiated its internal structure became, the more taxing the problems of integration it faced. Outward political success brought inward political strain. When a powerful dadia declined it was more commonly from weakness within than from pressure without.

As they grew, dadias developed within themselves subgroups of the same general order as themselves—that is to say, discrete sets of preferentially endogamous agnates making up ritually and politically ambitious corporate entities. But though corporate and independent of one another, these subgroups were not considered to be independent of the parent dadia, which had explicit jural, moral, and religious superiority over them. In case of conflict the interests of the larger group were supposed to take precedence; subgroup membership was considered to be derivative from and secondary to dadia membership, and subgroups had no legal right to deal directly with groups outside the dadia. Further, in any given dadia, not all members—in many cases, not even a majority—belonged to such a subgroup. Unlike a segmentary structure in which each individual belongs to a segment at every level of segmentation, membership in what we may call "sub-dadias" did not extend over the entire dadia membership; so a dadia was a collection both of members of this or that subgroup and of unaffiliated members-at-large. Finally, in the very largest or most important dadias a third level of differentiation sometimes occurred, in which subgroups ("sub-subdadias," so to speak) formed in turn within the sub-dadias, bearing the same general relation to them that the sub-dadias bore to the dadia. The whole structure was more like a set of nested Chinese boxes than a branching genealogical tree (see figure 1).

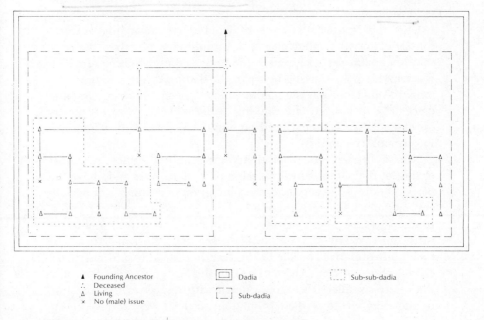

▲ Founding Ancestor ▢ Dadia ⌐⌐ Sub-sub-dadia
∴ Deceased
△ Living ⌐⌐ Sub-dadia
× No (male) issue

Figure 1. Model Dadia Structure (women omitted)

However, though in theory the smaller groups were subordinate to the larger, in fact authority was distributed along subgroup lines. As dadias competed for power within a region, so sub-dadias—smaller, more tightly knit, each seeking to become the inner focus of descent-group grandeur—competed for power within a dadia. But though inter-dadia competition was essentially unregulated by descent institutions, the competitors being unrelated, within the dadia it was very carefully regulated. Claims to authority within the dadia could not be left to the free play of political combat, a mere power struggle among autonomous factions, if the dadia was to be able to act with any unity and effectiveness at all on the larger political stage. As it was, internal integration was always a chancy matter: the parts threatened continually to swallow the whole. But without the comprehensive application of a descent-based system of subgroup ranking it is difficult to see how such integration could have existed at all.

— 3 —

The system that integrated the dadias internally was an institutional counterpart of what on the general cultural level has been referred to as "the sinking status pattern," expressed here in the more concretely sociological idiom of agnatic kinship and primogenitural succession.

Each upper-caste dadia was considered to have a core line of eldest sons of eldest sons, stretching back in unbroken purity to the original Majapahit-period founder, the present representative of which was viewed as the ranking figure of the dadia. At any one time, the ranking sub-dadia was the one to which the contemporary core-line descendant belonged; the ranking "sub-sub-dadia" was essentially his extended patri-family; and he himself was the dadia's nominee for exemplary kingship.

Now, as in each generation there were usually a number of younger sons of the paramount lord, there took place, over and above the perpetuation of the core line, the generation of a number of peripheral or cadet lines, each founded by one or another of these junior brothers. These lines, continued thenceforth by a primogenitural succession pattern of their own, formed separate sub-dadias, but their status relative to that of the core line steadily and automatically declined as time passed. Thus, in the first generation the cadet lines were considered to drop a notch with respect to the core line by the mere virtue of their formation; so if we were to give an arbitrary "status value" of, say, ten to the core line, the peripheral lines formed by the core lord's younger brothers would have a value of, say, nine. However, in the next generation the same process would reoccur. The core line would continue to have a value of ten; the new lines then formed by the younger brothers of the succeeding paramount lord would have a value of nine, and those cadet lines which had been formed in the previous generation would sink to eight, being outranked by the just-born cadet lines and the sub-dadias growing out of them. And so on to the third, fourth, and, in theory, nth generations (see figure 2).

This description is, of course, very overschematized, an ideal model. (A concrete example is developed below, in chapter 3.) But the main point is: *closeness to the reigning paramount lord, the contemporary core-line head, determined relative status within the ruling dadia.* The "older" the line out of which a sub-dadia grew, the further back in time it crystallized as a social entity, and therefore the lower its formal status vis-à-vis its fellows. It was this general principle, not any autonomous genealogical process, which was important; for, as in other descent-based political systems, genealogies could be, and continually were, manipulated in order to rationalize current power realities and justify current prestige claims.

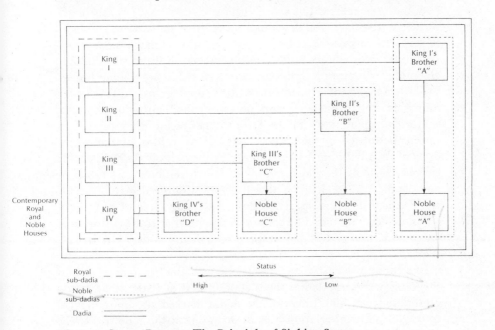

Figure 2. Gentry Descent: The Principle of Sinking Status

It was the notion of sinking status, of a positive correlation between rank and closeness to the living core-line head (notions completely absent in commoner dadias, where genealogies were not kept and sub-dadias not formally ranked), which gave an internal shape to the dadia and provided the social structural forms through which differences in authority were expressed. But the actual reasons for these differences, the causes which brought them into existence, had rather more to do with the workings of politics than with the logic of kinship.

The concrete outcome of the operation of these various principles of descent-group organization (if that is what it should be called) was that a politically important dadia came to be composed of a set of ranked "royal" and "noble" houses. Each such house had a certain quantum of authority of its own, but all the houses were considered as related to one another by agnatic ties and seen, for all the intensity of their actual rivalry, as inseparable parts of the larger descent-group whole.

The various houses were called either *puri* or *jero*, depending upon their rank. The core-line house was usually referred to as "the great puri" (*puri gdé*); the "closer," "more recent" noble houses as "*puri* such-and-such," the name itself being more or less arbitrary; and the (genealogically) more distant houses as "*jero* such-and-such." A great many other symbols of relative status were employed to give this formal structure an explicit cultural expression: subtle title differences among heads (and members) of the various houses; elaborate etiquette prescribing customs of deference among houses, including highly developed differential language use; precise inter-dining, seating, precedence, and marriage rules; enormously detailed sumptuary regulations for the layout, types of buildings, and decorations permitted in the house's "palace," as well as for the proper dress of its inhabitants; meticulously defined ritual rights and obligations, perhaps the most notable of which centered on cremation and death. And so on to an absolutely astonishing degree of invidious distinction. Here, as generally, the driving force of public life was status ceremonial. The assiduous ritualism of court culture was, once more, not merely the drapery of political order, but its substance.

In structural terms, then, the triwangsa dadia (or more precisely the Wesia or Satria dadia) was a state in and of itself, or at least a candidate state. The limits of the dadia marked the limits not, of course, of political relationships as such, but of those political relationships to which the institutions of agnatic connection gave a more determinate form. Between dadias there was intrigue, force, and artful bargaining; within them there was intrigue, force, artful bargaining, and the shaping power of family loyalties. Agnatic descent, preferential endogamy, the inhibition of segmentation, and subgroup ranking combined to make the dadia an integral power bloc, and in fact the only such bloc in the entire political cosmos. The units that competed both lengthwise and crosswise over Bali's tipped and corrugated landscape were not just lords and courts: they were the dadias of which these lords were the symbolic heads and their courts the cultural focus.

— 4 —

Yet, to say that the dadias were integral power blocs is not to say that they were well integrated. On the contrary, there were faction-ridden factions, the clash of units within the dadias was occasionally as intense and commonly more constant than clashes between them.

The dadia was essentially a descent-based federation of royal and noble houses, of puris and jeros which, though they could not secede or radically change the formal structure of authority, could nonetheless struggle for power and influence among themselves. The noble houses may have been viewed officially as the "hands" (*manca*) or even the "servants" (*parekan*) of the core-line lord; in fact, however, they were often more powerful than he. Legally, subordinate houses were not free to treat directly with houses of other dadias; yet in practice they did so whenever the temptations seemed greater than the dangers, conspiring to weaken enemies within their own camp so as to improve their own position. Nor did the necessity for close adherence to the formal etiquette of rank mean that core-line lords could not favor lower, and thus less threatening, houses over higher; could not appeal to outsiders for support against internal insubordination; or could not have recourse to extrakinship instruments of power.

The core-periphery descent pattern of status and authority provided a familistic framework within which political maneuver could take place in a more ordered and (usually) less openly violent manner. But it neither eliminated violence nor reduced politics to mere administration. The rules governing intra-dadia jockeying were somewhat more clearly defined and more regularly observed than those governing struggles between dadias. But rivalry was no less intense, ambition no less unbounded, jealousy no less implacable.

Clientship

There was, however, much more to state organization than title-group stratification and Chinese-box kinship. In addition to the bifurcation of the population into a triwangsa gentry eligible to wield supravillage authority and a Sudra peasantry ineligible to do so, and to the sinking status dadia system differentiating the gentry as such, there was yet a third social institution giving form and character to "national" politics: clientship. Although it operated within the general context that "caste" and kinship established, clientship differed from both in that it was not ascriptive but contractual, not diffuse but specific, not jural but informal, not systematic but irregular. Clientship provided a way in which to forge ties across the fixed boundaries of status and consanguinity as well as to realign relationships within them. It presupposed these more fundamental groupings and operated with them as its units. But without the escape from the rigidities of descent-based status which clientship provided, Balinese political organization could hardly have developed beyond the level of a disjunctive tribalism.

The first sphere within which clientship operated was the dadia itself. The growth and internal differentiation of a major dadia led, as we have seen, to the development of a reasonably well-ordered set of relationships between its subparts, the various royal and noble houses. Were this descent-based stratification hierarchy the only mode of relationship among the houses, the dadia would have been a sort of miniature bureaucracy; its form would have been given directly by the presumptive pattern of kinship ties, and political position would have been a simple reflex of real or imagined genealogical history. But in fact, though the vectors of deference and the graduations of prestige followed this pattern quite exactly, the flow of power and influence followed it in an only much more general way. The several houses formed cliques among themselves and practiced a more opportunistic Realpolitik, with a group of lower-ranking ones following the leadership of a higher-ranking one. A system of intra-dadia factions was thus built up which, though it was in loose congruence with the official structure of authority, had yet a form and dynamics of its own. Within the established framework of the core-periphery ranking pattern there remained a definite field for independent political maneuver—a field few lords omitted to deplore or hesitated to exploit.

Although clientship was important within the dadias, it played its most significant role *across* dadia boundaries. Three main sorts of such extra-kin-group but (for the most part) intraregional affiliation were found: (1) between more powerful dadias and less powerful ones; (2) between Satria or Wesia "political" dadias and Brahmana "priestly" ones; and (3) between powerful dadias and important minority groups, especially Chinese traders. Here, the units of affiliation were not, in theory anyway, the separate houses, but the dadia as a whole (or in the case of the Chinese, Bugis, Javanese, and so on, the minority community as a whole). Clientship thus produced a web of ties spreading irregularly over the entire region—a much more fragile web than that which held the individual dadias together, yet strong enough, at least at times, to give a certain political form to the whole area.

Naturally, clientship ties between more powerful and less powerful dadias were almost purely political in function; the latter were agents of the former within the actual system of domination still to be described. Military threat, economic pressure, personal friendship, bribery, and mere mutual interest all played a part in forging these ties. But perhaps their main institutional support was the practice of large-scale polygynous marriage in which the royal and noble houses engaged.

Though marriage was preferentially dadia-endogamous, title-group hypergamy—that is to say, marriage of a woman of lower title to a man of higher—was permitted. As a result, the higher it was in the title-group ladder, at least among the ruling gentry, the more endogamous a marriage could be, from the point of view of the women of the dadia; while, from the point of view of the men, and especially the lord, the larger the man's complement of endogamous and hypergamous wives could be. The degree to which a dadia could keep its own women and still bring in others from outside was an almost quantitative measure of its status. The lower, or less powerful, dadias were obliged to send some of their women to the higher, or more powerful, in order to secure their place in the polity. The relationship thus established was called *wargi*. That is, the lower dadia was wargi to the higher, by virtue of having given a woman to it in marriage and acknowledging thereby both its own inferiority and its loyalty to the higher. Wives were given as a form of tribute, an act of homage, and an oath of fealty (not, in fact, so terribly binding).

35

Such wargi relationships extended across the triwangsa-Sudra status divide, linking gentry dadias with locally powerful, strategically placed commoner ones and raising the latter to a kind of quasi-gentry status. Indeed, the lower in status a powerful local dadia, the more willing, even anxious, it would be to establish such wargi relations with the eminent. On the other hand, higher-status dadias were always dreaming of undercutting their rivals' position and becoming ascendant themselves some day; and so, to the extent it was practicable, they resisted claims on their women from the more powerful (in some cases even concealing their comelier girls when agents from the more prominent dadias came around) and attempted to remain as endogamous as possible, so far as their own women were concerned, while perhaps collecting a few wargis of their own. Since wargi ties, once set up, tended to be reinforced by subsequent marriages, the ascendant gentry dadias gathered around them a reasonably well-defined cluster of matrilaterally related client dadias of varying degrees of rank and importance, through the agency of which they exercised their authority over the general population. Again, these ties were very far from being unbreakable. In marriage politics, shifts and realignments took place almost continually, of a subtlety and shrewdness the Habsburgs would have envied. Women promised but not delivered, demanded but not given, or received but not honored were among the main provocations for subversion and war. But the wargi system—a product of a delicately balanced interaction of endogamy, hypergamy, and polygyny—allowed a network of intergroup loyalties to develop that tied powerful dadias at various levels into alliances which were, if not rigorously solidary units, at least loose, regionwide confederations.

— 3 —

The second sort of extra-dadia clientship, between ruling dadias and priestly ones, was rather different; for in this case prestige relationships were not even loosely congruent with political relationships, but on the contrary were a direct inversion of them. The Brahmanas in general, and the consecrated priests among them in particular, outranked everyone else so far as the varna system was concerned and, more important, so far as popular Balinese notions of spiritual worth, religious learning, and magical effectiveness were concerned. But, unlike Brahmins in India, no Brahmana, priest or not, seems ever to have held even local political power, at least directly and openly; and for the most part even economic power was denied them. The Brahmana-Satria (or Wesia) relationship—a matter which will be discussed more circumstantially later on—was thus always a peculiarly uneasy one. On religious grounds the Brahmanas felt superior to the lords, a superiority they maintained through a monopoly of scriptural tradition and esoteric ritual knowledge. On political grounds the lords felt superior to the Brahmanas, a superiority they maintained through a monopoly of the instruments of rule. Each distrusted the other, yet each needed the other. The Brahmanas needed the lords' political favor and protection to maintain their special status; the lords needed the Brahmanas' liturgical expertness to mount the ritual extravaganzas of the theatre state. As the ancient Balinese lawbooks say, ruler and priest were to one another as a ship to its helmsman. Neither could reach its common destination—the creation of a negara, a cosmologically based exemplary state—without the other.

There were two formal types of relationship between lords and priests. The first was that, as did every Balinese, each noble or royal house had a special teacher-disciple (siwa-sisia) tie with a particular priestly house; the priest (padanda) from that priestly house acted as the major adviser in ritual matters for the noble or royal house. When the royal house was the paramount one in a region, the attached priestly house was usually referred to as bagawanta, or purohita, and considered to be the ranking Brahmana house of the region (in a pure prestige sense only). Actually, when an important lord held a major ritual, or "work" (karya), as such productions were quite appropriately called, not only his own siwa (or bagawanta), but those of all the lesser houses of his dadia, and even sometimes those of the houses of dependent dadias, attended and assisted in directing the proceedings. The second type of formal relationship between lords and priests was that the lords' tribunals were commonly, though not inevitably, manned by Brahmanas on the grounds, whether accurate or not, that they were learned in Indic law.

In both these functions, as ritual director and royal judge, the Brahmana's main role was essentially advisory, preceptive, informative. He provided the lord with the religio-aesthetic guidelines along which he should shape the life of his court if he wished it, as of course he did, to be at once a microcosm of supernatural order and a paragon of civilized existence.

— 4 —

If the first sort of client relationship, that between higher and lower ruling dadias, was almost purely political in function, and the second, that between ruling and priestly dadias, was almost purely religious, the third, that between ruling dadias and minority communities, was even more purely economic.

Though small "morning markets" filled with Balinese women traders selling daily staples existed in nineteenth-century Bali, as did village-specialized artisan-peddler groups, the overwhelming bulk of significant trade was in the hands of non-Balinese minorities—especially Chinese, but also Muslims (Bugis, Javanese, Malays, Arabs) and, in one or two rather dramatic instances, Europeans. In particular, long-distance trade, and local trade dependent upon long-distance trade, was almost exclusively a preserve of immigrant groups. A few marginal figures aside, a developed indigenous bazaar class, such as is found in so many other parts of Indonesia, never appeared.

This ethnic insulation of the disruptive world of commerce was especially striking in the less isolated north, where at Singaraja, a typical Java Sea port of trade, one can still see the sedate Balinese court town, now a civil service complex, atop a small rise, looking down contemptuously, one imagines, though perhaps nervously and avariciously as well, on the crowded, disordered, casbah-like "Javanese" (i.e., Muslim) and Chinese quarters hugging the small waterfront below. But even in the south, away from the general flow of spice-route trade, this pattern was important; and in each main court town one still finds encapsulated Chinese and "Javanese" ghettoes—*Kampong Cina, Kampong Jawa*—whose inhabitants are almost entirely traders, storekeepers, and certain sorts of marketplace artisans.

The substance and organization of trade in nineteenth-century Bali will be described at length below, in connection with the functioning of the state. Here, the point to be made is: *within the negara*, trade that reached in any serious way beyond it was, a stray Dane or Englishman aside, under the control of large-scale Chinese entrepreneurs, who were granted commercial patents by one or another of the Balinese lords in return for tribute in money and goods. These Chinese (who, if their contract was with a powerful paramount lord, could themselves become quite splendid local figures, living in grand palace-like houses, affecting the upper-caste Balinese life style, and collecting a sizeable harem of Balinese wives) directed the activities of a fair number of agents and subagents—Chinese, "Javanese," and on the most local level Balinese—posted through the countryside. In less integrated realms, almost every petty lord would have his own Chinese. In more integrated ones, the paramount lord's Chinese, sometimes dignified with the office of *Su-bandar* (i.e., "trade master"), would have an almost complete monopoly, organizing all the other foreign traders into an elaborate syndicate centered upon himself. Such men, often entrenched as large-scale landholders as well (particularly of coffee groves and grazing lands), might in turn gain significant informal influence as backdoor advisers to their patrons.

As the spiritual business of the realm was contracted out to one or a number of Brahmana priests, so the commercial was contracted out, on a scarcely less traditional basis, to Chinese merchant gentlemen. In the one case, the lords bartered political favor for prestige; in the other, for wealth.

Alliance

There is, finally, one more level of state organization, one which, though it was the least substantial, the least stable, and except at passing moments the least consequential, was yet the most obvious, because the most dramatic to outside observers—so dramatic that what few descriptions of gentry politics we have but rarely penetrate beneath it. I mean the pattern of interregional, crosswise ties between or among the various locally dominant dadias—what we may call (so as to indicate the largely symmetrical rather than asymmetrical nature of the relationships involved) alliance rather than clientship. This was the peak of the acrobats' pyramid, the unsteady summit of the tottery house of cards.

Or, rather, it was that layer, perhaps even more crucial, just below the summit, from which each man schemed to hoist himself to preeminence on the shoulders of his most formidable rivals: the peak itself was never really scaled in nineteenth-century Bali. All alliances were, sooner or later (and rather more often sooner than later) failures; all islandwide ambitions thwarted; all public proclamations of "spiritual unity" and "brotherhood to the death" empty. Even in the face of increasing pressure from the Dutch, entrenched after 1849 at Singaraja, moves for a genuine political unity, though often enough proposed, never came to anything.

It was, in fact, the turn to the Dutch for military assistance by the Gianyar house in 1899 which marked the beginning of the end of the whole system. Located at the island's political epicenter and advised by two extraordinarily shrewd Sudra brothers ("They could capture a village in their sleep," one of my ancient informants remarked), this house perhaps came closer than any other, though even then not very close, to gaining overall hegemony toward the second half of the nineteenth century. As it grew in strength, all its neighbors, each sequestered in its separate jealousy, of course turned against it. And beginning to weaken from within as well, it made what turned out to be a fatal decision to appeal for help from outside the system, fatal because a local political struggle was thereby projected into a much wider complex of forces for which that struggle had no meaning and upon which it had no effect. The Balinese state was built from the bottom up. It crumbled from the top down.

— 2 —

The institutional framework within which alliances were formed was more cultural and symbolic than sociological and structural. In the first place, there was an elaborate status ethic of honor and politesse, a kind of chivalric code minus horses, homage, and romantic love (but not pride, pomp, and passion) which bound all the great and near-great figures into that sort of baronial community in which etiquette has the force of law and even maleficence must be drenched in courtesy. Formal and suitably ostentatious exchanges of gifts—of heirlooms, trade goods, artistic performances, and even, on occasion, of women—were also very important.

Second, and perhaps most important, there was a system of interregional religious observances centering on the so-called "Six Great Temples" (*Sad Kahyangan*). Precisely which temples were taken to be the transcendent six differed somewhat from region to region. But the mere notion that they existed and that the rituals performed in them were directed toward the welfare not of any one place or party, but of the land and people as a whole, added symbolic substance to the diffuse sense of the oneness of Balinese civilization which the theory of the exemplary state induced in even the most parochial of lords. The great "mother temple" of Besakih, secluded on the upward slopes of the sacred volcano of Agung, formed an especial, almost physical expression of the overall unity of Bali, of its unbroken connection with Majapahit, and of the ideal of the microcosmic state. Though it may in fact date from pre-Indic times, Kepakisan, the immigrant king, is said to have made it his ancestor shrine; the various sections of the rambling, open-court structure were specifically identified with the various regional negaras; and each year, in the fourth lunar month, the leading lords of the island made offerings there in the name of the entire society.

40

And third, there was, on this rather more conceptual than concrete level of integration, the series of formal and, in the nineteenth
century at least, written treaties contracted among various of the
major powers of the island. These treaties were hardly the most crucial element in that complex of symbols which maintained at least
the vision and promise of overall order, if not very much of its substance; both the status ethic and the Great Temple ritual pattern
were more consequential. Nor were the treaties so terribly binding as
documents, or directed toward such politically central issues as to
provide a structural backbone for a genuine "international" polity.
They were as purely ceremonial, in their juridical way, as were politesse, gift exchange, and cosmopolitan worship. (Treaty closings
seem to have been major ritual events in and of themselves, taking
place during the celebration of a royal marriage or tooth filing, under the sanctifying witness of the "official" Brahmana priests attached to the various signatories, and in the dadia temple of one or
another of the contracting lords.) Nevertheless, the treaties are perhaps the most useful of these cultural elements for deriving a picture
of what the shape of politics at this level must have actually been,
because they are so circumstantial and down-to-earth. Informed
with the Balinese version of the legal mind, they express, more clearly and more precisely, what the other crossregional institutions express in a diffuse, elusive, and even deliberately ambiguous manner.
In this regard they are rather like the Domesday Book: while from
an historical perspective they do not say a great deal, what they do
say is at least explicit.

— 3 —

Such treaties covered an extremely wide range of issues, most of
which must seem to us rather trivial concerns for international
diplomacy at the highest level. The disposal of thieves fleeing from
one region to the next and how many armed men are permitted to
pursue them; indemnities due to Chinese who have had their slaves
stolen by Balinese and to Balinese who have had their women stolen
by Chinese; payments necessary in cases of wife capture or elope-
ment; punishment scales for various "castes," especially the triwangsa; blood-money rules; the number of roofs allowed in palace
temples; commercial regulations governing the sale of cattle, pigs,
horses, and chickens, as well as principles for the disposition of such
animals when found wandering loose; salvage rights in wrecked
ships; problems of debt enforcement; foreign-trade regulations;

abduction of servants from one noble house to another to serve as concubines, dancers, or whatever; rules for hospitality due travelers journeying from one region to another; punishments for the sale of fraudulent goods (e.g., "false metals"); maintenance of roads between regions; and, perhaps most frequently, the extradition of refugees—all these issues and a great many more find a detailed consideration in the treaties. By and large, however, the big problems—military coalition, material support, settlement of head-on authority disputes, restitution of peace or declaration of enmity— do not. These evidently remained on the personal, inner-courtyard level of whispered intrigue. The treaties provided a broad consensual framework, built out of the accepted conventions of customary (adat) law, within which the real business of interregional alliance, the islandwide traffic in power, could proceed and take a certain degree of form. To glimpse this more vital process, politics properly understood, one must look beyond or, perhaps more accurately, through the treaties.

One thing that the treaties did do was to define in public terms who the official players in this superordinate game were, and thus to lay out the largest and most general political subclassifications on the island. Klungkung, Karengasem, Lombok, Bangli, Gianyar, Payangan, Mengwi, Badung, Tabanan, Jembrana, and Bulèlèng were, usually in groups of two or three at a time, the formally responsible contracting parties in all the treaties. On this penultimate level they were the certified negaras. (The ultimate level, the one on which all were but extensions of a unitary Klungkung, was also, rather perfunctorily, expressed: Klungkung was always placed first in any listing; the formal superiority of its line openly acknowledged; and vague protestations of loyalty to its leadership and admiration for its wisdom uttered.) And though Payangan fades from view at the beginning of the century (it was a temporarily important upland house soon dismembered by its downslope rivals), Bulèlèng in the middle of the century (after the Dutch conquest of north Bali), and Mengwi (the victim of Tabanan and Badung) at the end of it, in general the pattern is reasonably consistent from document to document.

Except in an ancillary fashion, the treaties did not create this pattern. They were conceptual in function, not causal. Upon what was, in social fact, a disorderly, far from even regionally integrated, and only minimally territorial network of political relations, they impressed a general categorial scheme, a cultural stereotype which, by dint of radical simplification and a free recourse to legal fiction, made that network look as though it had a much more clear-cut order than it ever even approached having. The view of the Balinese polity which emerges from these treaties (and, less clearly, from the all-Bali temple system as well) is a set of seven or eight bounded, more or less equally powerful states led by a *primus inter pares* Klungkung raj. Although too many scholars have accepted it as such, this is hardly an accurate picture of either structural realities or functional processes in the precolonial period. But, as ideas have consequences, in Bali or elsewhere, it is not less important for that.

One fact is clear from the treaties themselves: this "family of nations" picture of Balinese political reality is, on its most general level, sheer stereotype; politics on that level differed from those at the lower only in being a good deal more fluid and somewhat more violent. For although the lords of the "official" negaras were the nominal signatories of the pacts, they were acting not as sovereigns, but as heads of confederations, or even as mere delegates of them. In a 1734 treaty between "Bulèlèng" and "Tabanan," three lords were involved on the Bulèlèng side, six on the Tabanan. In a later one between "Badung" and "Tabanan," thirty-eight were listed on either side. "Mengwi" consisted of thirty-three separate lords in a pact with "Badung," "Gianyar" of thirteen in one with Badung, and so on. Rather than an agreement between two, three, or a half-dozen regional despots, these alliances involved an encounter of whole collections of separate, semi-independent, intensely rivalrous political figures joined at best in unstable blocs by ties of kinship and clientship.

And as for Klungkung's preeminence as the titular capital of all Bali, the core negara, the reality is perhaps well enough indexed by the story that the Sudra advisers of the prince of Gianyar hung a straw effigy of the king of Klungkung, that direct descendant of Kepakisan himself, in Gianyar's public square and invited all who passed by to give it a kick.

— 4 —

In fact, the treaties seem to have been designed more to codify the pretexts upon which alliances could be broken than to establish the bases upon which they could be built. By setting forth, reaffirming actually, what were not formal, contractual agreements at all, but long-established or even sanctified social usages concerning this or that specific yet politically peripheral concern—wandering cows or fleeing thieves—they provided a vocabulary of charges to justify assuming I can specify w/ some clarity what a dadia is - then ~~the~~ positing / individuals are determined by position / dadia in structure + ~~their~~ distribution of resources in their dadia.

POLITICAL ANATOMY

hostility, not a set of mechanisms to realize interregional unity. The participants agreed upon the already agreed, the common background of everyday custom by which they all in any case lived, and at most adjusted a few trivial differences. The un-agreed, the proper domain of diplomacy, they left to the play of the sort of Florentine closet politics at which they, or some of them, came to be such consummate masters.

The degree to which this chorus of concord on inessentials masked an almost Hobbesian discord on essentials is indexed by R. van Eck's (certainly quite partial) listing of the major interregional conflicts between 1800 and 1840 alone. In 1800 Klungkung and Gianyar (i.e., the royal dadias of Klungkung and Gianyar, together with as many of their clients as they could induce to support them) allied against Bangli, while Karengasem attacked Lombok and Bulèlèng. As for Bulèlèng, it fought Jembrana in 1804 and reattacked Karengasem a little later. In Badung, the major lords of the royal dadia fell out among themselves in 1813, leaving them prey to outside incursions from several directions; and after 1820 the would-be potentates of Gianyar fought wars not only with Badung, but with Klungkung, Mengwi, and Bangli as well. In Bangli one of three rivalrous brothers seized power and allied first with Karengasem to attack Klungkung and then with Klungkung to attack Bulèlèng. Tabanan fought with Badung around 1808; and Mengwi, allied with Klungkung, attacked Badung in 1813.

In such a context of institutionalized perfidy, treaties, like the other expressions of crosswise alliance, functioned in a peculiarly negative, almost perverse manner. Rather than creating political unity they provided a rich dictionary of "reasons"—a delicate insult, a neglected ritual observance, an inadequate gift, or a confiscated cow—by which the nearly complete lack of such unity could be justified and understood. The treaties maintained, in such a way, a sense that the perfect system of integration always lay just barely out of reach, prevented from realization only by the duplicity of this lord or the obstinacy of that one. Their far from unimportant contribution to Balinese political equilibrium was that they made inveterate turmoil seem but a recent lapse from order on the immediate verge of being corrected.

(dadia - individuals conceived as "sharing" some pool of resources.)
with kin ties
- like history, social structure is a seamless web)

CHAPTER 3

Political Anatomy: The Village
and the State

The Village Polity

The structural infirmity which kept the Balinese ruling classes fragmented—the tendency for the divisive effect of social institutions to predominate over the unifying power of cultural ones—was further aggravated by the mechanisms through which those classes actually attempted to govern. The ties between ruler and ruled, like those between ruler and ruler, were inherently dispersive, undercutting in their very form the autocratic ideals toward which they were ostensibly directed. Few political elites can have as intensely sought loyalty by means so ingeniously designed to produce treachery as did the Balinese.

This fact has been particularly obscured not only by the "oriental despotism" image of the Balinese state (an image which long predates Wittfogel's hydraulic society theories), but also by a seemingly contradictory yet in fact complementary image of the Balinese village as a bounded, self-contained, wholly autonomous *dorpsrepubliek* ("village republic"). The state—arbitrary, cruel, rigidly hierarchical, but in essence superfluous—was seen to ride above the "patriarchal communism" of village society, feeding upon it, now and then damaging it, but never really penetrating it. The village, the desa, was a self-contained, cosmologically based organic unit, shut in upon itself and growing out of the soil of indigenous ur-Balinese culture. The state, the negara, was a foreign import and an external irritant, always attempting to absorb the village but never succeeding in more than oppressing it. Though dynasties, kings, courts, and capitals came and went, a procession of distant spectacles, the unpretentious villager, hardly conscious of changing masters, went on, exploited but unchanged, in the settled path of centuries. An engaging vision, pleasantly romantic and suitably democratic, as well as comforting to a colonial elite which has just displaced an indigenous aristocracy; but for all that a false one. The state created the village as the village created the state.

Perhaps the clearest indication of this fundamental fact that the village and the state grew up concurrently, locked in a continual process of mutual influence which shaped each of them in response to the other, is the virtual absence of any urban settlements, properly understood, in pre-twentieth-century Bali. The most important noble houses of a powerful dadia tended to cluster in one or another strategic location, disposed, in accordance with a metaphysical blueprint, around the palace of their core-line king—their exemplary center. Secondary and tertiary noble houses, those conceived to have sunk furthest from royal status, were usually scattered about in less central villages, where their "houses" and "palaces," scaled down imitations of the houses and palaces of the capital, were set in the midst of local life to serve as models there. Even the capitals themselves, outside the high walls of the noble houses, were organized precisely as any other village, and in this type of system what was capital and what outlier was frequently neither clear nor stable. The Balinese great tradition, "Hinduism" (if that is what it should be called), was not supported by a differentiated urban social system. Rather, it was carried by a specially demarcated stratum of exemplary ruling houses that were distributed, with concentrations here and there, over the landscape generally. The relation between gentry and peasantry in traditional Bali cannot be formulated in terms of a contrast between town and country, but only in terms of two very different yet elaborately interwoven sorts of polity: one centered on regional and interregional political processes of a predominantly expressive cast, the other centered on local ones of a predominantly instrumental nature. It was not a matter of the totalitarian ambitions of a centralized urban elite contending against the libertarian stubbornness of a horde of encapsulated rustic republics. It was a matter of a detailed, complex, and extremely tenuous adjustment between the institutions of theatre-state pageantry and those of local government.

— 2 —

Something has already been said about the organization of the theatre state, and more will be. But at least a general outline of the forms of local government must now be presented if Balinese political processes at even the uppermost levels are to be properly understood.

Here, too, however, the dorpsrepubliek image of village society stands squarely in our way. For along with it goes an historical (or better, quasi-historical) theory of the progressive degeneration of the Balinese village from its pristine organic form, supposedly represented by some of the geographically more peripheral villages of today, into its present composite state as a result of the interference of the ruling classes in properly village matters. Despite the postulated autonomy of the peasant community, the exactions of the lords (it is said) tended to "rip apart" the "natural" ties within villages. Aboriginal village unity was seriously eroded, in the central regions at least, by the progressive imposition of state power. And so on.

A systematic critique of this theory, one which was designed, as I say, to save the dorpsrepubliek concept in the face of a flood of recalcitrant ethnographic data, would take us into ethnohistorical questions of fact, method, and concept which would be quite out of place in this context. All I am concerned to make clear is that, if I present a view of "the traditional Balinese village" at sharp variance with the assumptions of the encroachment-and-dissolution theory, it is not because I am ignorant of that theory's existence or unmindful of its influence. I simply read the evidence, both historical and ethnographic, quite differently. To my mind, it is not the heartland villages, in which virtually the entire population seems to have lived for centuries, which are atypical, eccentric outcomes of the play of special circumstances; it is the remoter ones, scattered along the margins of that heartland. What the "original," or "archaic," or "pre-Hindu" Balinese community was like I do not know. Neither, however, does anyone else, and to regard the mainstream of village social development as but a derangement of the eddies swirling along its edges seems to me merely odd.

— 3 —

There were three main spheres in which locally based political forms played a predominant role: (1) the ordering of the public aspects of community life, (2) the regulation of irrigation facilities, and (3) the organization of popular ritual. For each of these tasks there were separate (though not unrelated) institutions specifically directed toward their fulfillment: the hamlet (*banjar*), the irrigation society (*subak*), and the temple congregation (*pemaksan*). Around them were clustered a number of organizations in themselves non-political and also specifically focused—kin groups, voluntary organizations, and so on—which, at least at times, played important ancillary political roles within one or another of these contexts. The result was a composite political order composed, like chain mail, of overlapping and interlocking yet nonetheless distinctive and corporate groups, extending in virtually unbroken continuity over the whole of the Balinese countryside; an order on which a very broad range of governmental functions rested. Like *negara, desa* in Bali refers most accurately not to a single bounded entity, but to an extended field of variously organized, variously focused, and variously interrelated social groups—a pattern I have referred to elsewhere as "pluralistic collectivism."

The hamlet, or banjar, to begin with public life, was, in formal terms, a residential unit. This is not to say that it was always strictly territorial; for members of several hamlets were sometimes interspersed within a single settlement, and on occasion hamlet loyalties crosscut settlement boundaries. More often, however, members of each hamlet lived contiguously within one or another of the nucleated house clusters strung out down the narrow spurs, although it was uncommon for a settlement to contain only one hamlet. In any case, the hamlet was much more than a simple residential unit: it was an enduring public corporation regulating a very wide, yet also very sharply demarcated, area of community life. Where it had jurisdiction, it was supreme to the point of absolutism; where it did not, it was powerless.

But though the domain of its jurisdiction was precisely defined (often set out in elaborate detail in written "constitutions" called *awig-awig banjar*, "hamlet rules"), and though this domain was reasonably uniform from one hamlet to the next, it is rather difficult to summarize its nature in a phrase. Perhaps it is least misleading to say that the hamlet was the fundamental civil community in Bali. But it must then be made clear that by "civility" is meant neither "secularity" (for the hamlet was, as was virtually every institution in this ritualistic society, deeply involved in religious matters) nor, of course, "urbanity." What is meant is "public virtue," what the Balinese call *rukun*: the creation and maintenance of order, good relations, and mutual support among a group of neighbors. The purpose of the hamlet as a political body was civic in the broadest sense—the provision of the legal, material, and moral requisites of a healthy common life.

The hamlet was responsible for public facilities (road building and maintenance; the construction and upkeep of hamlet meeting houses, granaries, cockpits, market places, and cemeteries), for local security (night watch; the apprehension, judgment, and punishment of thieves; the suppression of violence), and for the settlement of civil disputes (inheritance conflicts; arguments about various sorts of traditional rights and obligations; contractual disagreements). It regulated the transfer of personal property (except for rice fields) and controlled access to houseland which, in most cases, it held corporately. It legitimized marriage and divorce; administered oaths; conferred and withdrew the rights of citizenship in itself; enforced a number of sumptuary laws designed to keep status relationships in order; and organized various sorts of collective work activities, both religious and secular, conceived to be of general rather than merely individual significance. It sponsored certain public feasts, supported certain common aesthetic pursuits, performed certain, mainly purificatory, rites. It could tax and fine, it could own property, and it could invest in commercial ventures. In brief, perhaps the bulk (though, as we shall see, far from the whole) of Balinese government, in the strict sense of the authoritative regulation of social life, was carried out by the hamlet, leaving the state free to dramatize power rather than to administer it.

The concrete expression of this formidable corporation was the *krama banjar*. This is an extremely difficult term to translate. Literally, *krama*, a Sanskrit loanword, means "manner," "method," "way," or even "style." But here it has the force of "member" or "citizen"; so *krama banjar* refers not only to the customs of the hamlet but to the actual body of men who at any one time are invested with the responsibility of maintaining those customs—the citizenry.

In most hamlets a man became a member of the krama banjar at marriage or after the birth of his first child and sometimes retired from it after the death of his wife or when all of his sons had in turn entered it. Thus, the krama banjar consisted of the adult heads of independent nuclear families of the hamlet. As a rule, it met once every thirty-five-day Balinese month in the hamlet meetinghouse, although special meetings could be called for special purposes. At this meeting all important policy issues were decided consensually, usually after extended discussion and, to judge by present practices, a good deal of preliminary ground laying. The krama banjar chose its own leaders (*klian banjar*), who were more its agents than its rulers. It decided its own modes of procedure, within the context of established traditions. And it was the sovereign body in all hamlet affairs, punishing any incorrigible resistance to its authority, no matter how apparently trivial, by ostracism. Small wonder that the Balinese still say that to leave the krama is to lie down and die.

Yet, for all the hamlet's scope and power, one of the most important aspects of Balinese peasant life fell outside its purview virtually altogether: wet rice agriculture. Here, another public corporation, the subak, usually translated somewhat lamely as "irrigation society," was sovereign. In one sense, the subak was a sort of agricultural hamlet, and indeed Balinese still on occasion refer to it as a "water hamlet" (banjar yèh). The members of the corporation (the krama subak) were, however, not coresidents, but coproprietors—the owners of terraces irrigated from a single artificial watercourse drawn off from one or another point along one or another of the hundreds of river gorges incised into Bali's tilted landscape.

Structurally, the similarity to the hamlet was also close. There were periodic meetings of the krama subak; there were official leaders chosen from among it (klian subak); and there were specific, often written, "constitutions" (awig-awig subak) laying down basic rules, collective work obligations, communal rituals, and so on. Like the hamlet, the irrigation society could levy fines, exact punishments, settle disputes, own property, and determine its own policies independently of any outside or superordinate authority. What differed was the content of these rights and obligations, the social domain over which they played, and the ends toward which they were directed. The hamlet shaped the everyday social interactions of a collection of neighbors into an harmonious pattern of civil attachments; the subak organized the economic resources of a company of peasants—land, labor, water, technical know-how, and, to a rather limited extent, capital equipment—into an astonishingly effective productive apparatus.

The main function of this apparatus was, of course, irrigation control. The creation and maintenance of waterworks and the allotment of water among users were the central concerns of the subak as a whole. The first of these tasks was effected through a precise organization and virtually continuous application of manual labor —that of the subak members themselves. The second was effected through discussion and group consensus under the guidance of established tradition and was, as may be imagined, a most ticklish business. But aside from these central concerns, matters of life and death to its members, the irrigation society engaged in purificatory ritual performances at special rice field and water-source temples; legitimated transfers of terrace ownership; gave or withheld permission for new terrace construction; and regulated the timing of the cultivation cycle, mainly by controlling the time of planting. As in the hamlet, the members of the irrigation society were not simply citizens, but also private persons with a distinct sphere of indefeasible private rights and interests into which the corporate group could not encroach: a man could sell, rent, or pawn to whomever he wished; employ whatever tenancy or other work patterns he wished; use whatever cultivation techniques he wished. But, as in the hamlet, in the sphere of life where public rights and public interests were conceived to be dominant its word was law, defiance of its word crime.

— 5 —

Finally, the third politically important institution in the desa system was the temple congregation, what I have referred to somewhat arbitrarily as the *pemaksan*. Though in essence religiously focused, this unit, also a highly corporate public body organized by explicit and precisely detailed jural rules, was at the same time an agency of government because of the indissoluble connection in Bali between religion and custom, the forms of worship and the patterns of social behavior. This connection can be seen in the Balinese version of the general Indonesian notion of *adat*. *Adat*, from the Arabic for "custom," does not mean "local usage" as contrasted to "divine command" (*hukum*), as it does in the Muslim parts of the archipelago, but rather the entire framework of social action in which both men and gods are enclosed. Applying equally to forms of etiquette, rules of inheritance, methods of agriculture, style of art, and rites of invocation, it is but another name for order.

Like everything else in Bali, however, adat varies. The variations are almost always in small, sometimes even trivial details: in recruitment to the hamlet council; in selection of its officers; in ownership of residential land; in the schedule of offenses and fines; in funerary practices; in the role the "upper-caste" (i.e., triwangsa) people play in social affairs; in what crafts can be practiced and what animals kept; and in a vast multitude of ritual technicalities. From the bird's-eye view of survey ethnography, these really quite marginal differences appear as but incidents in what is a generally homogeneous pattern of custom setting Bali off with marked clarity from its neighbors—Java, the Lesser Sundas, the Celebes, and so on. But for the villagers the variations are much more prominent, for they define the boundaries of the pemaksan—the group of people for whom adat customs are invariant, down to the very last detail. The pemaksan is at base, therefore, a moral community, standing beside the civil community, which is the hamlet, and the economic community, which is the irrigation society. Whereas these others rest on a common set of governmental institutions or on a common set of productive arrangements, it rests on a common set of religiously based social norms, sanctified customs.

The membership of a pemaksan may be composed of the members of anywhere from one to perhaps nine or ten hamlets, though three or four is (today, anyhow) most common. These hamlets are usually, though not inevitably, contiguous ones, and in its spatial aspect the pemaksan is called the *desa adat*—the "custom village." The desa adat is in essence not a social system at all, but a bit of sacred space, based on the Balinese belief that the world and everything in it ("the land with everything that grows on it, the water that flows through it, the air that envelops it, the rock it holds in its womb") belongs to the gods. But it is a bit of sacred space for which a defined social group, the pemaksan, is humanly responsible—responsible for following the moral laws (the adat customs, laid down for that space by the gods) and for worshiping the gods themselves. It is this latter obligation, the most imperative any Balinese has, which gives rise to the main institutionalized expression of this "custom village": the *Kahyangan Tiga*, or "Three Great Temples."

As in the case of the Sad Kahyangan, the "Six Great Temples" discussed earlier, the use of the elevated term for "temples" rather than the ordinary *pura* (though as with the Sad Kahyangan, the individual temples themselves are referred to as *Pura* This or *Pura* That) indicates that these particular places of worship are considered to sum up, in a way ordinary temples (agricultural, familial, market, etc.) do not, an entire social order of a certain type. Here it is the local rather than the translocal order that is ritually underscored, the village system rather than the state system. In both cases the set of temples, as a set, symbolizes and celebrates a particular kind of polity: that of the negara, the exemplary state, on the one hand; that of the desa, the composite village, on the other. Together, they mark the antipodes of traditional Balinese political life—the institutional limits between which, in classical times, it moved.

The Kahyangan Tiga are, by name, the Origin, or Navel, Temple (*Pura Pusèh*), dedicated to commemorating the human settlement of the area; the Death, or Underworld, Temple (*Pura Dalem*), dedicated to pacifying the not yet cremated and consequently dangerous dead; and what can be, literally but somewhat misleadingly, translated as "The Great Council Temple," (*Pura Balai Agung*), dedicated to ensuring the fertility of the desa adat area—both its fields and its women. There are, of course, not just one set of these, as with the Sad Kahyangan state temples, but hundreds: one for every half-dozen or so hamlets. The pemaksan is, then, the congregation which is saddled with the obligation of supporting the three temples associated with its desa adat, and which is gifted with the privilege of worshiping in them.

The actual forms of worship carried out in each of the temples need not be described here. Suffice it to say that both the secular work needed to maintain the temples and the actual ceremonies are at once elaborate and of very frequent occurrence. They thus demand great outputs of effort on the part of the pemaksan, which is, as a result, a social unit of marked prominence in the life of the individual Balinese. Like the hamlet and the irrigation society, the pemaksan is corporate; like them, it is specifically directed toward certain limited, well-defined ends; and, like them, it is essentially autonomous. Its political importance derives from its role as a ritual group, as theirs derives from their role as a governmental or productive group.

— 6 —

These three main constituents of the village polity—banjar, subak, and pemaksan—are noncoordinate: their memberships do not coincide. Rather, they intersect and overlap. Virtually any irrigation society has members from many different hamlets and many different congregations. The members of virtually any congregation come from several hamlets and several irrigation societies. The members of virtually any hamlet will belong to different irrigation societies. And, though all the members of any one hamlet will almost always belong to one congregation, they will belong to it together with members of other hamlets and are organized within it on the pemaksan's, not the banjar's, terms. Together, this triad of corporations forms, and so far back as we have reliable historical data has always formed, the political heart of the desa system. It is the core around which the other, also noncoordinate, components of "pluralistic collectivism" (kin groups, voluntary associations, and so on) cluster. It was to this sort of political system, this partly ordered assemblage of what Balinese refer to as seka(s), these disjunct groups with divergent functions, not to integral "village republics," that the explosion of privilege, ceremony, and pretension we have been calling the state had to relate.

The Perbekel System

The central agency of this relation between desa and negara was the
perbekel system. A *perbekel* was a state official linking the individual
villager, whether triwangsa or Sudra, to the individual lord. Any
lord of political importance had several such perbekels, and the
grander ones had dozens, each of whom was responsible for a certain number of the lord's subjects. Over Bali as a whole there must
have been several thousand of these political superintendents in the
nineteenth century. Tied upward to his lord or lordling and downward to the villagers "owned" by that lord, who were entrusted to
his immediate authority, the perbekel was the steward, bailiff, and
seneschal of traditional Bali.

This much of the perbekel system seems to have been uniform
over the whole of the island. Virtually everything else about it, including the medley of collateral administrative structures with
which it was intertwined, varied widely and reached extraordinary
levels of complexity. For expository purposes, I shall describe the
system as it existed, just before and just after the turn of the last
century, in Tabanan, the principality immediately to the west of the
present capital of Bali, Den Pasar (see map 1). Though the Tabanan
version is no more typical of the perbekel system generally than is
that of any other region of the island, it is in many ways the clearest
expression of it, the version in which the system's essential principles
appear in their most straightforward, readily visible form. State-
village relationships in traditional Bali were of such intricacy and
irregularity that almost anything one asserts in detail about any
particular example of them is false when applied to any other. Yet
such relationships were informed by a conception of the nature of
political loyalty, political obligation, and political purpose that was
everywhere the same. For all its surface variation, the interaction
of negara and desa had, at base, a definable form, a form produced
by centuries of history proceeding under the guidance of a set of
jural assumptions, which, were we to find it in a modern state, we
would call a constitution.

— 2 —

There were in the Tabanan of 1891-1906 about thirty to thirty-five
noble houses of political significance. These houses can be, and
were, classified into three main groups: (1) the Tabanan royal
"lineage" itself; (2) an independent, or semi-independent, outlying
lineage, Krambitan; and (3) two lineages removed by military

54

means from the Mengwi sphere of influence, one as early as the 1820s, the other in the climactic encounter of 1891. The approximate locations of these houses are shown on maps 2 and 3.

The houses belonging to the Tabanan royal lineage (that is, the dadia, though the term actually used in Tabanan was *batur dalem*) all considered themselves to be agnatically descended from Batara Hario Damar, one of Gaja Mada's field generals in the Majapahit Conquest. The paramount lord (*cakorda*, or, if you will, "king") in office at the time of the Dutch invasion (the one who killed himself in custody) was, according to the lineage genealogists, the eighteenth in the direct and unbroken line of primogenitural patrilineal descent from Batara Hario Damar. The eighteenth cakorda was crowned in 1903. His cosuicide son, the crown prince, would have been the nineteenth, but with his decease the direct line expired. Each of the other houses were considered direct-line descendants of some full- or half-brother of a once-reigning king; the earlier his reign the lower their current rank, according to the sinking status pattern described earlier (see figure 1 and chapter 2, under "Descent Groups and Sinking Status").

As for the Krambitan houses, they regarded themselves and were regarded as in some way or other related to the main Tabanan line (as, indeed, the Tabanan line regarded itself as distantly related to the royal line of Badung, and beyond it, to Klungkung), and as lying within its general sphere of influence. But for all intents and purposes they were a dadia of their own with the lord of Puri Gdé Krambitan as their paramount.

Of the four ex-Mengwi houses, the three detached in the 1820s—Marga, Blayu, and the core house, Perean—were related in a single dadia; the 1891 acquisition, Kaba-Kaba, was a branch of a dadia whose seat was at Kapal, a village in Badung, having been cut off from the rest of its line by the division of spoils between Badung and Tabanan.

Except for Kaba-Kaba, which continued to look eastward, all of these independent, or semi-independent, lines and sublines were tied to Tabanan proper by wife-giving (*wargi*) relationships of the sort described earlier. We can, therefore, center our analysis on the Tabanan royal lineage as such and consider the less powerful but structurally identical Krambitan and Perean dadias as semisubordinate, semiautonomous clients to it. The official "peace settlement" to the contrary notwithstanding, Kaba-Kaba was essentially client not to Tabanan but to Badung during the 1891-1906 period, and so can be ignored here altogether.

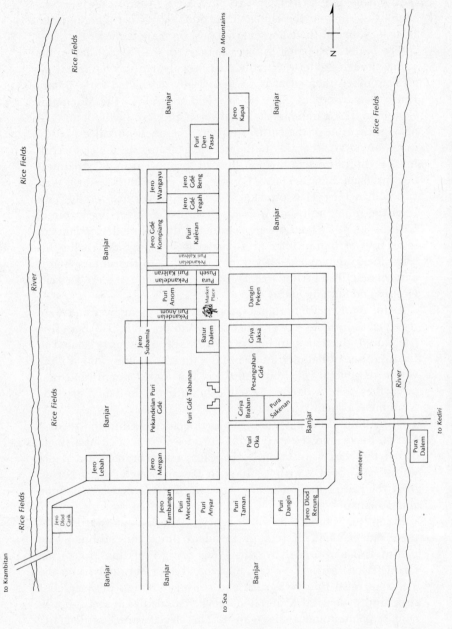

Map 2. Royal Houses of Tabanan and Allied Houses in the Capital, ca. 1900

Ruling Houses (33)
Puri Gdé—core-line royal house of Tabanan (1)
Puri—houses belonging to the royal sub-dadia—i.e., founded by brothers or
   father's brothers of the ruling king (10) or major allied lines (2)
Jero Gdé—houses founded by brothers of the grandfather or great-
   grandfather of the ruling king (4) or by branches of allied lines (2)
Jero—houses formed by brothers of yet earlier ruling kings (14)

Leading Priestly Houses (4)
Griya Pasekan—bagawanta to Puri Gdé
Griya Jambé—bagawanta to "second king," Puri Kalèran
Griya Jaksa—state judges
Griya Beraban—no special function, but locally important

Politically Important Sudra Houses (4)
Dangin Peken—"secretary" to Puri Gdé
Malkangin—"secretary" to "second king," Puri Kalèran
Kebayan Wangayu Gdé—house with regional ritual responsibilities in
   connection with Mt. Batu Kau
Pupuan—semi-independent highland house

Other Significant Houses
Jero Samsam—Klungkung connected Satria house, loosely allied with
   Tabanan
"Jero" Singkeh Cong—Chinese trademaster

Other
Pekandelan—residential quarters of permanent dependents of major houses
Pesangrahan Gdé—guest quarters for royal or noble visitors to the Tabanan
   court
Batur Dalem—royal core-line temple
Pura Puseh—village origin temple
Pura Dalem—village death temple
Pura Sakenan—a royal public temple
Mt. Batu Kau—regional holy mountain
Lake Bratan—sacred regional water source

approximate limits of wet rice growing area ——————

royal gate

sacred banyan tree

**Map 3. Royal Houses of Tabanan and Allied Houses
in Countryside, ca. 1900**

The Tabanan royal lineage is best seen (and the Balinese so see it) as a set of concentric circles, a nested structure of core and peripheral lines ranked in terms of their presumed distance from the core of cores in Puri Gdé (*gdé*—"great," "large"), which was, in fact, often merely referred to as *Dalem*—"Within" (see figure 3 for a simplified diagram of the genealogy involved).

First, there were the nine primary houses, *puri*, running from Gdé itself, through those founded by the brothers of the seventeenth Gdé lord, who forced them out of the Dalem at his accession to the cakorda-ship (Dangin, Mecutan, Den Pasar, and Taman), to those conceived to have been founded by the brothers of that cakorda's father when *he* was crowned (Kalèran, Kediri, Oka, Anom, and Anyar). Next around this wider core of primary houses there clustered in turn four secondary houses, *jero gdé*, founded, it was assumed, by the brothers of the grandfather and great-grandfather of the reigning king. And, finally there were fourteen tertiary houses, or *jero* (a word which, as I noted earlier, also means "within" or "inside"), whose founders were conceived to have "gone out (*jaba*) of the Dalem" at various earlier stages of the line's history, and so to have drifted further from it.

There was thus a four-tiered structure, a product of the workings of the sinking status pattern, running from the Puri Gdé, or Dalem, at the top or center, through the puris and the jero gdés to the plain jeros at the bottom or edge. But at the same time, the "lineage" taken as a whole was a unit. The meanest noble house in the most outlying village, the most peripheral line, could trace its ties, or thought it could, to Dalem, the innermost core itself; and so the lowliest jero shared, if dimly, in the power, the prestige, and the charismatic force that Dalem commanded as an exemplary center.

That at least was the theory. The practice, the administrative structure as it actually operated, given the nature of Balinese politics (or perhaps just of politics), was rather more complicated and not nearly so regular.

In the first place, just where the lines between Dalem, puri, jero gdé, and jero were to be drawn was less clear-cut than figure 3 suggests, and what their proper position was thought to be tended to depend on who was drawing them.

Members of the first five houses—Gdé, Dangin, Mecutan, Den Pasar, and Taman—tended to refer to *all* the other houses, at least when they thought they could get away with it, as "jero." The houses

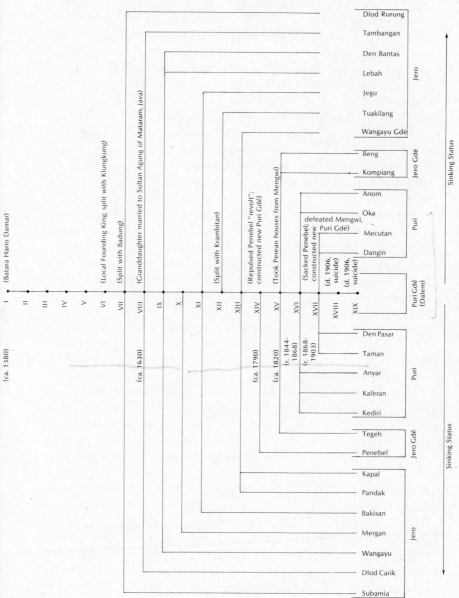

Figure 3. The Tabanan Royal Lineage

one notch "down" (or "back," or "out")—Kalèran, Kediri, Oka, Anom, and Anyar—resisted this, of course; but, like the first five houses, they also resisted referring to the Beng, Kompiang, Tegeh, Penebel group houses as "jero gdé," preferring to call them merely "jero." The reverse, self-upgrading, occurred as well. The king's brothers attempted to represent their houses as still part of Dalem, as having not yet really "gone out": and even the Kalèran group tried this on occasion, at least vis-à-vis the lower-status houses. (By the common people, the whole dadia and any house in it was commonly referred to as "Dalem": though the distinction between the "Dalem of Dalems," Puri Gdé, and the others, as well as between major houses and minor ones, was quite clear to the merest peasant.) Beng-group people tried to call their houses "puri," the further out jeros to call theirs "jero gdé," or, vis-à-vis outsiders, even "puri." And so on.

The intra-dadia ranking system, with its four classes of house names was not, as a pattern, questioned; nor was the sinking status principle which underlay it. But just who properly belonged where, who had a right to how much and what sort of deference, was a much more discussable question; just the sort of discussable question that could lead to bloodshed in the prestige politics of theatre-state Bali.

The second factor disturbing the regularity of core-periphery hierarchical relationships was that, in Tabanan as all over Bali, there was not just one king but two, a "senior" and a "junior"— what has been called, not quite accurately, a "double government."

In Tabanan, during the period under consideration, the second king (pemadé—"following," "junior"), the subparamount, as it were, was the head of the house of Kalèran. The other major houses were attached by intra-dadia clientship ties to one or the other of the leading houses and referred to as the punggawas. Thus were formed two major factions within the royal lineage as a whole. With Puri Gdé, the senior king, were affiliated as his punggawas the puris Dangin, Mecutan, Den Pasar, Taman, Oka, Anom, and Anyar, and the jero Subamia; with Kalèran, the junior king, were affiliated the puri Kediri and the jero gdés Beng, Kompiang, and Tegeh.

The fact that there were nine houses in the Gdé faction and only five in the Kalèran should not be taken to mean that the former was necessarily the stronger. Prestige aside, the really powerful (because large, rich, and vigorous) houses were Anom and Subamia on the one side, and Kalèran and Kediri on the other; so the balance was, if not exactly even, nearly so. What you had, in effect, was a vigorous internal rivalry for dadia leadership between the core-line house as such and the strongest house formed, or regarded as having been formed, from the brothers of the immediately previous paramount king. The former, the reigning (1868-1903) cakorda, maintained the loyalty, such as it was, of his brothers and gained that of a powerful outlying house (Subamia), as well as that of three members of Kalèran's own subdadia (Oka, Anom, Anyar). The latter, the junior king, was supported by the strongest of his cousins (his father's brother's son, the lord of Kediri) and by all of the houses formed at his grandfather's accession (i.e., his second patri-cousin), led by the lord of Jero Gdé Beng as a kind of junior king to his junior king, or *patih*. (Gdé's patih was Subamia.) The concrete political processes by which these alignments came into being and were maintained (until the decisive split of 1906, when Kalèran supported the Dutch and Gdé opposed them) and particularly the reasons for the against-the-genealogical-grain affiliations of Oka, Anom, and Anyar, for the "neutrality" of Penebel, and for the strikingly anomalous positions of Subamia are, unfortunately, largely unrecoverable. But they must have been tangled, delicate, stylish, and murderous.

Finally, the third irregularity in the Tabanan governmental system, at least regarding legitimacy, was that not all the houses playing significant roles in it were actually genealogically connected, even in theory, to the ruling line at all—that is, were not in the proper sense of the term "noble." In fact, a number were Sudras. Of these, one in particular—Dangin Peken, a very large Sudra house located in Tabanan proper (see map 2)—was of such importance as to be counted among the leading houses of the realm, its power and influence rivaling that of all but Gdé and Kalèran themselves. Often referred to as "the right hand of the king," it was firmly attached to the core house, Gdé, to which it served as "secretary" (*penyarikan*); and, as its position depended upon that attachment rather than upon its ancestry, it was considered—along with Subamia, a quite peripheral house brought into the very center of political life also by Gdé's favor—the most unquestioningly loyal.

At less elevated levels, other Sudra houses and nonnoble Satria and Wesia houses (houses, that is, genealogically unconnected with any of the major lines in the region) also played roles in the system equivalent to that of the tertiary houses (the jeros) of the royal line itself. If Dangin Peken and, in a somewhat different way, Subamia were, so to speak, "jero gdés" by appointment to the court, so perhaps were twenty-five or thirty less powerful houses "jeros" by similar appointment, though not all of them to the same court.

These hundred or so houses—the ranked and rivalrous subparts of the ruling lineage; the major client courts, only very reluctantly subservient; and the unrelated, semi-independent lines, loyal when necessary, rebellious when possible—thus formed the pyramid of power in late nineteenth-century Tabanan, an area, it might be remembered, of some three hundred square miles and perhaps eighty or ninety thousand people. It was in this tremulous, constantly readjusting, intricately balanced pyramid of power, not, again, in some centralized, Pharaonic despotism, that the state, the negara, consisted.

The negara was, in Weber's now standard sense of the terms, neither a bureaucratic, nor a feudal, nor a patrimonial state. That is, it was not a functionally differentiated, systematically graded administrative structure, à la Confucian China or Imperial Rome. It was not a system of contractual law propped up by domanial organization, service tenancy, and the chivalric ethic, à la northern Europe in the Middle Ages or Japan before Meiji. And it was not a distended and militarily developed household *oikos*, à la Islam under the Umayyads or Persia under Darius. There was, as we shall see, just enough of a trace, perhaps embryonic, perhaps incidental, of each of these more familiar forms of traditional political organization in the negara to mislead scholars into regarding it (in Java and Sumatra, or in Cambodia and Burma, as well as in Bali) as essentially but one more example of one or another of them. But, as we shall also see, it was in fact something quite different from any of them: a ceremonial order of precedence imperfectly impressed upon a band of sovereigns.

If one looks at the classical state in Tabanan as a cultural hierarchy defined by the exemplary center and sinking status image of governmental authority; that is, if one considers it in terms of political legitimacy, it appears to be organized from the top down—to descend from the paramount lord, or king, through the varying grades of lesser lords, related and unrelated, to the lowly villager, the hapless object of its arbitrary exactions. But if one examines it as a system of domination, a structure of command and compliance, it does not look that way at all. Rather than flowing down from a pinnacle of authority or spreading out from a generative center, power seems instead to be pulled up toward such a pinnacle or to be drawn in toward such a center. The right to command was not delegated from king to lord, lord to lordling, and lordling to subject; rather, it was surrendered from subject to lordling, lordling to lord, and lord to king. Power was not allocated from the top, it cumulated from the bottom. This is not to say the system was democratic, which it certainly was not; nor that it was libertarian, which it was even less. It is to say that it was—radically, pervasively, inveterately—confederate.

— 5 —

There were, to simplify somewhat, four general orders of political being in precolonial Tabanan: *parekan, kawula, perbekel,* and *punggawa.*

A *parekan* was a man (or, more exactly, a family) completely dependent upon a lord or, much less frequently, upon a Brahmana priest. He was landless, he lived in a quarter called a *pekandelan* (see map 2) next to or near his lord's house, his food was provided by the lord, and he was obliged to do just about anything the lord asked him to do. He was not precisely a slave; for parekans were not, so far as I can tell, bought and sold (actually there was no traffic in them of any sort), nor were they legally forbidden from leaving the lord's employ if they could manage some way to do so and continue to clothe, feed, and house themselves. But he was certainly the next thing to it: a totally resourceless servant.

The *kawulas* were far and away the most numerous among the Balinese, making up perhaps ninety percent of the population. A *kawula* was a man, not a member of the ruling elite, who, owning land or practicing a craft or both, was obligated to perform certain quite carefully defined and narrowly limited services for one or another lord: a subject.

A *perbekel* was, as mentioned, a man who had a larger or smaller number of kawulas directly attached to him; he was responsible for their duties as subjects: a political foreman.

And finally, a *punggawa* was, as also mentioned, a lord of the realm, insofar as there was a realm, to whom were attached a larger or smaller number of perbekels and, through them, anywhere from a few hundred to several thousand kawulas. Though he was not usually called a punggawa (except when his relation to Klungkung was in mind), the paramount lord—the "king"—was in fact but one punggawa among others: one with a higher prestige standing, but not necessarily a stronger power position. In fact, the heads of Kalèran, Subamia, Kediri, Anom, and perhaps Beng all "owned" more kawula subjects than did Gdé during the 1891-1906 period.

From the point of view of political structure (we shall come to the even more interesting matter of content shortly), the critical thing about the kawula "holdings" of perbekels, and thus those of the punggawas the perbekels served, is that they were not territorially concentrated. That is to say, any given perbekel did not have his kawula subjects in any one hamlet, or even in any group of adjacent hamlets, but rather in a number of dispersed and unrelated ones: a few here, a few there, a few in a third place, and so on.

For example, one of my informants, who had been perbekel under a punggawa in Jero Subamia, held four houseyards (the local unit according to which kawulas were allotted) in one hamlet high up in the mountains directly north of Tabanan proper, seven in another mountain hamlet about five miles farther down the slope, ten in a hamlet perhaps fifteen miles northeast of Tabanan proper over toward Marga, four in an isolated forest hamlet up in the northwest coffee area, forty in another hamlet out to the arid west near the Jembrana border, ten in a hamlet only about a half a mile from Krambitan, two in a hamlet directly south of Tabanan proper about halfway to the sea, and about a dozen in one off to the southeast toward Kediri—an almost perfect scatter through the general Tabanan sphere of influence.

As the other perbekels under Subamia, perhaps some fifteen or twenty of them, had holdings equally scattered, the subjects of the punggawa were in no sense a concentrated group. And the same was true of every other punggawa, up to and including Puri Gdé, whose holdings were, it is said, the most widely and evenly distributed of all: two or three houseyards in almost every hamlet, but not very many in any one. Neither perbekels nor punggawas, nor even the king himself, held territories. Nor did they hold village political units (hamlets, irrigation societies, temple groups), to which they had no defined relationship *as lords* at all. They held, or as they put it "owned," the real political resource in classical Bali: people.

If we look at the matter from the village side of things, this system meant that the population of any hamlet (or irrigation society, or temple group) was distributed, so far as supralocal political obligations were concerned, among several punggawas and commonly an even larger number of perbekels. The basic local political unit so far as the negara was concerned (this unit had no meaning in the desa system at all) was the *bekelan*—all those "belonging" to one perbekel. And as the assortment into bekelans was not by descent group but by houseyard, even close kinship connections could be, and frequently were, crosscut. In fact, no structural divi-

64

sion of importance in the desa system had any reality whatsoever so far as the alignment of supralocal political loyalties was concerned.

In some cases a villager might even have two loyalties, to two perbekels, and thus (though not necessarily) to two punggawas, each demanding a slightly different service. Thus, Korn reports that, of the 1,500 or so houseyards attached to one or another of the Krambitan punggawas, 700 were also attached to one or another of the Tabanan punggawas, in both cases through the appropriate perbekels. To the Tabanan lords they had the usual obligations (which will be described presently); for the Krambitan lords they had only to work, from time to time, on the outer walls of the lords' puris. The remaining 800 houseyards were attached, in the more normal fashion, only to Krambitan.

From the peasant's point of view, his obligations to the state were a matter only between him, or more exactly the members of his houseyard, and (via his perbekel) his lord, not between any desa group to which he belonged and an overarching state administration, of which his local group would have been a co-opted part. The negara and the desa were organized along different lines and directed to different ends. They were linked by neither a common structure nor a common purpose, but by the simple fact that each person who belonged to the one belonged as well to the other.

— 6 —

Turning to the content of the kawula's obligations to his lord, we find that what is most striking about *them* is how altogether specific and narrowly defined they were. Rather than diffuse loyalty, a kind of general subjection to an all-sovereign lord, there was a very limited rendering unto rajah of those things explicitly his. And of these there were essentially two, and those two were but analogues, cultural equivalents: ritual service and military support. Beyond these obligations, which could of course be onerous enough, the kawula was not bound. He was not a tenant, a serf, a servant, or a slave. He was not even what, *faute de mieux*, I have been calling him, a subject. He was stagehand, spear carrier, and *claqueur* in an endless political opera.

As were the kawulas themselves, so were the functions of government: they were not concentrated, but dispersed; not focused through a hierarchical system of executive institutions, but scattered through a plurality of such institutions, each one to a high degree independent, autonomous, and differently organized. The confed-

erative nature of the Balinese power system did not consist only in
the self-assertiveness, the cultural ambitiousness, of the men who
headed it, great as that was. Nor did it consist only in the awkward
fragility of their elephantine social organization, severe as that was.
It penetrated to the very marrow of government: the administrative
apparatus through which these men had to act.

— 7 —

Perhaps the most striking example of this sort of segregation—of the
separation of other types of socially significant relationships between
lords and villagers from the properly political (penggawa-perbekel-
kawula) relationship—is the autonomy of the landlord-tenant tie in
classical Bali. Western feudalism may have come down to a collection of domains which were also dominions; but that was not true
of the negara, where control over land and control over people expressed themselves in distinct and uncoordinate institutions.

In Tabanan, irrigated rice land was, with a few exceptions, in-
dividually owned. The overwhelming bulk of the owners were
peasants, village-dwelling kawulas. But the lords also owned such
land, from which they drew most of their subsistence, for themselves
and for their landless parekan servants. Most holdings, noble and
commoner alike, were divided into a greater or lesser number of
quite small and usually scattered parcels, a half to perhaps two-and-
a-half or three acres each. In legal terms, the rights of lords and
villagers in such land were precisely the same. There was no difference whatsoever in the forms of tenure. The only difference was
that the lords commonly had a greater amount of land scattered
more widely through a larger number of irrigation societies. (Even
that was not inevitably the case. At least two of the largest landholders in late nineteenth-century Tabanan, with holdings rivaling those
of all but the richest lords, were Sudra kawulas.)

But although the holdings of the lords were for the most part
larger than those of the commoners, they were in themselves quite
unequal in size. The great landlord houses in Tabanan seem to
have been Anom, Kalèran, Kediri, and Krambitan. The other punggawa houses, though hardly without significant holdings, were much
less landed. The correlation between political power and agricultural wealth was thus very partial at best. And this was true not
merely in Tabanan but in Bali generally. One of the most consequential powers on the island, the southeastern kingdom of Karengasem, had very little rice land at all; while Kaba-Kaba, the old
Mengwi house, had very extensive holdings, but never seems to have

been able to translate its land into very much in the way of military strength. Differential access to agricultural property was certainly not irrelevant to political power in Bali. But it was not the sum and substance of it either.

Tenants worked the lords' lands on the same basis that village tenants worked for village landlords. As the lands were scattered in small parcels, so the tenants were also scattered; and any given lord had a multiplicity of both parcels and tenants. Tenants were chosen mainly for their residential proximity to the land concerned (they usually owned land themselves in the same irrigation society, thus being, like the lord, proper members of it) and for their reputation for agrarian virtue: farming skill, industry, honesty. Once in place as tenants they tended to remain in place permanently, sons often inheriting a father's rights, so long as they performed satisfactorily, even if the land changed hands from one lord to another.

So far as I can discover, there was no effort to choose one's kawulas as one's tenants. Nor, on the other hand, was there any particular effort to avoid them. The criteria of tenancy and those of subjecthood were simply different; apparently, the two matters were hardly thought of as having anything to do with one another. As a result, by far the greater number of tenants were not kawulas of their landlords, and by far the greater number of a landlord's kawulas were not tenants of his. In fact, as plots were small, and as good farmers without sufficient land of their own were far from numerous in this still relatively uncrowded period, many tenants worked land for more than one lord, and perhaps for a villager or two as well.

There was, in short, no systematic congruence (though there was, here and there, some more or less accidental overlap) between the structure of political authority, the structure of land tenure, and the distribution of land tenancy.

— 8 —

The noble landlord's share of the rice crop was collected for him at the harvest by an official known as a *sedahan*—"rent master," "tax collector."

Most lords had several such sedahans, chosen usually from among lesser members of their own house or from members of houses attached to them by perbekel or other loyalties. (There were a few cases in which one man was both a sedahan and a perbekel. However, this was rare and was deliberately avoided when possible.) Over all the sedahans of one lord, one noble house, there was usually a *sedahan gdé*—a "great," or "big" sedahan. Almost always a member of the noble house itself, he was responsible for the rent- and tax-gathering operations for the lord: for checking on the sedahans, for keeping the appropriate records, for storing the grain, and so on. But he was responsible too for making a certain number of on-the-spot collections himself, precisely as were the ordinary sedahans, among whom he was thus rather more a first among equals than a true chief. And where the rice lands for whose rent and tax collection the individual sedahans were responsible were territori- ally concentrated, consisting of the lord's lands in one or, more com- monly, a number of neighboring irrigation societies, the sedahan gdé's responsibilities were again scattered in such a way that he had one or two fields under his immediate surveillance in virtually ev- ery place that the lord had holdings.

As noted, taxation (*pajeg*) also fell under the responsibility of the sedahans, great and plain. It too was organized on a basis peculiar to itself, coordinate neither with the perbekel system of authorita- tive command nor with the land tenancy system.

Tax areas (*bukti pajeg*) were formed which consisted, in the majority of cases, of a single irrigation society. The right to collect the tax for a given tax area "belonged" to a particular lord, whose sedahans then collected it, in kind (i.e., husked rice), at harvest time or shortly thereafter. The tax was considered to be not a land but a water levy, and was therefore assessed in terms not of field size but of the quantity of water used by the peasant for irrigation. Fi- nally, the tax areas "belonging" to one or another lord were, as one might suspect by now, not concentrated but distributed about the landscape. From the fiscal point of view, as from the proprietary and the political, the Balinese countryside was something of a check- erboard. One of the more exotic results of this was that it was pos- sible for a man to be a kawula of one lord, to be a land tenant of a second, and to pay taxes to a third.

The ground from which grew what V. E. Korn, who took it as self-evident that a proper state ought to have a proper sovereign, called "the great failing" (*de groote kwaal*) of the Balinese king- doms, "the lack of a powerful government over the whole realm," should now be coming fairly clearly into view. There was no unitary government, weak or powerful, over the whole realm at all. There was merely a knotted web of specific claims usually acknowledged.

The Politics of Irrigation

There remains, however, the vexed and critical problem, in light of

"Asiatic mode of production" theories affirming the inherently power-centralizing effects of hydraulic agriculture, of the relation of the lords to the organization and management of irrigation as such. Insofar as such organization and management existed, here also it was composed of the sedahans; so the issue comes down to the role of the sedahan, or more exactly the sedahan gdé, in the internal functioning of the irrigation societies. Was he, and the lord behind him, the administrative axis of the whole system—its planner, initiator, and general overseer, a kind of rice-field rajah? Or was he, and the lord behind him, essentially peripheral to it—a rent gatherer and tax collector who on occasion performed certain auxiliary functions of coordination, arbitration, and adjudication, these functions being entrusted to him by the irrigation society members, in whose hands effective and final control over agricultural decisions really lay?

There is, in my opinion, a short answer to these questions: the second view, a marginal exception here and there aside, is accurate; the first, an anomalous situation here and there aside, is not. But to see why this is so, and what the role of the negara in irrigation really was, and what it was not, something more needs to be said about the ecology of Balinese agriculture in general and about the social and technical organization of the irrigation society, the subak, in particular.

—2—

Technically, the Tabanan subak was entirely self-contained. It depended on no facilities over which it did not have direct control. There were no state-owned or state-managed waterworks of any sort, nor were there waterworks that were the property or responsibility of autonomous super-subak bodies of any sort. The whole apparatus—dams, canals, dikes, dividers, tunnels, aqueducts, reservoirs—upon which any particular landowner depended for his water supply was built, owned, managed, and maintained, sometimes exclusively, sometimes in partnership, by an independent corporation of which he was a full and, in legal terms anyway, equal member. Whatever else may be said about Bali from a Marxian point of view, there was no alienation of the basic means of production. The result was hardly primitive communism. But it was not primitive state captitalism—"total terror-total submission-total loneliness"—either.

As a productive unit, a subak may be defined (and the Balinese so define it) as all the rice terraces (*tebih*) irrigated from a single major water canal (*telabah gdé*). This canal, the property of the subak as a corporation, ran down from a single mud and stone dam (*émpelan*). In the case of the larger subaks, this dam might also belong wholly to the subak. Often, however, it was the property of several together, each of which presumably played a part in its construction, sometime in the more or less distant past, and now had a main canal running off from it. In such cases, responsibility for the dam's maintenance was allocated among the subaks concerned by some simple rotation scheme, and the share of each in the total water supply (that is, the relative size of the main canals) was fixed by custom.

As the dam, whether single or jointly owned, inevitably lay a fair distance upslope from the terraces it served (ten or fifteen kilometers in some cases), the main canal ran, often with the aid of very ingeniously constructed aqueducts and water tunnels, through, over, under, and around a good deal of intervening "foreign" territory. In very small subaks this canal might flow directly to the terraces, but in the overwhelming majority of the cases a major water divider (*temuku aya*) intervened as the canal approached the terraces and split it into two smaller canals (also called *telabah*). Farther downstream, these smaller canals were usually again divided in halves or thirds by a second rank of dividers (also called *temuku*), a process which in some cases was repeated yet another time. The final result of this preliminary, before-the-terrace water distribution was the creation of anywhere from one up to perhaps a dozen separate inlets to the terraces themselves. Each such inlet defined a distinct subsection of the subak, these subsections being called *tèmpèk*. How much such branching of the overall, main-canal water supply prior to its arrival at the terraces occurred, and thus how much internal division of the subak into subsections there was, depended primarily on the size of the canal, and secondarily on the topography of the area plus, to a certain extent, mere historical accident.

A schematic summary of preterrace irrigation works for a more or less typical subak is given in figure 4.

After the water reached the tèmpèk (that is to say, the terraces), it was further divided into halves, thirds, fourths, or very occasionally sixths. The canals thus produced defined the main sub-tèmpèk unit, usually called a *kecoran*. Within the kecoran, which could consist of anywhere from a half-dozen to as many as seventy or eighty terraces, smaller dividers were capable, given the mere rivulets they were by this stage faced with, of divisions as fine as a tenth; they

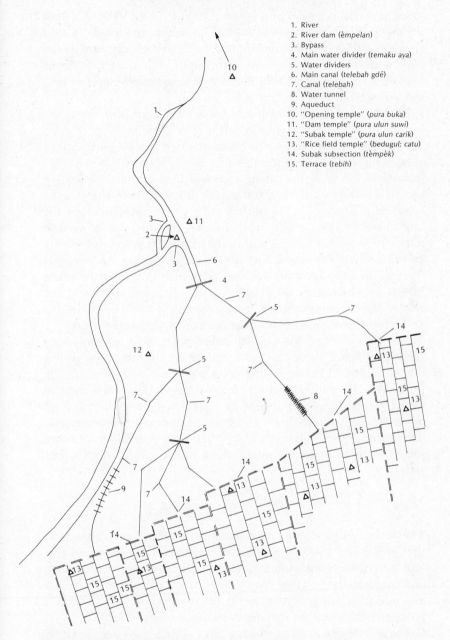

1. River
2. River dam (*èmpelan*)
3. Bypass
4. Main water divider (*temaku aya*)
5. Water dividers
6. Main canal (*telebah gdé*)
7. Canal (*telebah*)
8. Water tunnel
9. Aqueduct
10. "Opening temple" (*pura buka*)
11. "Dam temple" (*pura ulun suwi*)
12. "Subak temple" (*pura ulun carik*)
13. "Rice field temple" (*bedugul; catu*)
14. Subak subsection (*tèmpèk*)
15. Terrace (*tebih*)

Figure 4. Schematic Diagram of Preliminary Waterworks for a "Typical" Tabanan Subak

segmented the water out into terminal canals. These terminal canals then defined the fundamental unit of the subak: the *tenah*. Within any one subak, one tenah represented, in theory anyway, exactly the same share of the subak's total water supply, whatever that might be, either in general or from moment to moment; the overall grid was arranged to produce this equal division.

Figure 5 shows, again in model form, such a grid for the subak whose preterraced structure was outlined in figure 4.

This figure represents, however, an observer's, not a participant's view of the system. For a member of a subak, it was not a matter of looking at the whole as having a certain large number of parts— 240, or whatever—and then tracing the distribution of them downwards to the tenah, but of starting with the tenah, which was the immediately known reality, and moving upwards. Assuming that distribution among terraces within the tenah had been satisfactorily arranged, the member was first concerned to see that the proximal (that is, the intra-kecoran) divisions were just; then that they were just at the kecoran, or intra-tèmpèk level; then that they were just at the tèmpèk, or intra-subak level; and finally that they were just at the subak level as a whole—that is, at the main canal dividers.

The formal resemblance, which anthropologists at least will have noticed, of figure 5 to a chart of a segmentary kinship system is thus not accidental. The organizing principle is the same, though the idiom and the field of application are different: there is a complementary opposition of units (divider-and-canal-defined) at each level of the system, from the most elemental to the most comprehensive. The whole system is one in which *structurally* equivalent units are joined in an ascending pyramid of, in this case, jural rights over water.

— 3 —

The social, political, and religious organization of the subak, and thus of wet rice agriculture generally, paralleled this technical pattern of irrigation with some exactness. The structure of the subak as a corporate body was given by (or if that be too deterministic a way to put it, was congruent with) the structure of the subak as a physical mechanism for moving water from rivers to fields.

The immediate tasks of wet rice agriculture—plowing, flooding, sowing, transplanting, weeding, watering, harvesting, and so on— were organized and carried out at the lowest level of the system, that of the individual, privately owned terrace or complex of ter-

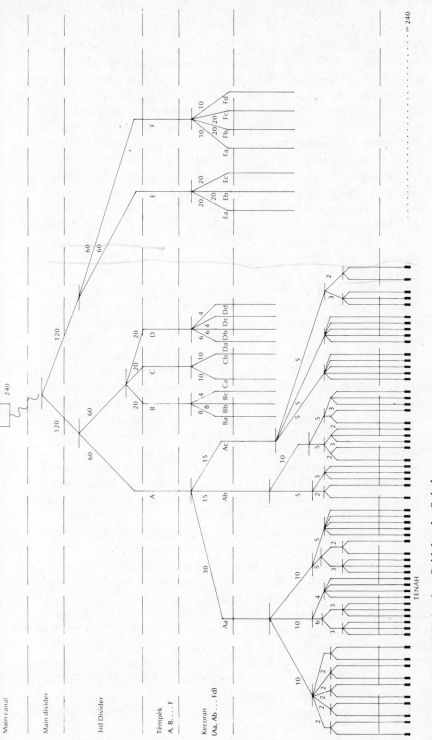

Figure 5. A Model Irrigation Grid for the Subak

races (that is, more or less, the tenah, the "minimal segmentation" level in figure 5). So too were the social arrangements necessary to accomplish them—sharecropping, land renting or pawning, exchange labor, group work, and so on. At this elemental level, the subak as a corporate unit played no active role; it merely set the context within which the individual peasant, on his own land his own master, was obliged to work. The subak never acted (and this seems to be one of the few flat statements one can venture about Bali) as a productive organization in the proper sense. It regulated irrigation, and in order to do so it exercised important constraints on the decisions of the individual cultivator. But the actual process of cultivation within those constraints has always been a matter beyond both its competence and its interest. The subak was, and is, a technically specialized, cooperatively owned public utility, not a collective farm.

The routine, day-to-day technical work required by this kind of irrigation system was mainly accomplished on what one might call, following out our segmentary-system image, the medial levels of organization—that is, the tèmpèk and kecoran levels. At these levels were formed what the Balinese call *seka yèh*, "water teams"—groups of men, members of the subak, who were delegated by the subak membership as a whole to carry out these everyday duties and recompensed accordingly—either in kind, in cash, or by exemption from various subak taxes and contributions. Balanced in their location within the subak, and usually rotating their duty days, the members of the water team performed what must have been, by a conservative estimate, ninety percent of the labor connected with water control in the subak. The water-team members, headed by an official elected from among them, the *klian seka yèh*, formed the technical heart of the subak.

The subak level of organization was mainly concerned with policy matters and with (very) occasional mass labor efforts. The former had to do with such things as setting and collecting subak taxes; levying fines for rule infractions; paying the water team and generally governing its activities; deciding to add or subtract terraces; rearranging the canal grid (virtually always minor changes); recording and regulating land transfers; settling disputes among members; and conducting "foreign relations" vis-à-vis other subaks in the same drainage. The latter had to do with repairs to the main dam and the preterrace canal system that were too extensive for the water team to accomplish unaided.

The social expression of this level of organization was the *krama subak*—the group of all persons owning terraces in the subak. The krama subak, all of whose members had the same legal rights no matter what the size of their holdings, usually met once a Balinese month, in plenary session. The head of this body, and thus of the subak as a whole, was, as has already been mentioned, the klian subak, a man chosen (usually by formal election) from among the subak membership. The krama subak, headed by its klian subak, was thus the operative government of the subak. It was here, no higher and no lower, that effective sovereignty over "the water hamlet" resided. As the water team, with its klian, was the technical heart of the subak, so the krama subak, with its klian, was the political heart.

— 4 —

With each of the three levels of organization so far discussed—the terrace, the intra-subak, and the subak—were associated as well certain ritual activities. At the terrace level, these activities consisted mainly of small flower and food offerings placed at the terrace corners on calendrically appropriate days, at certain points in the cultivation cycle, or even as mood and circumstance suggested; and also of certain rites in the terraces themselves connected with planting, harvesting, and so on. The rituals were, again, "individual"— that is, directed toward the welfare of the owner, the productivity of the particular terrace or terraces in question. At the tèmpèk/ kecoran level they consisted of similar activities conducted at small stone altars, called *bedugul* (see figure 4, above), by the klian seka yèh and the water team, on behalf of the relevant subgroup. Placed near important water dividers (that is, ones defining important sub-subak units), beduguls were considered "way stations" or "reduced versions" of the main subak temple—the *Pura Ulun Carik*; and it was at the subak level that the ritual center of gravity, like the political, really lay.

The *Pura Ulun Carik*, literally "head of the rice (fields) temple," was usually located either near the preterrace grid as in figure 4— that is, above the fields as such—or in a clearing toward the upper end of the fields. It was a temple, a pura, rather than merely an altar, because it had a once-a-Balinese-year celebration day, a day when the gods descend to be feted—and had attached to it a regular temple priest, or *pemangku*. Again, the ritual details need not be described here, save to note that, from the bottom of the system to the top, from the terrace level to that of the still-to-be-described drainage-region level, the essential elements—versions of the rice-mother/rice-wedding cult—were basically the same, differing mainly in degree of elaboration, in manner or performance, and, most significantly, in range of social reference. Here, that range was the subak as a whole. The Pura Ulun Carik ceremonies spread their beneficence over the subak generally and were conducted by the temple priests in the subak's name, with the support and assistance of its entire membership. The Pura Ulun Carik was thus the subak temple par excellence. It was the expression of its moral unity and the symbol of its material purpose.

There were, however, two other temples of immediate relevance at the subak level of organization. One, which has already been mentioned in connection with hamlet religious life, was the Pura Balai Agung, a "village temple" which was dedicated to the fertility not only of irrigated fields and unirrigated (that is, gardens, coconut groves, and other plots lying outside the subak) alike, but also of the women of the "custom village" area as well. From the point of view of the subak, then, the Pura Balai Agung symbolized the general connection of what went on in the subak, irrigated agriculture; and what went on in the hamlet, everyday social, political and economic life. It, and the ceremonies given in it, formed a bridge between the "wet" hamlet and the "dry" one, the banjar, and thus placed the subak within the general "composite," "pluralistic," or "overlapping and intersecting planes" village system of Bali already described. Second, there was the "head of the waters" temple, the *Pura Ulun Suwi*, located at or near the main dam of the subak (see figure 4). It was at this temple that the gods of water resided, or more accurately, resided when they visited; and here, as we shall see presently, a "season opening" ritual meshed the individual subak into a drainagewide ecological system.

Thus, the three subak temples, like the three hamlet temples (the Pura Balai Agung being a member of both sets) symbolized and, even more important, *regulated* different aspects of the relevant social unit's activities. The Pura Ulun Carik symbolized the subak as a set of rice terraces, a cultivation unit. The Pura Ulun Suwi symbolized it as part of a larger, regional ecological system. And the Pura Balai Agung symbolized it (from the subak perspective) as part of the overall local social-political-jural-economic system, the "desa" in the broadest, most general, "not-negara" sense of the term—as a *moral* community.

All this discussion of temple types and levels of ritual activity is not, however, just so much ethnological detail, for the activities in those temples (or altars or terraces) provided the subak system as a whole with the mechanisms of coordination it needed in order to function. It was not highly centralized political institutions controlling massive waterworks and huge gangs of coolie labor, "Hydraulic Bureaucracies" run by "Asiatic Despots" pursuing "Total Power," which enabled the Balinese irrigation system to work and which gave it form and order. It was a sociologically stratified, spatially dispersed, administratively decentralized, and morally coercive body of ritual obligations. It is at the supra-subak, drainage-area (what the Balinese usually call the *kesedahan*) level, where problems of coordination reached their maximum scale, that this fact becomes particularly clear and, for an understanding of the Balinese state, particularly important.

To give a more concrete sense of what the relation "on the ground" among subaks is like in Tabanan, I have diagrammed, in figures 6-10, five local areas at different altitudes, ranging from the seacoast, with its large, densely packed subaks, to the upper edge of the rice-growing area, with its small, scattered ones.

— 5 —

The kesedahan level of irrigation organization differed from the levels which we have been discussing, subak and sub-subak, in several critical respects. In the first place, there was no corporate group, like the water team or the subak membership, associated with it. There was just the collection of sedahan and sedahan-agung rent masters and tax gatherers already described, their loyalties running off to different lords and their bailiwicks scattered irregularly over the landscape. Second, at least in part as a result of this scattering, there were no genuinely bounded units at this level, merely a general sense that subaks sharing water from a single river system faced a certain necessity of at least minimally coordinating their activites. And third, there were, some special exceptions which will be touched on later aside, no established, well-organized, and repetitive technical tasks at this level. If ninety percent or so of Balinese irrigation labor was performed by the water team, probably another nine percent was performed by the subak members as a body, leaving, say, one percent or so, and that intermittent, to be performed by a plurality of subaks in concert.

In short, what there was at this apical level of the system was a set of state revenue officials—the sedahans, ordinary and "gdé"—and an elaborate, regionwide, largely self-propelled ritual system, a highly

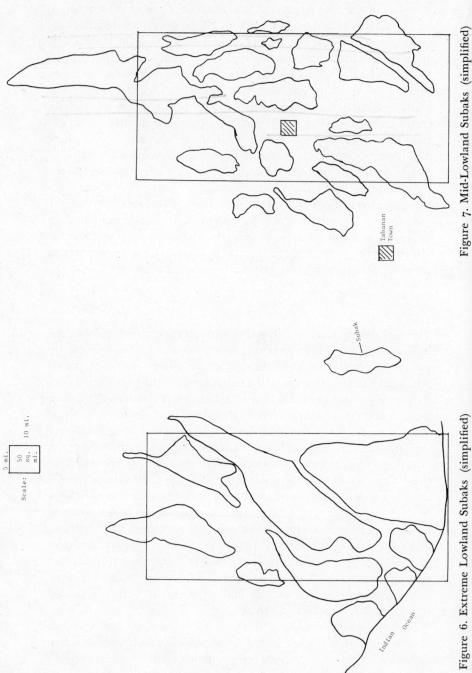

Figure 7. Mid-Lowland Subaks (simplified)

Tabanan
Town

Subak

Scale: 5 mi.

50 sq. mi. 10 mi.

Indian Ocean

Figure 6. Extreme Lowland Subaks (simplified)

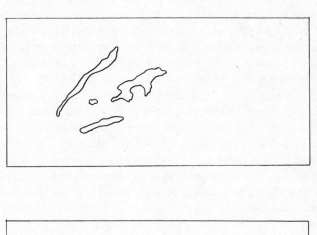

Figure 10. Extreme Highland Subaks (simplified)

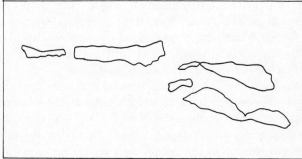

Figure 9. Mid-Highland Subaks (simplified)

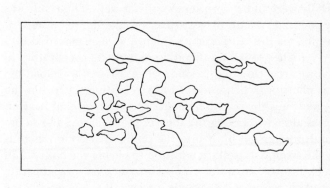

Figure 8. High-Lowland (or low-highland) Subaks (simplified)

traditionalized rice-field cult, of which, in a quite symbolic and almost incidental way, these officials were the formal leaders.

In nineteenth-century Tabanan (and, with some adjustments, still today) this rice-field cult consisted of nine major, named stages, these stages following one another in a fixed order at a pace generally determined, once the first stage was initiated, by the ecological rhythms of growing rice. This cult was uniform over the whole of Tabanan (that it so say, uniform in its *structure*; there were, as usual, wide variations in ritual content); and it refracted to all levels of the system, from the terrace to the supra-subak. The nine stages were: (1) Water Opening; (2) Terrace Opening; (3) Planting; (4) Purifying the Water; (5) Feeding the Gods, a once-a-Balinese-month celebration in which holy water from the subak temple, the Pura Ulun Carik, was taken by each owner to his fields, and various flower and food offerings were made. (As this ceremony was repeated every thirty-five days through the whole cultivation cycle, it was perhaps not properly a separate stage.); (6) Budding of the Rice Plants (which occurs about a hundred days or so after planting); (7) Yellowing (that is, approaching fruition) of the Rice; (8) Harvest; (9) Placing the Harvested Rice in the Granary.

Now, the Water-Opening day for the various subaks in the drainage—that is, the day on which water was diverted, at the dam, into the subak's main canal—was staggered in such a way that the higher the subak along the mountain-to-sea gradient, the earlier the opening day. Subaks at the top of the system thus began the ceremonial cycle, and with it the cultivation sequence, in December; subaks at the bottom, near the coast, began it in April; and those in between topographically were in between temporally as well. The result was that, at any one time, the drainage area as a whole showed a step-by-step progression in the cultivation sequence as one moved downslope. When a higher subak was flooding its terraces preparatory to plowing, a lower was clearing its land; when a lower was flooding, a higher was planting; when a lower was celebrating the Yellowing of the Rice, and thus the promise, about a month hence, of harvest, the higher was already carrying the sheaves to the barns; and so on. The temporal progression built into the ceremonial cycle was thus laid out on the ground as well: in addition to pacing the cultivation sequence in each subak separately, it also intermeshed those separate sequences in such a way as to provide an overall sequence for the region as a whole.

The main ecological effect of this system (and, though it must have evolved, like the American city or British common law, in a fairly unselfconscious, case-to-case adjustment fashion), its main ecological purpose, was to stabilize the demands upon the central resource, water, over the crop year, rather than allowing its use to fluctuate widely, as it would in the absence of such a system. Simplifying somewhat, terraced wet rice growing requires maximum water input at, or just after, the initiation of the cycle, and then a steadily decreasing input as the cycle proceeds, until, at the end, harvesting is carried out in a fully drained, dry field. If the cycles of the various subaks in a single drainage (or, worse yet, along a single river) were coincident, the result would be that water resources would be enormously overtaxed during the earlier phases of the cycle and about as enormously underutilized during the later one, especially as, again simplifying slightly, the amount of water naturally available does not vary widely over the year, particularly over the half of the year in which rice is grown. Indeed, as water is the central limiting factor in the subak ecosystem, if the subak cycles were not staggered, wet rice cultivation in Bali could never have attained a fraction of its nineteenth-century extent.

The initiation of the whole cycle began with an all-Tabanan Water-Opening ritual at the most important "all-Bali" temple in the region, far up the forested sides of the sacred mountain which dominates the Tabanan area both physically and spiritually: Batu Kau. Under the symbolic leadership of the sedahan gdé from Puri Gdé (that is, the ranking sedahan of the ranking house), a ceremony —attended by all the sedahans, all the heads of the subaks in the region, all the priests of the subak temples, and any individual subak member pious enough to make the arduous journey up the mountain on his own, as well as, of course, by the appropriate god and goddess invited down for the occasion from the skies—was conducted in order to secure sufficient and "effective" water for all the terraces in the realm during the coming season. With this "Opening of Openings," also of course calendrically determined, the cycle for the whole region was set in motion; for the various Water-Opening temples in each subak, the Pura Ulun Suwis, then followed at the appropriate intervals with their own, by and large, identical ceremonies. The sedahans, as a loose, noncorporate (indeed, internally rivalrous) group, thus set the water-use sequence for the region in motion in the act of consecrating it. But after it was so set in motion, the system ran by itself, by its own momentum, and produced its own, quite local, quite independent, replica ceremonies of consecration.

In sum, if one took a Balinese god's-eye view of this system (that is to say, from somewhere above the Mount Agung crater, where the gods live), one would see a set of structurally similar (indeed, some content variations aside, identical) ritual sequences proceeding simultaneously in various parts of the landscape and at various levels of organization from the drainage region to the individual terrace.

But though these sequences would all be proceeding at approximately the same pace and through the same stages, they would not all be in phase with one another. On the supra-subak level they would be staggered temporally, from the top of the drainage system to the bottom. On the subak level and below they would be coordinate temporally: when the Budding of the Rice Plants was being celebrated by the subak priest in the subak temple, it was also being celebrated by the water-team members at the tèmpèk and kecoran altars, and by the individual landowners in their separate fields. The resultant picture would thus reveal a collection of locally phased agricultural cycles locked into an overarching regional cycle. For all-Tabanan there would be the paradigmatic, state-legitimized, purely ceremonial cycle at Pura Batu Kau, which, as it lay above the rice-growing line, was unconnected with any particular subak and thus any particular cultivation cycle. And in each subak, on all its levels, there would be the appropriately timed replication of this "exemplary center" ceremonial cycle, tied now to a specific cultivation cycle. In such a way, a complex ecological order was both reflected in and shaped by an equally complex ritual order, which at once grew out of it and was imposed upon it. The comment of the second-century *Chinese Record of Rituals*, "rites obviate disorder as dikes prevent inundation," finds an exact application in Bali.

— 6 —

Yet it would clearly not do to take a too "preestablished-harmony" view of inter-subak relationships, especially since in fact they were often very far from harmonious. From our god's-eye view, the whole cycle of cultivation might look like one huge, ceremonially paced process refracted over and over throughout the whole region. From a peasant's-eye view, however, the larger rhythm, taken, like the very workings of nature, more or less for granted, would be less apparent than local disturbances of it.

The ceremonial system provided a general coordinating frame within which the subaks could regulate their work without intensive applications of coercive power from a centralized state, but it did not in itself resolve the day-to-day problems of adjustment which inevitably arose within that frame. Just as, in a particular subak, a particular cultivator had to adjust his activities to those of his immediate neighbors, either personally or through the mechanisms of subak government; so also, among subaks, each subak had to adjust its activities to those of its immediate neighbors. Indeed, it was only because the mechanisms for such subregional adjustment were so well developed, and, an exception now and then aside, so effective, that regional coordination could be accomplished through the agency of a ceremonial system which was only minimally reinforced by superordinate political authority. Anyway, most of the political tension generated by the intensely particulate structure of the subak system was absorbed in parochial, case-by-case, ad hoc settlements between the subaks themselves, rather than rising to more exalted, and more explosive, levels of the system.

Here, rather as with the treaties between states already discussed, the main framework for such case-by-case adjustment was a very highly developed, almost obsessively specific collection of customary practices—established precedents which, though there was no superordinate political body to enforce them, had nonetheless the force of law, if only because they provided a dictionary of legitimate, agreed-upon grievances one subak might have against another.

The number of these "customary laws" was extremely great, and their content varied widely from place to place. They covered such matters as the quantity of water which must at all times be allowed to flow past the dam (that is to say, even at terrace-flooding time the river could not be completely diverted, the reason for the permanent bypass shown in figure 4); prohibitions against polluting the water; ways and places in which dams, tunnels, aqueducts, canals, reservoirs, and other works could be built; water divisions and labor obligations when two or more subaks were linked to a single dam; rules for borrowing, lending, pawning, renting, and selling water among subaks; rules for the disposition of overflow and for redrainage into the river; fishing regulations; rights of human and animal passage across "foreign" fields; procedures for negotiating disputes; fines for infractions of all these various rules; dates of temple festivals; and so on and so forth down, it often seems, to a nearly all-eventualities level of detail. The Balinese seem rarely to have been faced with a situation without an applicable "law," or at least some sort of rule from which they could plausibly draw an analogy.

For routine cases, which were of course the vast majority, intra-subak arrangements were conducted in terms of these rules by the appropriate subak heads and their staffs, perhaps with a few other leading citizens of the subak—larger landholders, especially knowledgeable elders, men of general influence and standing, or whatever —in attendance. Occasionally, for more important issues—adding new terraces, changing the water distribution, and so on—the entire membership of each subak might meet in joint session and talk the matter out in the usual "sense of the meeting" manner. Occasionally, too, one or another sedahan, especially if he was a liked, trusted, and intelligent one, might be prevailed upon to act as a neutral mediator, or even an arbiter. But in no way did the sedahans act as judges in the proper sense, as individuals with authority to offer binding, enforceable decisions. When and if they were asked, they merely gave advice, which might or might not be accepted by the parties involved. Whether conducted among members of the subak elites directly, between the subak members as a whole, or with the assistance of a sedahan as a go-between and counselor, the process was one of mutual adjustment in terms of an established body of indefeasible custom, a process the Balinese call *rukun*—a potent, virtually untranslatable term which means something like: "the creation of concord," "the harmonization of wills," "the establishment of peace," "the attainment of unity."

All this is not to say that subak politics were absolutely democratic or that they led inevitably to equitable solutions, even in Balinese eyes. Certainly wealth, social status, personal power, and so on played critical roles in the actual determination, both between subaks and within them, of who got what, when, where, and how. But these familiar realities played their role in the subak and intersubak legal-political system, not in the state apparatus, which, beyond the points already mentioned (taxation, ritual, occasional mediation) and one or two others still to be touched upon, was not officially concerned with these matters. In fact, it was explicitly excluded from them.

Also, and even more important, to describe how rukun was pursued is not to say that these local mechanisms of adjustment, as elaborate and carefully designed as they were, worked to anything approaching perfection. On the contrary, physical violence between whole subaks or certain members of them seems to have been very common, as the inclusion, in the customary "water laws," of indemnities for property damage and for personal injury resulting from such violence attests. Pitched battles between groups of peasants, often enough wielding their hoes as weapons, occurred with some regularity. Less often but still frequently enough, so did chronic feuds, extended incidents leading one to the next. And, when such conflicts spread beyond local confines, they could and did involve the higher reaches of the political system, whose mutually rivalrous members were usually more than willing to fish in troubled paddies, thereby bringing on genuine wars—military encounters among the adherents of competing lords. Conflicts between subaks, or at least conflicts that began as such, were far from the least significant sources of the steady hum of political violence which plagued the Balinese state all through the nineteenth century and, on the evidence of inscriptions, probably through the whole course of its history.

— 7 —

As a polity, then, or part of a polity, the subak system was what anthropologists have come to call acephalous—"headless." Rather than centering on a concentrated locus of power and authority, which would be at once its axis and its anchor, it consisted instead of an ascending set of social tiers balanced, at each level and in each dimension, one against another. The most important of such social tiers, or levels, were in the individual terrace or terrace complex; the intra- or sub-subak; the subak proper; and the inter- or supra-subak. As one moved from the bottom of this system toward the top, one moved from a narrower range of social relevance to a wider one; from a more explicitly technical focus on cultivation or irrigation to a more integrative focus on what were essentially ritual-legal rather than bureaucratic-administrative matters; and from solid, well-equilibrated social forms to more fragile and explosive ones.

The political center of gravity sat very low in this system, as it does in all such systems, and as it did in the Balinese state generally. As the negara was stretched taut between the centripetal forces of state ritual and the centrifugal ones of state structure, so the subak system, one of the bases on which the negara rested, was stretched tight between its dispersive, segmentary, particulate nature as a concrete socioeconomic institution and the integrative demands placed upon it by the rice cult. Here too culture came from the top down (given the location of Batu Kau, it came down both physically and literally), while power welled up from the bottom.

I have sought to diagram this system, and thus to summarize the preceding discussion, in table 1.

Table 1

The Irrigation-Society (Subak) System

	Structural Level			
	Inter-Subak (kesedahan)*	Subak	Intra-Subak (tèmpèk, kecoran)	Terrace (tebih, tenah)‡
Corporate group	None	All the landowners of the subak (krama subak)	Water team (seka yèh)	Privately organized cultivation groups
Responsible officer	Tax/rent collector (sedahan, sedahan gdé)	Subak chief (klian subak, pekasih)	Water-team chief (klian seka yèh)	Peasant/owner (tani)
Main work tasks	None†	Setting general policies; occasional collective work on dam, major canals, etc.; collection and disbursement of subak funds; enforcement of rules	Steady, day-to-day labor controlling water flow, repairing works, etc.	Cultivation (including regulation of water within terrace, etc.)
Main institutional mechanisms	Customary water laws (adat yèh); mutual adjustment (rukun); mediation; violence	Written constitutions (awig-awig, kertasima); subak meetings; chief's staff (section heads, heralds, temple priests, etc.)	Duty rotation; payment for work	Exchange work, share tenancy, wage labor, collective labor, etc.
Associated ritual activities	Regionwide: staged coordination rites, centered on all-Bali temple (Pura Batu Kau)	Temple celebrations in subak temples (Pura Ulun Carik, Pura Ulun Suwi, Pura Balai Agung)	Periodic offerings at grid-marking altars (bedugul, catu)	Rice field offerings and celebrations

* Only the most common vernacular terms for the Tabanan area are given. Where no terms are given, there either are no special terms or usage is too varied and complicated to be easily summarized.

† Very occasionally, joint work on joint facilities was undertaken by two or three subaks in concert, but this was rare. Subak unions, also rare, occasionally were found as well.

‡ Tebih is the literal term for terrace. Tenah refers to the final water-division unit and may include one or several terraces, or very occasionally a fraction of a terrace.

The Forms of Trade

As has been suggested earlier, commerce in classical Bali, though definitely in the negara, was not altogether of it. Not only was the bulk of it in foreign hands (Chinese, Javanese, Buginese, on occasion European), but also it was connected to political life eccentrically—through a set of extremely specialized institutions designed at once to contain its dynamic and to capture its returns. The lords were not unmindful of the material advantages to be got from trade; but they were not unmindful either that, in reaching for them, they risked the very foundations of their power. Grasping by habit, they were autarchic by instinct, and the result was a certain baroqueness of economic arrangement.

Essentially, there were four main institutional complexes channeling the flow of trade in nineteenth-century Bali: (1) rotating markets, (2) traditionally fixed exchange relationships, (3) redistributive ceremonies, and (4) politically insulated "ports of trade." From the point of view of the negara as such, though not necessarily of the population as a whole, the first two were relatively unimportant, and the third is more naturally treated under the rubric of state ritual. I shall therefore concentrate here on the fourth, and in particular on its role within the life of the negara.

— 2 —

The port of trade is a site usually, but not necessarily, coastal or riverain, set aside as a politically neutral meeting place for foreign traders. It is about as old and about as widespread in Indonesia as the negara itself. Indeed, most of the earliest Indonesian negaras— Sriwijaya, Jambi, Taruma, Sindok's unnamed kingdom in Eastern Java—were "thalassocratic" bazaar states, built upon their capacity to defend and administer such ports. Long-distance, high-margin trade is, as J. C. van Leur has demonstrated, "an historical constant" in Indonesia; the spice-trade explosion of the sixteenth and seventeenth centuries, which brought on colonial rule, is merely that "constant's" most visible and dramatic representation. From very near the time of Christ until very near our own, the sort of adventurer merchantry that Gibbon characterized as "splendid and trifling" gave to the archipelago a unity in commerce it lacked in language, culture, politics, race, or religion.

So far as Bali is concerned, the critical fact is that in large part it looked away from this trade. It faced south toward the Indian Ocean, where, given poor harbors and rough seas, there was hardly any traffic, rather than north toward the Java Sea, the Asian Mediterranean around which Chinese, Indian, Arabic, Javanese, Buginese, Malay, and European merchants shuttled like so many itinerant street peddlers. Much of Bali's reputation for seclusion and isolation stems from this fact. In an international sea-rover's world, where the great names are Malacca, Jambi, Palembang, Bantam, Banjermasin, Japara, Tuban, and Makassar, it seems almost not to exist.

— 3 —

There was one north-coast harbor, of course: Singaraja, the port of trade for Bulèlèng. And, though it never seems to have been of major significance in the life of the Indonesian sea emporium, it does become faintly visible now and then in the history of that life. "Balinese from Bulèlèng" are referred to as allied with the Javanese port kingdom of Surabaya in its war against the Dutch East Indies Company in 1718 (though they are also said to have gotten sick and gone home) and are said to have controlled Blambangan, the Javanese kingdom guarding the far side of the Bali Strait, between 1697 and 1711. B.J.O. Schrieke refers frequently to the importance of Balinese cloth in the Java-Moluccas trade of the sixteenth and seventeenth centuries, as well as to the export of rice eastward from the island.

In 1814, T. S. Raffles, in place as (lieutenant) governor general as a result of the Napoleonic wars, is said to have been "forced to act in Bali" (though, in the event, he did not) because the "Rajah of Baliling" had seized an East Indies Company ship. In 1846 the Dutch did act, in response to a similar opportunity (the plundering of a stranded Dutch ship), and, after a series of ultimatums and expeditions, established a fort-cum-factory there in 1849. Finally, in 1859, P. L. van Bloemen Waanders, the Dutch governor of the place, described the Bulèlèng-Singaraja port of trade as the entrepôt for the whole island, exporting about 300,000 and importing about 500,000 florins' worth of goods a year. The trade was leased by "the king" (i.e., the lords) to seven Chinese "trade lords" (subandar) according to "trade realms" (kebandaran), within which they were granted monopoly privileges; actual trading was carried out by them, other Chinese dependent upon them, and by Bugis and Madurese proa drivers contracted to them. The exports were mainly rice (36% by value); coffee (13%); tobacco (12%); soya beans (11%); animals (9%)—beef mainly, some pigs and horses; with the remainder accounted for by cotton, coconut products, and various odds and ends. The imports were mainly opium (87%!) and cotton textiles (6%), the rest being taken up by iron, chinaware, gold work, and various sorts of spices.

— 4 —

But although the Singaraja port of trade was the only commercial center of any importance on Bali throughout most of the island's history (and, in the context of the larger Indonesian bazaar-state economy, of distinctly minor importance at that), after the Dutch established themselves there in the mid-nineteenth century the world of international trade finally began to penetrate the heartland of the country, the south, and to do so with gathering force. By 1876, Bangli, a place which "thirty years ago was the poorest on the island," is said to have reached an annual turnover of 300,000 florins. A quarter of a century later, in 1900, Karengasem had a hundred Chinese importing opium and exporting coffee, sugar, indigo, and kapok (i.e., Java-type "plantation products," only here grown, small-holder style, on rice terraces during the off-monsoon). Kasumba, a small fishing village on the south coast of Klungkung, had already begun to develop into a proper port. And the Chinese population of our type case, Tabanan, had risen to over four hundred, some of whom actually owned private coffee plantations, having bought them outright, as "wastelands," from the lords.

But of all the port-of-trade developments of the nineteenth century, the most significant, the most dramatic, and, fortunately, the most vividly described is that which took place at Kuta, on the coast south of Badung, between 1839 and 1856 under the leadership of the Danish merchant adventurer Mads Lange.

Lange, who first shipped to the Indies at the age of seventeen and spent the remainder of his life there, actually began his operations in the Balinese-dominated region of the neighboring island of Lombok. Appointed subandar to one of the two major lords there in 1834 (he displaced a Chinese, a sign in itself that things were changing), he soon found himself counterposed to an English equivalent, a certain George King, who was appointed within the year to the other lord. When the two lords, urged on by their respective "white rajahs," plunged into war with one another, the Europeans advanced their careers by running arms to their patrons, until, his man defeated, Lange fled to Bali, established his factory at Kuta in 1839, and maintained it until his death, at forty-nine, in 1856. For fifteen years—its prosperity did not outlive him—Kuta became south Bali's first genuinely significant port of trade, even rivaling Singaraja, where, during the same period, the Dutch were getting themselves solidly established.

Kuta lay five miles south of what was, during this period, probably Bali's largest and certainly its most extravagent court, Badung, on the pinched thread of land by which Bukit, the desolate, clubfoot plateau that forms the country's southern extremity, somehow hangs on to the rest of the island (see map 4). There were two harbors, each about a mile from Lange's headquarters, on either side of this thread, which he used alternately according to the change of the monsoons. By 1843, he had fifteen ships of his own, some as large as 1,500 tons, which he kept constantly moving around in the eastern

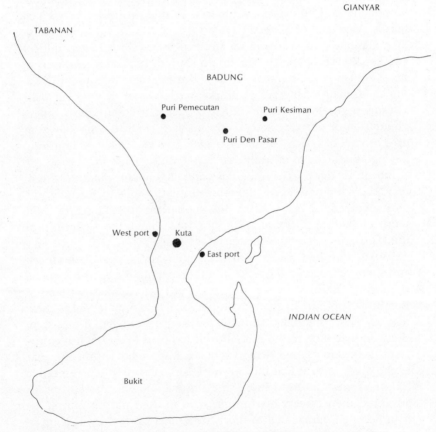

Map 4. The Kuta Port of Trade (after Nieuwenkamp, 1906-10, p. 169)

archipelago, buying here and selling there. But, more important, "hardly a day passed [writes Lange's young assistant, Ludvig Helms] in which some [foreign] vessel did not turn up"—Dutch, French, English, Chinese, Arab, Buginese, Malay—loading coffee, rice, tobacco, coconut oil, ponies, oxen, dried beef, pigs, and "all sorts of poultry and fancy birds," and leaving, so far as one can make out from Helms's description (which, reflecting the mentality of the port, is infinitely more attentive to exports than imports), largely Chinese opium, Chinese porcelain, and Chinese coins.

The coins (the already mentioned *kèpèng*, small bronze discs with a hole in the center) were the immediate currency of the whole local trade, and their handling was one of the most prominent, most laborious, and most profitable activities of the port. They were bought in China, by weight, at about 1,200 to 1,400 for a Dutch dollar. Carried to Kuta in Chinese ships, "thousands of bags" at a time, they then had to be recounted and put on strings, 200 to a string, by Balinese women. So parceled, they were used as means of payment at the rate of 700 per dollar (hence the profit) in a system of essentially fixed equivalencies: "so many measures, so many pice." "It may be worth mentioning," says Helms, who knows very well it is extremely worth mentioning, "that the great staples . . . were received at a uniform price . . . and this price seldom varied, whatever might be the state of European markets or the fluctuation of prices in other places."

Thus, in addition to the most remarked general features of port-of-trade enclaves (political insulation, an international orientation, and domination of commerce by "minorities" or "foreigners," *marchands protégés* to local powers), Kuta also possessed the less remarked but equally diagnostic features of customary equivalencies, administered prices, and interiorized money. Customary equivalencies, in that relative values of major goods (coffee and rice, oxen and opium) were settled in terms of locally established expectations that, once in place, were not readily upset by overall market changes. Administered prices, in that the monetary expression of these equivalencies ("so many measures, so many pice") was merely decreed by Lange, in terms of his estimate of what it cost him to provide the place with coins, and what profit he might make out of doing so (prices were, in Polanyi's phrase, the preconditions of trade, not the results of it). And interiorized money, in that kèpèngs, though purchased from abroad and found all over Southeast Asia, functioned as the means of payment in this particular port of trade independently of their (or any other moneys') functioning in others.

Kuta was, then, for all its cosmopolitan connections and its local dependencies, an economic cosmos all its own. Men came—in ships from overseas, on foot or horseback from around the island—to procure goods there, and the double protégé Lange (whom both the Dutch East Indies government and the lords of Badung referred to as "our subandar") tried to arrange matters so that they could. When he was able to, the port prospered, and so did he; when he was not, it languished, and so did he.

— 5 —

While Kuta's prosperity lasted, however, it was an element (for a few years perhaps the most dynamic element) in the general explosion of commercial life that, long after it had taken place in most other parts of the archipelago, brought Bali out of the fifteenth century and the negara and into the twentieth and the *Binnenlandsch Bestuur*. Helms is doubtless all too accurate when he says, "we had little social intercourse with the Balinese; indeed they lived in so poor a way as not to hold out much inducement to visit them." But the impact of Kuta, and of the trade expansion generally, upon the lives of those unvisited multitudes, was nonetheless profound and, in the *puputan* end, a half century on, revolutionary.

For the lords "protecting" it, Kuta was a source of tribute, of luxuries to decorate the theatre state. For the merchants visiting it, it was the teats through which the substance of the countryside was sucked (as an unceremonious Portuguese navigator, comparing Java to a mother pig, described that island's sixteenth-century ports of trade). For Lange, with "more of the bold Viking than the prudent trader in his nature," it provided an opportunity to play Lord Jim rather later in time than was practicable in most other places in the archipelago. But for the negara as such it was the beginning, or better the middle, of the end. Like Singaraja, and to a much lesser extent Kasumba, Kuta was the unwitting *voorlooper* (way paver, ground layer) for the political force—Disraelian Europe—to which the Old Order, having withstood Islam, the East India Company, and plantation colonialism, finally surrendered.

The impact of Kuta upon the general population took place both through the involvement of natives in the work of the port proper and through the spreading of what one can only call, to avoid more colloquial terms, "the Spirit of Commerce" throughout the whole of southern Bali.

Most of the Balinese who were directly involved in the work of

92

the port were women. Not only did they count and string the kèpèngs; they also were entrusted ("of course, under careful supervision") with measuring and paying for the produce brought into the port by local traders. And those traders who were not Chinese— as were the more considerable ones, whose traffic Helms handled himself—were also women, a matter on which he is even more eloquent than usual:

Meanwhile [that is, during Helms's breakfast; he is describing his daily round] strings of ponies had been converging from different parts of the country towards our factory, each carrying four baskets filled with the produce of the island. Each little caravan was attended by the owner, usually a woman, and the day's work now fairly commenced; by seven o'clock all were at work. Measuring, weighing and packing went on rapidly, and long rows of carts carried bags, bales, and casks to the seashore. . . .

But a more exciting branch of our commerce was that dealing with live cargoes. . . . When the order was given for the loading of one of these vessels [French animal ships—"veritable Noah's arks"—from Mauritius], it was only necessary to send a few days in advance to a dozen or so of the Balinese ladies, who acted as our agents in such matters, and on the appointed day the beach near which the vessel lay would be crowded with many times the number of animals wanted, from which the selection was then made.

The leading part taken by the women in all these transactions was a peculiar feature in Balinese life; but their business capacities justified the confidence of their lords and masters . . . and when shipments of live stock had to be got ready, it required some discretion to distribute patronage amongst our friends to their satisfaction.

When a half-a-dozen ladies arrived, each with a following of slaves, who, on such occasions, would carry propitiary offerings on their heads, in the shape of baskets of delicious fruit, it was difficult to hold the scales so as to satisfy all. Here, for instance, is a fat, insinuating little woman, commonly called by us Anak Agung, "Child of the Great One" [in fact, it is a noble title, literally meaning "Great Personage"]. She is the wife of Gusti Mate [properly, "Madé"; "Gusti" is also a triwangsa title], a noble of rank. She has come many miles this morning with her ponies and attendants, and wants to contract for the delivery of a number of oxen and pigs, not to mention innumerable geese, ducks and fowls. How can her pleading be resisted? But on the other hand, there is Meme Kingtang, a tall, thin woman, who, I am sorry to say, is addicted to opium, but who pleads her long business relations with energy, while a third screams that, last time her oxen were shut out in favor of her sister merchants. And so the argument goes on.

Possibly at this juncture Mr. Lange makes his appearance, when they all in chorus appeal to him, who, most likely, in his usual offhand way, consents to take all, to the great embarrassment of the unfortunate clerk, who, when the day of the shipment arrives, finds that he has two or three times as many animals on his hands as the ship will hold, and does not know what to do with the rest. With that day comes the tug of war. The beach is, of course, crowded, and the lowing of cattle, screeching of pigs, and crowing of cocks, mingled with the shouting of the natives, make a very lively scene indeed.

— 6 —

For the spread beyond Kuta of the disturbance in which, for fifteen brief years, it was the forward tremor, it is useful to look once again at Tabanan, where external trade was in the hands not of a "white rajah," but a "yellow" one, and was centered not on a coastal anchorage, but an upland counting palace.

From some time after 1880 until the Dutch arrived in 1906, the chief subandar in Tabanan was a certain Singkeh Cong. A China-born Chinese, Cong lived about ten miles north of the capital, in the approaches to the coffee highlands, the master of a great compound of residences, courtyards, sheds, and storehouses all laid out in the manner of a Balinese royal house and called, in fact, "Jero Singkeh Cong" (see map 3). A large-scale landholder, both of coffee lands and wet rice fields; official head of the by now quite large Chinese community; periodic host of grand ceremonies in the curious syncretistic style (part Sino-Buddhist, part Bali-Hindu) still characteristic of the island's Chinese; and patron-patriarch, surrounded by a small army of brothers, wives, cousins, servants, employees, and hangers-on—he was a merchant prince in no merely metaphorical sense. Far more than Lange, who remained a passing adventurer, he was a power in the state.

Formally, Cong held his subandar-ship from the "senior" and "junior" kings, Gdé and Kalèran jointly, to whom he paid a large

annual rent. How large is impossible to say; the precise figure is unrecoverable. In the first place, it was not exactly a public matter.
("They put you in a sack and dropped you in the ocean for asking
questions like that," one of my informants said.) In the second, as it
was a variable outcome of local political-cum-commercial circumstances, it was not in fact precise.

This was true not only of the size of the payment, but of its destination as well. Though in theory the payment was made to Gdé
and Kalèran as the "owners" of the realm's trade, in fact it was distributed among the houses of the royal line, and even on occasion
among client houses. And this was not done in accordance with
some fixed and regular system of division, an established charter of
rights, but in response to the pull and haul of theatre-state competition.

Whenever a lord undertook to hold a ceremony, he advanced a
claim for a certain contribution from the subandar, a claim against
the latter's general obligation. The factors determining how much,
at any particular time and for any particular purpose, a particular
claimant got, were multiple. The lord's formal status, his real political strength, his previous record of claims, the concurrent demands of others, his inherent shrewdness, the importance of the
occasion, the current state of Cong's affairs, the accidents of immediate history—all played a part. But in any case the distribution
was not an administrative process, but a deeply political one: one
in which Cong himself, as often in the royal puris and jeros as in his
own, was an active, quite direct, and far from ill-positioned participant.

Cong's lease actually gave him the right not so much to monopo-
lize trade in the direct sense as to control the channels through
which it flowed into and out of Tabanan. As the client of Gdé and
Kalèran (the latter was, by all accounts, the richest house in the
royal dadia), he was very deeply involved in such trade, with dozens
of agents, a large staff of coolies, warehouses scattered about the
countryside, and so on. But he was only the leading subandar, not
the only subandar. Other houses in the royal line had their own
Chinese on contract. Not all the traders, not even a majority of
them, fanned out over the countryside buying up export goods or
peddling imports, were agents of his. A number were important
rivals, even candidates to replace him; for the Chinese community
was not without a politics of its own. Over and above his own trading activities, what raised Cong to his central position in Tabanan
commercial life was the decree, promulgated by the king, that all

traffic in the two major commodities—coffee on the export side, opium on the import—had to pass through his station.

All coffee, whether grown by the Chinese directly, or, as was more common, bought up from Balinese peasants, had to be carried first to Jero Cong. Inspected, weighed, recorded, and taxed (i.e., by Cong), it was then carried by jogging Balinese coolies, shouldering balanced baskets on a pole, to the coast directly south of the capital. From there (i.e., the strand; there was no harbor), it was taken in very small Balinese boats either the ten miles southeast to Kuta, or, more frequently, the thirty northwest to Jembrana (i.e., Negara —see map 1) for shipment overseas. For opium, the process was the same, but reversed. Whoever was importing them, the cases were carried from the beach to Jero Cong, were recorded and so on, and were then taken off by their owners to be retailed.

— 7 —

Thus, despite its inland location, and despite its manager's own deep involvement in the countryside traffic that swirled around it, Jero Cong was also a port of trade: a place set aside, through which valuable commodities were pumped in and out of the country in such a way as to enable the lords to share in the returns of trade while not actually pursuing it themselves. What Lange did for the lords of Badung—he made them mercantile without making them merchants—Cong did for those of Tabanan.

The main difference was that, by Cong's time, "the Spirit of Commerce" had penetrated so far into south Bali that containing it within the confines of a foreign enclave had become increasingly difficult. By the turn of the century there were opium peddlers, many of them Balinese, in just about every village in the kingdom, and in the coffee areas the concentration of buyers grew so large that their trade became feverish. Weaving, once a specialized craft, became very widespread; cotton to supply the looms began to be grown in Krambitan; and several land-poor hamlets in the southwest of Tabanan turned almost entirely to the itinerant peddling of cloth. The market in the capital was transformed into an everyday affair. And, though Balinese women were still important in it, it began to be dominated by Bugis and Javanese who clustered in a residential community, the earlier mentioned *Kampong Jawa*, just below it. Some of the Chinese, joined shortly by an Arab and a "Bombay" (i.e., an Indian Muslim), set up permanent shops between the market area and the "Javanese hamlet," providing the place with a business district. Netherlands East Indies money, silver "ringgits," began to circulate alongside kèpèngs, progressively displacing them in the more sizeable transactions.

It is too simple to say that the Balinese *ancien régime* collapsed because trade expanded to so large a scale that the commercial institutions of that regime were no longer capable of dominating it. Other motives were afoot, other forces engaged. But that the pretext for the Dutch destruction of the south-Bali negaras should have been a series of free-enterprise lootings of stranded merchant ships, lootings that the lords could neither stop, nor gain personal control over, nor lease out either to passing Vikings or self-made Mandarins, has a certain symbolic appropriateness. Mutually parasitic, the lord and the subandar, the negara and the port of trade, political splendidness and commercial isolation—all went out together.

CHAPTER 4

Political Statement: Spectacle

and Ceremony

The Symbology of Power

While I [Helms] was at Bali one of these shocking sacrifices took place. The Rajah of the neighboring State died on the 20th of December 1847; his body was burned with great pomp, three of his concubines sacrificing themselves in the flames. It was a great day for the Balinese. It was some years since they had had the chance of witnessing one of these awful spectacles, a spectacle that meant for them a holiday with an odour of sanctity about it; and all the reigning Rajahs of Bali made a point of being present, either personally or by proxy, and brought large followings.

It was a lovely day, and along the soft and slippery paths by the embankments which divide the lawn-like terraces of an endless succession of paddy-fields, groups of Balinese in festive attire, could be seen wending their way to the place of burning. Their gay dresses stood out in bright relief against the tender green of the ground over which they passed. They looked little enough like savages, but rather like a kindly festive crowd bent upon some pleasant excursion. The whole surroundings bore an impress of plenty, peace, and happiness, and, in a measure, of civilisation. It was hard to believe that within a few miles of such a scene, three women, guiltless of any crime, were, for their affection's sake, and in the name of religion, to suffer the most horrible of deaths, while thousands of their countrymen looked on.

But already the walls which surround the palace of the King of Gianjar are in sight. Straight avenues, up the sides of a terraced hill, lead to the . . . palace; and, higher still, on the centre of an open space, surrounded by a wooden rail, a gaudy structure with gilded roof, rising on crimson pillers, arrests the attention. It is the spot where the burning of the dead man's body is to take place. Upon closer inspection the structure is seen to rest upon a platform of brick-work four feet high, upon which is a second floor, covered with sand. In the centre stands the wooden image of a lion, gorgeous with purple and gold trappings. The back is made to open, and is destined to receive the body of the king for burning. The entire building is gaudily decorated with mirrors, china plates, and gilding.

Immediately adjoining this structure is a square surrounded by a wall four feet high, the whole of which space was filled with a fierce, bright fire, the fatal fire which was to consume the victims. At an elevation of twenty feet a light bamboo platform is connected with this place, a covering of green plantain stems protecting it against fire. The center of this bridge supports a small pavilion, intended to receive the victims while preparing for the fatal leap.

The spectators, who, possibly, did not number less than 40,000 or 50,000, occupied the space between these structures and the outer wall, inside which a number of small pavilions had been erected for the use of women. This space was now rapidly filling, and all eyes were directed toward the kraton whence the funeral procession was to come. Strange to say, the dead king did not leave his palace for the last time by the ordinary means. A corpse is considered impure, and nothing impure may pass the gateway. Hence, a contrivance resembling a bridge had been constructed across the walls, and over it the body was lifted. This bridge led to the uppermost storey of an immense tower of a pagoda shape, upon which the body was placed.

This tower, called the "badi," [*badé*] was carried by five hundred men. It consisted of eleven storeys, besides three lower platforms, the whole being gorgeously ornamented. Upon the upper storey rested the body, covered with white linen, and guarded by men carrying fans.

The procession marching before the "badi" consisted first of strong bodies of lance-bearers, with [gamelan orchestra] music at intervals; then a great number of men and women carrying the offerings, which consisted of weapons, clothing, ornaments, gold and silver vessels containing holy water, siri-boxes, fruit, meat-dishes, boiled rice of many colours, and, finally, the horse of the deceased, gaily caparisoned; then more lance-bearers and some musicians. These were followed by the young [newly installed] king, the Dewa Pahang, with a large suite of princes and nobles. After them came the pandita or high priest, carried upon an open chair, round which was wrapped one end of a coil of cloth, made to represent a huge serpent, painted in white, black, and gilt stripes, the huge head of the monster resting under the pandita's seat, while the tail was fastened to the badi, which came immediately after it, implying that the deceased was dragged to the place of burning by the serpent.

Following the large badi of the dead king, came three minor and less gorgeous ones, each containing a young woman about to become a sacrifice or "bela." The victims of this cruel superstition showed no sign of fear at the terrible doom now so near. Dressed in white, their long black hair partly concealing them, with a mirror in one hand and a comb in the other, they appeared intent only upon adorning themselves as though for some gay festival. The courage which sustained them in a position so awful was indeed extraordinary, but it was born of the hope of happiness in a future world. From being bondswomen here, they believed they were to become the favourite wives and queens of their late master in another world. They were assured that readiness to follow him to a future world, with cheerfulness and amid pomp and splendour, would please the unseen powers, and induce the great god Siva to admit them without delay to Swerga Surya, the heaven of Indra.

Round the deluded women stood their relatives and friends. Even these did not view the ghastly preparations with dismay, or try to save their unhappy daughters and sisters from the terrible death awaiting them. Their duty was not to save but to act as executioners; for they were entrusted with the last horrible preparations, and finally sent the victims to their doom.

Meanwhile the procession moved slowly on, but before reaching its destination a strange act in the great drama had to be performed. The serpent had to be killed, and burned with the corpse. The high priest descended from his chair, seized a bow, and from the four corners of the compass discharged four wooden arrows at the serpent's head. It was not the arrow, however, but a flower, the champaka, that struck the serpent. The flower had been inserted at the feathered end of the arrow, from which, in its flight it detached itself, and by some strange dexterity the priest so managed that the flower, on each occasion hits its mark, viz. the serpent's head. The beast was then supposed to have been killed, and its body having been carried hitherto by men, was now wound round the priest's chair and

100

eventually round the wooden image of the lion in which the corpse was burned.

The procession having arrived near the place of cremation, the badi was thrice turned, always having the priest at its head. Finally it was placed against the bridge which, meeting the eleventh storey, connected it with the place of cremation. The body was now placed in the wooden image of the lion; five small plates of gold, silver, copper, iron and lead, inscribed with mystic words, were placed in the mouth of the corpse; the high priest read the Vedas, and emptied the jars containing holy water over the body. This done, the faggots, sticks striped in gold, black, and white, were placed under the lion, which was soon enveloped in flames. This part of the strange scene over, the more terrible one began.

The women were carried in procession three times round the place, and then lifted on to the fatal bridge. There, in the pavilion which has been already mentioned, they waited until the flames had consumed the image and its contents. Still they showed no fear, still their chief care seemed to be the adornment of the body, as though making ready for life rather than for death. Meanwhile, the attendant friends prepared for the horrible climax. The rail at the further end of the bridge was opened, and a plank was pushed over the flames, and attendants below poured quantities of oil on the fire, causing bright, lurid flames to shoot up to a great height. The supreme moment had arrived. With firm and measured steps the victims trod the fatal plank; three times they brought their hands together over their heads, on each of which a small dove was placed, and then, with body erect, they leaped into the flaming sea below, while the doves flew up, symbolizing the escaping spirits.

Two of the women showed, even at the very last, no sign of fear; they looked at each other, to see whether both were prepared, and then, without stooping, took the plunge. The third appeared to hesitate, and to take the leap with less resolution; she faltered for a moment, and then followed, all three disappearing without uttering a sound.

This terrible spectacle did not appear to produce any emotion upon the vast crowd, and the scene closed with barbaric music and firing of guns. It was a sight never to be forgotten by those who witnessed it, and brought to one's heart a strange feeling of thankfulness that one belonged to a civilisation which, with all its faults, is merciful, and tends more and more to emancipate women from deception and cruelty. To the British rule it is due that this foul plague of suttee is extirpated in India, and doubtless the Dutch have, ere now, done as much for Bali. Works like these are the credentials by which the Western civilisation makes good its right to conquer and humanize barbarous races and to replace ancient civilisations.

I have little more that is interesting to tell of Bali. . . .

— 2 —

The ceremonial life of the classical negara was as much a form of rhetoric as it was of devotion, a florid, boasting assertion of spiritual power. Leaping alive into flames (and, so it was thought, directly into godhood) was only one of the grander statements of a proposition that royal tooth filings, royal temple dedications, royal ordinations, and, in the puputans, royal suicides made in other, no less categorical ways: there is an unbreakable inner connection between social rank and religious condition. The state cult was not a cult of the state. It was an argument, made over and over again in the insistent vocabulary of ritual, that worldly status has a cosmic base, that hierarchy is the governing principle of the universe, and that the arrangements of human life are but approximations, more close or less, to those of the divine.

Other aspects of Balinese ritual life had other statements to make, some of them in partial conflict with the point that the state ceremonies made: Status is all. As the negara was but one among many social institutions in classical Bali, so its obsession, rank, was only one among many obsessions. But that obsession, and the cluster of beliefs and attitudes that grew up around it, was about as pervasive in the general population as it was in that small part of it immediately absorbed in the affairs of the negara as such. "The king was the symbol of the peasantry's greatness," Cora Du Bois has written about Southeast Asian Indic monarchs generally; and, somewhat more carefully phrased, the comment applies with special force to Bali. The ritual extravaganzas of the theatre state, its half-divine lord immobile, tranced, or dead at the dramatic center of them, were the symbolic expression less of the peasantry's greatness than of its notion of what greatness was. What the Balinese state did for Balinese society was to cast into sensible form a concept of what, together, they were supposed to make of themselves: an illustration of the power of grandeur to organize the world.

The Balinese, not only in court rituals but generally, cast their most comprehensive ideas of the way things ultimately are, and the way that men should therefore act, into immediately apprehended sensuous symbols—into a lexicon of carvings, flowers, dances, melodies, gestures, chants, ornaments, temples, postures, and masks—rather than into a discursively apprehended, ordered set of explicit "beliefs." This means of expression makes any attempt to summarize those ideas a dubious business. As with poetry, which in the broad, *poiesis* ("making") sense is what is involved, the message here is so deeply sunk in the medium that to transform it into a network of propositions is to risk at once both of the characteristic crimes of exegesis: seeing more in things than is really there, and reducing a richness of particular meaning to a drab parade of generalities.

But whatever the difficulties and dangers, the exegetical task must be undertaken if one wants to be left with more than the mere fascinated wonderment—like a cow looking at a gamelan orchestra, as the Balinese put it—that Helms, for all his responsiveness and powers of description, displays. Balinese ritual, and most especially Balinese state ritual, does embody doctrine in the literal sense of "teachings," however concretely they are symbolized, however unreflectively they are apprehended. Digging them out for presentation in explicit form is not a task in which the Balinese, aside from a few modernists nowadays, have ever had any interest. Nor would they feel, any more than a translated poet ever feels, that any such presentation really gets to the heart of the matter, gets it really right. Glosses on experience, and most especially on other people's experience, are not replacements for it. At the very best they are paths, twisted enough, toward understanding it.

Practically, two approaches, two sorts of understanding, must converge if one is to interpret a culture: a description of particular symbolic forms (a ritual gesture, an hieratic statue) as defined expressions; and a contextualization of such forms within the whole structure of meaning of which they are a part and in terms of which they get their definition. This is, of course, nothing but the by-now-familiar trajectory of the hermeneutic circle: a dialectical tacking between the parts which comprise the whole and the whole which motivates the parts, in such a way as to bring parts and whole simultaneously into view. In the case at hand, such tacking comes down to isolating the essential elements in the religious symbolic suffusing the theatre state, and determining the significance of those elements within the framework of what, taken as a whole, that symbolic is. In order to follow a baseball game one must understand what a bat, a hit, an inning, a left fielder, a squeeze play, a hanging curve, or a tightened infield are, and what the game in which these "things" are elements is all about. In order to follow the cremation of a Balinese king, one needs to be able to segment the torrent of images it generates—cloth snakes, arrows turning into flowers, lion-shaped coffins, pagodas on litters, doves rising from the brows of suiciding women—into the significant elements of which it is composed; and, one needs to grasp the point of the enterprise to begin with. The two sorts of understanding are inseparably dependent upon one another, and they emerge concurrently. You can no more know what a *badé* tower is (as we shall see, it is an *axis mundi*) without knowing what a cremation is than you can know what a catcher's mitt is without knowing what baseball is.

The state ceremonials of classical Bali were metaphysical theatre: theatre designed to express a view of the ultimate nature of reality and, at the same time, to shape the existing conditions of life to be consonant with that reality; that is, theatre to present an ontology and, by presenting it, to make it happen—make it actual. The settings, the props, the actors, the acts the actors perform, the general trajectory of religious faith that those acts describe—all need to be set against the background of what the devil was going on. And that background can only be perceived, and perceived in the same measure, as those theatrical components are perceived. Neither the precise description of objects and behavior that is associated with traditional ethnography, nor the careful tracing of stylistic motifs that is traditional iconography, nor the delicate dissection of textual meanings that is traditional philology are in themselves enough. They must be made to converge in such a way that the concrete immediacy of enacted theatre yields the faith enclosed within it.

— 4 —

Behind the tendentious dramaturgy of state ritual, then, and in fact behind the unchanging plot that animated it, lay two fixed conjunctions of imaged ideas. First, *padmasana*, the lotus seat (or throne) of god; *lingga*, his phallus, or potency; and *sekti*, the energy he infuses into his particular expressions, most especially into the person of the ruler. Second, *buwana agung*, the realm of being; and *buwana alit,* the realm of sentience: the "big world" of what there is and the "little world" of thought and feeling.

Surrounded by a swarm of related, ancillary ideas, also deeply sunk in the pomp and ornament which Helms describes, these two symbol packets formed the content of what is usually all too casually referred to as "divine kingship" in Bali. The message the negara was designed to convey, and in its ritual life did convey, is ill-described by the mere statement, correct enough in itself, that the king was a kind of corporeal god. To the degree that it can be abstracted at all from the vehicles of its expression, the message was that the king, the court around him, and around the court the country as a whole, were supposed to make themselves into facsimiles of the order their imagery defined.

Like dream symbols, religious symbols are richly polysemic (that is, have multiple senses), their significance spreading out profusely in an embarrassment of directions. And this is as true for Balinese religious symbols as for any in the world. They reek of meaning.

Literally, *padmasana* means "lotus seat." It is used to refer to the throne of the supreme god, Siva (or Surya, the Sun), who sits unstirring in the center of a lotus (*padma*), surrounded on four petals to the north, east, west, and south by Wisnu, Iswara, Mahadewa, and Brahma, each associated with a particular color, day of the week, part of the body, weapon, metal, magical syllable, and form of supernatural power. It is used to refer to the small stone column, surmounted by a high-back chair (also of stone) set cater-cornered on the most sacred spot in Balinese temples, upon which offerings to the supreme god are placed during temple ceremonies, when, enticed out of one version of heaven into another by his dancing worshipers, he comes there to sit. It is used to refer to the posture, a kind of infolded squat, one adopts when meditating upon the divine. It is used to refer to the act and the experience of meditation itself. It is a coital position, it is the base of a lingga, it is one of the many names of the supreme god, it is an iconic picture of the cosmos, it is the receptacle upon which the remains of a high priest are conducted to his cremation. And it is the innermost reaches of the human heart.

Lingga is a symbol no less ramifying. Strictly, of course, it refers to Siva's phallus—the "marvellous and interminable" one by which he established his superiority over Brahma and Visnu. Beyond that, it refers to the rough-hewn stone representations of that phallus—mere oblong rocks, suitably rounded at the top—found in temples and other sacred spots all over Bali. More abstractly, it is the prime symbol of divine kingship as such. Not only is the king referred to as the lingga of the world; but also, since "on earth, the ruler acts on behalf of Śiva, and the essence of his royal power is embodied in the lingga [which] the brahman . . . obtains . . . from Śiva and hands . . . over to the founder of the dynasty as the palladium of his royalty," the image summarizes the deep spiritual connection (Hooykaas calls it an "indivisible trinity") between the supreme god, the reigning king, and the state high priest. The small, whisk-like sprinkler made of grass stalks and plaited leaves from which priests shake drops of holy water over worshipers at the sacramental high point of practically all Balinese rituals is also addressed as a lingga. The kris (dagger) all noble personages wear thrust into the back of their sarongs, the crystal bar set into the ceremonial headdress of a high priest, the upper tip of a noble's cremation tower, the vehicle that transports the cremated soul to heaven, and the scaffold from which those widows threw themselves so dutifully onto their lord's pyre are also conceived to be linggas.

Finally, *sekti* is the Balinese word for the sort of transordinary phenomenon that elsewhere is called *mana, baraka, orenda, kramat,* or, of course, in its original sense, charisma: "A divinely inspired gift or power, such as the ability to perform miracles."

At bottom, however, sekti rests on a distinctive view of how the divine gets into the world; and most particularly on an elusive and paradoxical conception (and not only to external observers) of the relation between, on the one hand, the subsistent "forms" or "shapes" the divine takes (the Balinese word is *murti*, "[a] body," "bodily," "physical," from the Sanskrit *mūrta*, "settled into any fixed shape") and, on the other hand, the dynamic "manifestations" (the Sanskrit is *śakti*, "the energy or active part of a deity") that, in those forms and through those shapes, it variously has. Brahma and Visnu are said to be sektis—that is, roughly, "activations"—of Siva. So is Siva's wife. So, indeed, are all the gods and goddesses. The king, the lord, the priest, and the ascetic are all said to be sekti (*not*, as often has been said, "to possess" it) to the extent that they are, in turn, instances of what they adore. Royal regalia, priestly ritual objects, sacred heirlooms, and holy places are all sekti in the same sense: they display the power the divine takes on when it falls into particular shapes. Sekti is "supernatural" power well enough—but supernatural power which grows out of imaging the truth, not out of believing, obeying, possessing, organizing, utilizing, or even understanding it.

Padmasana/lingga/sekti, the first set of apposed symbols (that is, ritual figures conjoined by the rhetorical structure of court ceremonial), provide the image of what it is, in that ceremonial, that is to be imaged; buwana agung/buwana alit, the second set of such symbols or figures, provide the image of what that imaging consists in. This is, perhaps, an odd way to put the matter. But if one is going to describe in words, and English ones besides, that abandoned piling of mirrorings upon mirrorings upon mirrorings that turned Balinese religious life, and, for that matter, Balinese social life generally, into a dazzle of reflecting reflections, it is more or less unavoidable.

The usual translations given for *buwana agung* and *buwana alit*, beyond the literal "big world" and "little world," are "macrocosm" and "microcosm." As I have several times indicated, this is not wrong. The Balinese conception is indeed that felt experience replicates, or can ritually be made to replicate, the general structure of reality; and in so doing it sustains that structure. But, for all that, such a formulation taken abstractly is rather too neo-platonic, and thus overintellectual, for Balinese thought. It suggests a tendency toward metaphysical miniaturization a heaven-in-a-grain-of-sand turn of mind, which is not quite the philosophical temper that the details of ceremony, more sensuous than visionary, actually convey.

"Material world" and "immaterial world" are also frequently used as glosses. In some ways, they are better, because they at least draw the line in the right place: not between the infinite and the infinitesimal, but between what there is to be experienced and experience as such. In other ways, they are further away; for the Cartesianism of such a contrast, opposing self to world, mind to matter, or consciousness to object, is even more foreign to Balinese thought than is the great-and-small mystagogy.

Perhaps the best renderings, ones which take us much more directly into the whole notion of exemplary statecraft as the theatre-state negara in fact practiced it, are the "outside" and "inside" conceptions we have encountered, as jaba and jero, at so many other points in Balinese culture. Buwana agung is what lies outside the immediate precincts of the soul, away from the center of experience: jaba. Buwana alit is what lies within them and toward it: jero.

As can be seen from the discussions of "political anatomy" already presented, jaba/jero imagery runs through a great part of

Balinese social structure. The Sudra commoners are called jabas, the triwangsa gentry are called jeros. The noble houses are jeros. The "sinking status" cadet lines "go out" (jaba) of the core line, which itself remains (jero) in the middle of the dadia. And there are many other uses not thus far noted. The forecourt of a temple, where the gamelan plays and the dancers perform, is (the) jaba; the rear court, where the altars are located and obeisance is made, is (the) jero. The same pattern is found in a royal or noble house; so the innermost living quarters of the lord of such a house comprise a jero within a jero. (And he, himself, a jero within that.) The rest of the world is jaba to the jero of Bali; and most especially jaba is Java, from which so much that is Indic has been taken in so eagerly, and so much that is Islamic has been kept out so resolutely. So is body to mind, countryside to settlement, circle circumference to circle center, word to meaning, gesture to sentiment, sound to music, coconut shell to coconut juice, and so, most critically for us here, is lotus petal where Siva's manifestations sit to lotus heart where he (or his lingga) himself sits.

The symbolic fusion of buwana agung and buwana alit, to which all royal ceremonies reduce, amounts, therefore, to the assertion of a sweeping metapolitical claim: the cultural forms that the negara celebrates in rituals and the institutional ones that it takes in society are the same forms. Lingga and royalty, royalty and lordship, lordship and commonality; padma and palace, palace and kingdom, kingdom and village; sekti and status, status and authority, authority and deference—all are represented through the rites of state as so many jero and jaba counterparts of one another. All the enormous gorgeousness was an attempt to set up, in terms of drama and decoration, an authoritative pattern of political analogy. As Siva was to the gods, the gods were to the kings, the kings were to the nobles, the nobles were to the perbekels, and the perbekels were to the people: "inside" and "outside," "little world" and "big world," or *murti* to *sekti*; all were versions of the same reality.

Whether it centered on burning a corpse, or filing down a row of teeth, or consecrating a palace temple, a state ceremony transformed the lord whose corpse, teeth, or temple were being labored over into an icon, a figuration of the sacred in itself sacred. He became one more of the "activations" of the "divine shapes" at the same time that he himself became such a shape, from which further activations automatically arose. The meaningful structure of the rituals was constant, however varied the symbolic detail. The "little world" of the experienced and the "big world" of the experienceable were matched in two directions; on the inward side toward the lingga in the lotus; on the outward, toward the state in the society. And in being so matched, they represented the lord as at once an image of power—that is, as *murti*—and (or, rather, therefore) as an instance of it—as *sekti*. The basic idiom is again emulative. Seeing Siva as the exemplary shape and the king as its activation, the people see the king as exemplary shape and the state as its activation, the state as exemplary shape and society as its activation, society as exemplary shape and the self as its activation.

The Palace as Temple

As the king or lord was turned into an icon by state ceremony, into a depiction of power by that token powerful, so his palace, his dalem, or puri, or jero was transformed into a temple, a setting for the icon. The hundreds or even thousands of people who swarmed there to participate (if Helms's guess of 50,000 "spectators" at Gianjar in 1847 is even approximately correct, that would have been about five percent of the entire population) came because the puri was a stretch of sanctified space, a fit place in which to confront the mysteries of hierarchy. It was in the lord's residence (and around it—for all Balinese temples are but the foci of the sprawling pageants which swirl in and out of them), in "the place where he sits," that the doctrine of the exemplary center was made socially real.

Like so many traditional palaces the world around, and most notably like Indic ones, the puri was itself, in its sheer material form, a sacred symbol, a replica of the order it was constructed to celebrate. A squared-off, walled structure of courts within courts within courts, its layout reproduced in yet another medium the deep geometry of the cosmos. The pattern varied somewhat in detail from palace to palace, depending upon tradition, accident, and lordly whim. But everywhere the distinctions between outside and inside; between the cardinal directions and the directionless center, which sums them up; and between the remote forms out of which power wells up and the nearby ones in which it is manifest—everywhere these distinctions are found, cast in a vocabulary of walls, gates, passageways, sheds, and furniture. What the padmasana expressed sculpturally, the lingga metaphorically, and the cremation theatrically, the puri expressed architecturally: the seat of the king was the axis of the world.

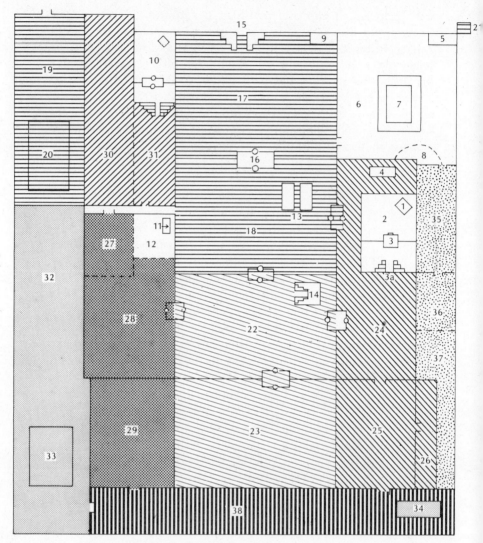

Figure 11. Plan of Palace of the King of Klungkung, ca. 1905

THE PALACE AS TEMPLE

I. SACRED AREAS ☐

1. Lotus Seat Altar (Padmasana)
2. Royal Dadia Temple (Pemerajan Agung)
3. Covered Gate to Inner Court of Royal Temple (Paduraksa)
3a. Split Gate to Outer Court of Royal Temple (Candi Bentar)
4. Demon's Pond (Taman Puyung)
5. Pavilion where Royal Judges met (Kertagosa)
6. Sacred Garden (Taman Agung)
7. Sacred Pond (Taman Alit)
8. Artificial Mountain (Gunung)
9. King's Public Seat (Balai Tegeh)
10. Royal Sub-Dadia Temple (Pemerajan Luk Melaya)
11. Heirloom Storage Place (Giri Suci)
12. World Axis (Ukiran)
13. Twin Pavilions for Displaying Corpses before Cremation (Balé Summanggèn; Balé Lunjung)
14. King of Mengwi's Origin Temple (Pemerajan Mengwi)
15. Split Gate Outer Entrance to the Palace (Candi Bentar)
16. Covered Gate Inner Entrance to the Palace (Paduraksa)

II. PUBLIC ASSEMBLY AREAS ▤

17. Outer Entrance Court (Bancingah)
18. Inner Entrance Court (Summanggén)
19. Public Kitchen (Guba Raja)
20. Public Rice Barn (Lumbung Roban)
21. Slit Gong (Kulkul)

III. ROYAL CHAMBERS ▨

22. Outer Royal Chamber (Penandakan)
23. Inner Royal Chamber (Rangki)

IV. KING'S "HOUSE" ▩

24. King's Living Area (Sarèn Kangin)
25. Living Area of King's Chief Wife and King's Mother (Rajadani)
26. Living Area of King's Secondary Gentry Wives (Sarèn Gianyar)

V. KING'S (deceased) FATHER'S "HOUSE" ▨

27. Living Area of (secondary) Gentry Wives of King's Father (Kaniya Bawa)
28. Living Area of King's Spinster Sister (Sarèn Gdé)
29. Living Area of King's (maternal) Grandfather (Balé Mas)

VI. KING'S BROTHER'S "HOUSE" ▨

30. King's Brother's Living Area (Semarabawa)
31. Forecourt of King's Brother's House (Suci)

VII. KING'S SERAGLIO ▦

32. Living Area of King's Commoner Wives (Pemangkang)
33. King's Kitchen (Paon Raja)
34. King's Rice Barn (Lumbung Raja)

VIII. NOBLE "HOUSES" ▦

35- Houses of Various (Patri-)
37. Cousins of the King (Jero)

IX. IMPURE AREA ▥

38. Impure Area (Teba)

⯊ split gate (candi bentar)

⊶ covered doorway (paduraksa)

⌐ ⌐ open passage way (pemedal)

111

If one looks at figure 11, a simplified plan of the king of Klung-kung's palace around 1905—that is, just prior to the Dutch arrival and the *puputan* court suicide which it occasioned—this master-place symbology can be seen in concrete form.

Aside from its generally square layout (it measures about five hundred feet on a side), the most obvious feature of the puri, indi-cated by the shadings on the diagram, is that it is qualitatively di-vided into several large blocks. There are the sacred areas: the temple and ceremonial places, where, at the appropriate times, the gods are induced to descend. There are the public areas, where, also at the appropriate times, and for the most part the same times, the people assemble to acknowledge and confront what the palace stands for. There are royal chambers, where the king treats with the notables of his realm and others: the places where all those treaties were signed, those marriages arranged, and those plots hatched. There are the living quarters of the king, of his recently deceased father, of his brother, and of various of his (patri-) cousins. There is the King's seraglio, the confine for his commoner wives. And fi-nally, there is the impure area, where menstruating women seclude themselves, where pigs and other animals are kept, where the lat·ine is, and where garbage is dumped.

Each of these blocks is at once a unit in itself, a composite of smaller units, and a component part of a larger unit. From the arrangement of altars in the dadia temple, or of pavilions in the entrance court, up to the arrangement of functional spaces within the whole palace and the relation of the whole palace to the realm around it, a fixed structural pattern is constantly repeated: the more sacred/central/interior/private/formal/elevat-ed/primary/hermetic/mysterious . . . against the less; the point at which meanings are gathered for the sort of presentment phrased as murti, against the plane upon which they are spread out for the sort of actuation summed up as sekti; the image against the instance of power.

In these terms, the padmasana (1) in the royal dadia temple stands in relation to the whole temple (2) as the whole temple stands in relation to the totality of the sacred regions of the palace (1-16), as the totality of the sacred regions stand to the palace as a whole, as the palace as a whole stands to the public square in which it sits, and as the public square stands to the countryside around it. Similarly, the pattern holds with the other sections and complexes

of the palace: the king's public seat (9) to the outer entrance court
(17); the inner entrance court (18) to the totality of the public assembly areas (17-21); the funeral pavilions (13) to the inner entrance court in which they are found; the king's courtyard (24) to
his immediate "house" (24-26); the king's immediate house to the
royal core-line house generally (24-34); the royal core-line house
generally to its peripheral branches still remaining within the palace (35-37); all the houses still in the palace (24-37) to those which
have "gone out" and are located at various points around it, either
in the capital proper or scattered strategically through the realm.

And so on. The detailed isomorphism reaches downward to the
smallest details of furnishing and decoration and upwards to, ultimately, the whole universe. The endless reexpression of a fixed set
of symbolic relations created, in the classical palace, a collection of
larger and smaller stages upon which larger and smaller celebrations
of hierarchy could be appropriately conducted. From a small offering on a minor holiday by the priest in charge of the royal temple
at its padmasana, a bare ritual gesture routinely observed, to the
mass festivals on major occasions in and around the palace as a
whole, great public enterprises involving the entire society, the
props and settings of the theatre state were, like its dramas, at base
the same. What varied was the number of people caught up in the
performance, the elaborateness with which the unchanging themes
were developed, and the practical impact of the event upon the
general course of Balinese life.

— 3 —

Looking at the palace as a collection of stages, and as a stage itself,
upon which exemplary dramas of ascendancy and subordination
were over and over again played out, clarifies its spatial layout:
why the more sacred spots were to the north and east, mountain-
ward, and the more profane to the south and west, seaward; why
the less prestigious areas rimmed the more prestigious; why there
was a public to private gradient from the front of the palace toward
the back. It also clarifies the specific meaning of the various sorts of
spaces themselves and the relationships that obtained among them.
The five major types of space—religious (1-16), civic (17-21), cameral (22-23), residential (24-37), and profane (38)—defined both a
set of contrasts that distinguished them and a pattern of resem-
blances that connected them.

Of the sacred spaces, the most significant ones were the royal core-line temple (2), the king's public seat (9), the display pavilions for the royal corpses (13), and the world axis (12).

The core-line temple was the family temple for the entire Klungkung ruling group, and its reconsecration after each accession to the throne, after repairs or alterations had been made in it, or after some natural misfortune (a rat plague, a volcanic eruption, an epidemic) had befallen the realm was, along with royal cremation and tooth filing, one of the most common occasions for the largest, kingdomwide mass ceremonies held at the palace. The King's public seat was a raised stone platform, covered with a roof, where he sat to observe and be observed during the festivities (dances, dramas, and so on) accompanying the great ceremonies, as well as to receive, on fixed occasions, also ritualized, ordinary petitioners seeking one thing or another. The funerary pavilions were for the display of noble corpses prior to their cremation; it would have been from them that the procession Helms saw emerging over a wall bridge (to avoid polluting the split gate) originated. But by far the most intriguing, as well as the most obscure, of the palace's sacred spaces is what, borrowing a term from comparative religion, but not all the theories that usually go with it, I have called the world axis—the *ukiran*. It is in the ukiran, even more than the core-line temple, that the sekti of the puri, its truth-imaging mimetic force, is concentrated.

Ukiran literally means "mountain," or, more accurately, "place of the mountain." It also means talismanical carving in wood or metal, especially on weapons. And finally, perhaps derivatively, perhaps not, it is one of the thirty 7-day "weeks," *wuku*, which make up the 210-day Balinese year. The intermingling of these meanings—iconographic, magical, calendrical—makes of the ukiran the point of points, not merely in the palace but also in the whole realm, the place at which the religio-cosmological and power-political aspects of hierarchy are brought most exactly together.

The sacred-mountain motif has played, of course, a prominent role in Indic mythology from the very earliest times. Mount Meru, the center, navel, and pivot of the world, is the point where heaven, earth, and hell conjoin, a kind of landbridge across which gods, men, or demons can travel back and forth between the major realms of being. In Indonesia, it is no less conspicuous a theme, finding iconographic representation in a wide range of forms, from shadow-play figures to commensal offerings. And in Bali, where the towering volcano in the center of the island, Mount Agung, is considered to *be* Meru—the place where the gods dwell, where the paramount temple is situated, and with respect to which the entire country is directionally arranged—the mountain motif is almost omnipresent. With Water and the Sun, it is one of the three great nature symbols of religious life.

In our Klungkung puri, the mountain motif appears again and again, like some stuttering effort after total utterance. After the padmasana, itself incised with such motifs, the most important altar in the core-line temple, as in all high-caste temples, is the "Gunung Agung"—that is, Mount Agung—located next to the padmasana. Next, in turn, to the "Gunung Agung" is the largest structure in the temple, the Meru as such: a Chinese-pagoda-type construction with a pyramid of (here, eleven) tiered roofs of decreasing size representing the stratified heavens. The artificial mountain (8), built out of the earth excavated in constructing the sacred pond (7), is yet another of its representations. The gates, both split (3a, 15, etc.) and covered (3, 16, etc.), are also explicit Meru images, passageways between less holy regions and more. And finally, the ukiran (and within *it*, yet more deeply "inside," the *giri suci* [11]) is, purely and simply, Meru-Agung locally emplaced: axis of palace, realm, Bali, and universe.

In the *giri suci*, which, it will be no surprise to discover, also translates as "holy mountain," are kept the magical weapons— krises, spears, lances and the like—which ensure and, in some sense, incorporate the dynasty's power. These heirlooms, what the Balinese call *waris*, are, so to speak, the charismatic inheritance of the house to which they belong, and most particularly of its head, who is entrusted with their safekeeping. Carved or incised with occult designs (called *ukiran*) having transordinary force, the weapons are associated with elaborate legends of divine origin (usually having to do with their having been forged for some god in the depths of a volcano), with mysterious occurrences of the most fantastic sort, and with military miracles rescuing the dynasty from its enemies. They are the king's *potentia*, without which, as without the phallus they quite explicitly stand for, he would be incapable.

Once a year, on the last day before the beginning of the "week" also called *ukiran*, these weapons are brought out by the king to be blessed with holy water by the high priest; and Siva is worshiped in the form of Pasupati, "whose name is also that of the finest of all weapons, the sword which Arjuna, after paying homage to Siwa, was given to use in battle against Niwatakawasa." On the following day, the first day of ukiran proper, Siva is worshiped again, but in the form of Batara Guru and at the core-line temple, "because in Guru one also sees one's own guru or father, and thus in him pays homage to the origin of one's family." Called *tumpek landep*—literally, the "closing of sharpness" (no sharp objects may be used anywhere in the realm on this day)—this holiday is celebrated with a symbolism that connects at once the instruments of violence, the energies of virility, the emblems of authority, and the vehicles of charisma. It provides a fair synoptic picture of what sovereignty, if that is even approximately the right word, meant in the metaphorical politics of classical Bali.

— 4 —

Given the sacred spaces, which summarize what palace architecture has to say—namely that to mirror a reality is to become it—the other sorts of spaces then fall naturally into place. Designed for different functions, but roughly similar in shape and layout, the various regions are stages, or arenas, on which the head-on status encounters, which form the substance of political life, are punctiliously played out. In the sacred spaces, the encounter is between gods and men; in the public spaces, between lords and subjects; in the cameral spaces, between lords and lords; in the residential spaces, between brothers, cousins, wives, spouses, parents, children—the inmates of the royal ménage; in the impure spaces, between men and demons.

More than anywhere else in classical Bali, more than the village, more than the household, more even than the temple, the palace (which was, of course, a bit of all of these, plus something of a coliseum) was where the vanities of Bali all came together, the conflux of the pretensions upon which the society turned.

Cremation and the Struggle for Status

Still, so far as the theatre state was concerned, all this was but *mise-en-scène*: it was in the court rituals that the negara came alive. The ideas carved onto padmasana reliefs or laid out in royal compounds became—in the temple consecrations, the tooth filings, and the cremations—great collective gestures, mass enactments of elite truths. The throngs of lookers-on and joiners-in that turned even a minor state ceremony into a kind of choreographed mob scene gave to the negara an expressive power that neither palaces as copies of the cosmos, nor kings as icons of divine authority, could themselves produce. "With a little imagination," Gregory Bateson has written

Twentieth-century painting by a Balinese artist
of a traditional cremation procession.
Collection of Clifford Geertz.

of a Balinese painting of a cremation—a tangle of bodies, leaves, towers, and offerings (e.g., see color plate)—"we could see the picture as a symbolic representation of Balinese social organization in which smooth relations of etiquette and gaiety metaphorically cover the turbulence of passion." Except that the arrow is reversed—the turbulence is the metaphor and the relations are what the metaphor covers—we could say the same thing of the event itself.

Though practiced as well by priests and commoners, cremation (*ngabèn*) was, in fact, the quintessential royal ceremony. Not only was it the most dramatic, splendid, sizable, and expensive; it was the most thoroughly dedicated to the aggressive assertion of status. What was, from one point of view, a suspiciously puffed up rite for the dead was, from another, a headlong attack in a war of prestige. Goris's suggestion that it might be an Indicised survival of a pre-Hindu potlatch is perhaps not very acceptable as ethnology. But it catches well enough the spirit of the thing: conspicuous consumption, Balinese style.

Beginning with the death of the king, stretching through the actual incineration, and continuing into a string of curious after-ceremonies, the ritual was a protracted matter, taking months to accomplish. The heart of it consisted of three great holy days: The Purification (*Pabersihan*); The Obeisance (*Pabaktian*); and The Annihilation (*Pabasmian*). But, as with most Balinese rituals, these central events were bracketed on the one side by a long crescendo of gettings ready and on the other by a dying fall of finishings-up. It was almost as much in the prologue (the constructing of the paraphernalia, the putting together of the offerings, the organizing of the feasts) and in the reprise (the obsessive reenactments, with effigies, ashes, designs, or flowers, of the burning of the corpse) as in the ceremony proper that the significance of the affair seems to have lain. From beginning to end, it was what the Balinese call *karya ratu*, "king work," a kind of religious corvée in which service and worship come down to the same thing.

— 2 —

Of the three "great days," the first, The Purification, was dedicated to the washing of the body (or what remained of it) by the relatives of the deceased, by the other lords of the realm, and, for a really major figure, by lords of allied realms; to the adornment of it with various devices (mirrors on the eyelids, flowers in the nostrils, wax in the ears, a ruby in the mouth, iron on the arms); and, most especially, to the sprinkling of holy water on it by the high priest. On the second day, The Obeisance, the body was moved to the display pavilions (number 13 in figure 11) where, set amid the family heirlooms (the krises, lances, and so forth from the giri suci) and among elaborate mountains of leaves and rice, it was viewed by dependents, clients, allies, and even some of the more prominent subjects, who came to pay their hands-to-forehead prayer of respect. But it was on the final day, The Annihilation, that the stream of status markers, here still but a freshet by Balinese standards, swelled to a torrent that swept even solemnity away.

As the Helms description makes clear, the outstanding features of the cremation proper were three enormous outbreaks of symbolic energy—a social one, the procession; an aesthetic one, the tower; and a natural one, the fire. The excitement of the crowd, the magnificence of the bier, and the abandon of the pyre fixed the tone of the event, which was (as Helms also notes) more like an outing than a lament.

The procession was a clamorous and disorderly affair throughout. It began with a mock battle between the men trying to carry the corpse over the palace wall to place it on the tower and the crowd outside seeking to prevent them from doing so. It ended, a half mile or so farther on, with a series of similar battles as the corpse was brought down from the tower to its animal coffin and set upon the pyre. In between, there was near-hysteria: the wild spinning of the tower "to confuse the spirit"; the pushing, shoving, and tumbling in the mud; the laughing scramble for coins and baubles; the relentless clanging of the war music.

Yet, for all that, the procession had a rigorous order: it was as calm and unruffled at its apex and center as it was tumultuous and agitated at its base and edges. At its head came the orchestras, the dancers, the carriers of sandalwood, the bearers of animal coffins. Behind them were the lance bearers and the carriers of the heirloom weapons; and then, containers and trays balanced on their heads, came the women with the holy water; then the doll-like effigies of the dead, the offerings to the demons and the lord of hell, and the king's regalia (clothes, jewelry, betel boxes, parasols). Next, half-entranced, chanting mantras, rode the high priest, borne aloft on his padmasana open chair. Behind him, but attached to him by the cloth serpent which Helms was so taken by, and which the immediate relatives of the deceased, also somewhat dissociated, carried strung out across their shoulders, came the funerary tower, looming grandly above the whole confusion. And finally, trailing like a shadow, came the funerary entourage of the sacrificial wives, the women as expressionless in their towers as the corpses they already were; following them, the Sudras, often hundreds of them, dozens to a tower, whom their families had disinterred to be cremated with their lord. The scene (which, so far as its general aspect is concerned, has not changed that much today) was a bit like a playful riot—a deliberated, even studied, violence designed to set off a no less deliberated and even more studied stillness, which the variously imperturbable priests, agnates, widows, and tributary dead contrived to gather about the central tower.

The tower itself, the eye within the eye of this manufactured storm, was again a cosmic image. At its base, the world of demons was invoked by the usual winged serpents and flattened out turtles. The world of man was represented in the middle by a protruding platform, shaped like a houseyard pavilion, and indeed called "the house," on which the corpse was placed. And at the top appeared the world of gods, symbolized in the familiar tiers of Meru roofs, their number indicating the level of heaven to which the departing soul aspired: a single one for the commoner, who was lucky enough to be ascending at all; three or five for the lesser gentry; seven or nine for an ordinary lord; and eleven, topped at the apex by a sculptured lingga, for a king; an uncovered padmasana seat, open directly to the Sun, Surya-Siva, was for a high priest.

The animal coffins also reflected the status of the deceased. Priests were burned in bulls, high lords in winged lions, lesser lords in deer, commoners in a mythological beast with the head of an elephant and the tail of a fish. The height of the tower (which could get up to sixty or seventy feet), the number of men carrying it (who had to be of lesser rank than the deceased), the elaborateness and fineness of its decorations (which were plundered by the crowd in a wild frenzy just before it was burned, on a separate fire from the coffin), and the number of sacrificial widows and disinterred Sudras —all expressed the status claims of the deceased, his dynasty, and his negara: the degree of exemplariness they professed to have achieved. In the whole tumbling day, with literally hundreds of ritual acts and thousands of ritual offerings, there was hardly one, from effigies and rice mounds to sacred hymns and fluttering doves, that did not have an explicit, delicately modulated status meaning.

The scene at the pyre . . . the flowered-arrow "killing" of the serpent by the priest; the bringing down of the body to the coffin on the burning platform; the priest, still almost as if somnambulant, climbing up to the platform to drench the corpse in great quantities of holy water; the placing of the corpse in the coffin, buried under piles of textiles, effigies, Chinese coins, and as many different

Helm; very [?] pyre as metaphor & for different interpretations of same material base —

sorts of offerings as could be somehow crammed in; the ceremonial igniting, with a fire drill, of the blaze by the priest; the priest, now fully in trance, performing a flowing last rite, a sort of seated dance with head, trunk, arms, and hands, amid smoke and clamor; the great collapse as the coffin's legs give way and it crumbles into the fire, disgorging the half-burned body; the silent drop of the widows into the flames; the gathering up of the ashes to be carried to the sea, the priest wading in to scatter them on the waves . . . all this was merely more of the same—the serenity of the god-like transcending the furor of the animal-like. The whole ceremony was a giant demonstration, repeated in a thousand ways with a thousand images, of the indestructability of hierarchy in the face of the most powerful leveling forces the world can muster—death, anarchy, passion, and fire. "The king is annihilated! Long live his rank!"

— 3 —

Thus the royal rituals (and in this the tooth filings, ordinations, realm cleansings, and temple consecrations were no different from the cremations) enacted, in the form of pageant, the main themes of Balinese political thought: the center is exemplary, status is the ground of power, statecraft is a thespian art. But there is more to it than this, because the pageants were not mere aesthetic embellishments, celebrations of a domination independently existing: they were the thing itself. The competition to be the center of centers, the axis of the world, was just that, a competition; and it was in the ability to stage productions of an eleven-roof scale, to mobilize the men, the resources, and, not least, the expertise, that made one an eleven-roof lord. The ascriptive nature of the Balinese ranking system, the fact that one's place in the hierarchy was in a broad way inherited, should not be allowed to obscure the in many ways more important fact that the whole of the society, from top to bottom, was locked in an intricate and unending rivalry of prestige, and that this rivalry was the driving force of Balinese life. The scale on which the rivalry was conducted was larger at the top, perhaps more unremitting, and certainly more spectacular. But the struggle of the lower placed to narrow the gap between themselves and the higher placed by imitating them, and to widen it between themselves and the yet lower placed by dis-imitating them, was universal.

A royal cremation was not an echo of a politics taking place somewhere else. It was an intensification of a politics taking place everywhere else.

Bali and Political Theory

Now this is quite a strange brand of imitation which
comprises and constructs the very thing it imitates!

Paul Ricoeur

That master noun of modern political discourse, *state*, has at least
three etymological themes diversely condensed within it: status, in
the sense of station, standing, rank, condition—*estate* ("The glories
of our blood and state"); pomp, in the sense of splendor, display,
dignity, presence—*stateliness* ("In pomp ride forth; for pomp becomes the great/And Majesty derives a grace from state"); and
governance, in the sense of regnancy, regime, dominion, mastery—
statecraft ("It may pass for a maxim in state that the administration
cannot be placed in too few hands, nor the legislature in too many").
And it is characteristic of that discourse, and of its modernness, that
the third of these meanings, the last to arise (in Italy in the 1540s;
it was not even available to Machiavelli), should have so come to
dominate the term as to obscure our understanding of the multiplex
nature of high authority. Impressed with command, we see little else.

As noted above, *negara*, too, catches up a various field of meanings, but a different field than *state*, leading to the usual misconnec-
tions of intercultural translation when it thus is rendered. But whatever matters distinct to us it may collapse—palace, town, capital,
realm, civilization—the sort of polity it designates is one in which
the interplay of status, pomp, and governance not only remains
visible, but is, in fact, blazoned. What our concept of public power
obscures, that of the Balinese exposes; and vice versa. And so far as
political theory is concerned, it is there, in exposing the symbolic
dimensions of state power, that the use of attending to decaying
rank, dispersed prerogative, ritualized water control, alien-managed
trade, and exemplary cremation lies. Such study restores our sense
of the ordering force of display, regard, and drama.

Each of the leading notions of what the state "is" that has de-

veloped in the West since the sixteenth century—monopolist of violence within a territory, executive committee of the ruling class,
delegated agent of popular will, pragmatic device for conciliating
interests—has had its own sort of difficulty assimilating the fact that
this force exists. None has produced a workable account of its
nature. Those dimensions of authority not easily reducible to a
command-and-obedience conception of political life have been left
to drift in an indefinite world of excrescences, mysteries, fictions, and
decorations. And the connection between what Bagehot called the
dignified parts of government and the efficient ones has been systematically misconceived.

This misconception, most simply put, is that the office of the
dignified parts is to serve the efficient, that they are artifices, more
or less cunning, more or less illusional, designed to facilitate the
prosier aims of rule. Political symbology, from myth, insignia, and
etiquette to palaces, titles, and ceremonies, is but the instrument
of purposes concealed beneath it or towering over it. Its relations
to the real business of politics—social domination—are all extrinsic:
"State Divinity that obeyes affections of persons."

For those "great beast" views of the state that, from Hobbes's
Leviathan to de Jouvenel's Minotaur, locate its power in its threat
to harm, the function of the parade and ceremony of public life is
to strike terror into the minds that threat confronts. Like an Aus-
tralian's bull-roarer or Oz's wizard machine, it is a dark noise to
impress the impressionable and to induce in them a trembling awe.
For those "great fraud" views, Marx-left or Pareto-right, where the
stress is on the capacity of elites to extract surpluses from the less
well-placed and transfer them to themselves, the conception of state
ceremony is more one of mystification, in the sense of the spiritual-
izing of material interests and the fogging over of material conflicts.
Political symbology is political ideology, and political ideology is
class hypocrisy. Populist conceptions of the state, those which see it
as an extension of the spirit of community out of which it comes,
naturally tend toward more celebratory formulations: as government is the instrument of the nation's will, its ritual trumpets that
will's immensity. And for pluralistic theories—the interest balancing
of classical liberalism and its pressure-group successors—the trappings of state are so many devices to clothe received procedures in
moral legitimacy. Politics is an endless jockeying for marginal advantage under settled ("constitutional") rules of the game, and the
role of the wigs and robes that everywhere attend it is to make the
rules seem settled, to raise them above—or insert them beneath—the

partisan struggle they are supposed to regulate. But, in all these views, the semiotic aspects of the state (if, foreshadowing an alternative approach to the issues at hand, we may now begin to call them that) remain so much mummery. They exaggerate might, conceal exploitation, inflate authority, or moralize procedure. The one thing they do not do is actuate anything.

It is not difficult, indeed it is fatally easy, to fit the Balinese state as here described to one or another of these familiar models, or to all of them at once. No one remains dominant politically for very long who cannot in some way promise violence to recalcitrants, pry support from producers, portray his actions as collective sentiment, or justify his decisions as ratified practice. Yet to reduce the negara to such tired commonplaces, the worn coin of European ideological debate, is to allow most of what is most interesting about it to escape our view. Whatever intelligence it may have to offer us about the nature of politics, it can hardly be that big fish eat little fish, or that the rags of virtue mask the engines of privilege.

— 2 —

Much about the character of classical Balinese culture and the sort of politics it supported is disputable, but surely not that status was its ruling obsession and splendor was the stuff of status. *Linggih*, literally "seat," generally rank, station, position, place, title, "caste" ("Where do you sit?" is the standard request for status identification), was the axis round which the public life of society revolved. Defined in terms of varying distance from divinity, as already explained, and, in theory at least, one of life's givens, not one of its contingencies, status and the compulsions surrounding it animated most of the emotions and nearly all of the acts which, when we find their like in our own society, we call political.

To understand the negara is to locate those emotions and construe those acts; to elaborate a poetics of power, not a mechanics. The idiom of rank not only formed the context within which the practical relationships of the major sorts of political actors—punggawas, perbekels, kawulas, and parekans—took their shape and had their meaning; it permeated as well the dramas they jointly mounted, the *décor théâtral* amid which they mounted them, and the larger purposes they mounted them for. The state drew its force, which was real enough, from its imaginative energies, its semiotic capacity to make inequality enchant.

Before all else, the Balinese state was a representation of how reality was arranged; a vast figure within which objects like krises, structures like palaces, practices like cremation, ideas like "inside," and acts like dynastic suicide had the potency they had. The notion that politics is an unchanging play of natural passions, which particular institutions of domination are but so many devices for exploiting, is wrong everywhere; in Bali, its absurdity is patent. The passions are as cultural as the devices; and the turn of mind—hierarchical, sensory, symbolistic, and theatrical—that informs the one informs the other.

This is clear throughout. But it is perhaps most clear in what was, after all, the master image of political life: kingship. The whole of the negara—court life, the traditions that organized it, the extractions that supported it, the privileges that accompanied it—was essentially directed toward defining what power was; and what power was was what kings were. Particular kings came and went, "poor passing facts" anonymized in titles, immobilized in ritual, and annihilated in bonfires. But what they represented, the model-and-copy conception of order, remained unaltered, at least over the period we know much about. The driving aim of higher politics was to construct a state by constructing a king. The more consummate the king, the more exemplary the center. The more exemplary the center, the more actual the realm.

The distinctive feature of Indic kingship in Southeast Asia is inevitably said to be its "divineness"—a hazy formulation, as earlier noted. Kings here had not two bodies, but one. They were not Defenders of the Faith, Vicars of God, or Mandatories of Heaven; they were the thing itself—incarnations (Hindu, Buddhist, or some eclectic mixture of the two) of the Holy as such. The rajas, maharajas, rajadirajas, devarajas, and so on were so many hierophanies; sacred objects that, like stupas or mandalas, displayed the divine direct.

This concept of divine kingship is not incorrect, any more than it is incorrect to say that the American president is a popular leader or that the king of Morocco is an autocrat. It is just insufficient. It is the content of the "divineness" (or of the "popularness" or the "autocracy") that matters. Even more important, what matters is how that content was created, how it was materially brought about. If a state was constructed by constructing a king, a king was constructed by constructing a god.

There are a number of implications for the shape of politics in this, but among the more important is that sovereignty, like divinity, was both one and many. The landscape, not just in Bali, but

throughout Southeast Asia, and over the course of at least fifteen
hundred years, was dotted with universal monarchs, each represented, in the declamations of his cult, as the core and pivot of the
universe, yet each quite aware that he was emphatically not alone in
such representation. From the pettiest rajas in the Celebes or the
Malayan Peninsula to the grandest in Java or Cambodia, the pronouncements of overlordship were total in their claims; it was the
scale on which those pronouncements could be mounted that varied.
Kings were all Incomparable, but some were more Incomparable
than others, and it was the dimensions of their cult that made the
difference.

— 3 —

It is this combination of an essentially constant cultural form, the
divine king cult, with an enormous variability in the people and
resources available for constructing that form, in this place or that
time, that turned "the struggle for power" in classical Bali into a
continual explosion of competitive display. The more prominent
features of that display, in myth, rite, art, and architecture, have
already been described. So has the political mentality it sustained
and which sustained it. But beyond both symbology and ethos, and
giving them a tangible expression in the actual course of state affairs,
were a number of social paradigms of royal authority, concrete ex-
emplifications of what being the lord of creation actually came down
to, in practical terms. Of these, three were especially important: the
relations of kings to priests, of kings to the material world, and of
kings to themselves.

The complementary pairing of king and priest, the Perfect Satria
and the Perfect Brahmana poised in antiphony at the apex of society, is at once the most characteristically Indian of Balinese political institutions (it appears already in the Code of Manu) and the
most conspicuous example of the sea change such institutions suffered in their passage south and east. In India, as scholars from
A. M. Hocart forward have shown, the function of the Brahmin (or
at least of the court Brahmin) was to conduct sacrifices in the name
of a ritually disqualified, blood-shedding, meat-eating king. In Bali,
where nonviolence and vegetarianism were at best but incidental
ideas, the function of the Brahmana was to stage mysteries and raise
incantations around which the cult of royal divinity could gather.
The complex differentiation and reintegration between hierarchy
and dominance—*dharma*, the realm of value; and *artha*, the realm

125

of force—that underlies the caste system in India did not occur in Bali, nor, for that matter, in Southeast Asia generally. The court-connected Brahmana was not ambassador to the gods for a secular ruler; he was celebrant-in-chief for a sacred one.

There were, in the traditional hierarchial states of the Mideast and Asia, three main forms of kingship. In such archaic bureau-cracies as those of Egypt, China, or Sumeria, the king was himself the head priest; the welfare of the realm turned upon the magical force of his liturgical activities, and other priests were but his sacerdotal assistants. In India, itself of course as much a continent as a country, the king was what Louis Dumont has called a "con-ventional" rather than a "magico-religious" figure—a ruler "dis-possessed of religious functions proper," whose priests ritually con-nected him to the other world as his ministers administratively connected him to this one. And finally, in Bali, as in most of the rest of Southeast Asia (as well as, interestingly enough, in the more developed polities of Polynesia, and, in a somewhat different way, in Japan), the king, no mere ecclesiarch, was the numinous center of the world, and priests were the emblems, ingredients, and effec-tors of his sanctity. Like the heirlooms already mentioned, like his sarongs, his umbrellas, his palanquin, and his jewelry, like his palace, his wives, his linggas, his cremation tower, his fetes, his wars; indeed, as we shall see, like the realm as a whole—priests were parts of the king's regalia.

That is not to say that they were mere appurtenance, trinkets of power. The royal chronicle of Bulèlèng that explicitly describes the court's priest as "the foremost of the king's jewels" also identifies him with the hilt of the king's kris, with the instruments of the king's orchestra, and with the whole of the king's elephant. He is learned in religious lore, adept in ritual, well read in Vedic law, an accomplished diviner, wondrously virtuous, and a skilled forger of sacred weapons. The king, hearing of his fame, has summoned him to court, settled him in an *asrama* in sight of the palace, attached three thousand retainers to him, and bestowed an exalted title on him, echoic of the king's own. As P. J. Worsley, the chronicle's editor and translator, well says: "[He] is not simply a royal adorn-ment, a symbol of royal authority, but rather an embodiment of part of that authority, and extension of the king's official person."

In short, although the priest stands here as he does in India for *dharma*, a word equally well and equally badly translated as "law," "norm," "duty," "right," "virtue," "merit," "good actions," "cus-tomary observance," "religion," "order," and "justice," the relation between him and the king is less one of pure and impure, or even righteous and practical, as of excellent and superexcellent. The priest's illustriousness reflects the king's, is part of it, and contributes to it; and the unshakable tie of loyalty that binds them, a tie demonstrated on every possible public occasion and in every possible way, is again exemplary. It is, Worsley writes, "a mirrored image of an ideal relationship. . . . In this very special relationship . . . is reflected the ideal relationship between the ruler and subject, for the relationship is regarded . . . as a model for the whole world." As a social paradigm, king and priest showed the realm how it was that to serve one's lord was to become an aspect of that lord, just as he, in serving God, became an aspect of God; and it showed also what sort of thing—the higher mimicry—that service was.

— 4 —

The general relationship between the king and the material world was summed up in a deceptively prosaic word whose apparent ease of translation has been the chief bar to scholarly understanding of it: *druwé. Druwé (madruwé, padruwèn)* means "owned" ("to own," "possess"; "property," "wealth"). That is not itself the problem. The problem is that, used in connection with the king, it was applied to virtually everything: not just to his private lands and personal possessions, but to the country as a whole, all the land and water in it, and all the people. The realm, the whole of it, was in some sense his "possession," his "property," which "belonged" to him. It is the "in some sense" that contains the complexities and that has engendered the debates.

The long, hundred-year argument between those who, confusing idiom with law, saw all the land, water, forests, and so on in the Indic states of Indonesia as the personal property of the king and those who, confusing peasant custom with it, regarded domanial claims as so much pretense and usurpation was essentially misdirected. It was based, on both sides, on the lawyer's assumption that "ownership" is a yes-or-no matter with a fixed and uniform definition and that, though proprietors might be persons, groups of persons, or even institutions viewed as persons, there can be, finally, but one legitimate claim to a particular right in a particular property. When one considers that not only "kings," but also "gods," "villages," "families," and "individuals" were said to own "everything"—the same "everything"—the necessity for a less elementary view of "possession" becomes apparent. In particular, if the relation between ruler and realm is to be understood properly, the notion that, however translated, *druwé* had to do with the use of resources (that is, with their appropriation and their enjoyment) must be given up. It had to do with their role in the symbology of power.

Viewed that way, the question of who "owned" Bali takes a less Lockean form, and we are faced once again with a society stretched taut between cultural paradigms conceived of as descending from above and practical arrangements conceived of as rising from below. The rules governing the immediate control and disposition of resources were, as we have seen, complex and irregular, a tangle of crosscutting particularities. And, as we have also seen, they were more a product of the hamlet, the irrigation society, and the household than they were, certain carefully specified matters aside, of the negara. But the quality and abundance of such resources, and thus the world's prosperity, issued from less mundane realities; and it was to these that *druwé* pointed. It signaled yet another hierarchy of exemplars, each lower one a coarser version of the next above, each higher one a finer version of the next below, cast this time in proprietary terms. The gods' "ownership" of the realm was approximated in the king's as best the king was able; the king's was approximated in the lord's; the lord's in the peasant's. Not only *could* such "possessings" exist together, but they *had* to exist together in order for any one of them to make sense. The king owned the country as he ruled it—mimetically; composing and constructing the very thing he imitated.

In concrete terms, the king was not only the paramount punggawa, at the apex of the status hierarchy we have already traced, but he was also, and for that reason, at the center of what we called, discussing the "spiritual" dimension of local community, "sacred space." He fused, in his person, the double representation of power we have seen running through the entire structure of Balinese public life: as a gradation of excellence scattering downward from a divine unity and as a radiation of it dispersing outward from a divine core. These are but two expressions of the same reality, like the height of a tower and the length of its shadow. But where the king-priest relation modeled the first, ascendancy as such, the king-realm relation modeled the second, its reach.

Beyond the multitude of local "custom communities," the desa adat, the realm as a whole was itself conceived of as such a custom community, a negara adat. Like the desa adat, the negara adat was a stretch of sacred space: "the land with everything that grows on it, the water that flows through it, the air that envelops it, the rock that holds it in its womb." Like the desa adat, all those living within its bounds, and therefore benefiting from its energies, were collectively responsible for meeting the ritual and moral obligations those energies entailed. And, like the desa adat, the negara adat was at base not a social, political, or economic unit, but a religious one, an assemblage of celebrants. In the same way that local populations secured local well-being, regional populations secured the regional, and, where possible, supraregional secured the supraregional—through grandly mounted collective ceremony.

It was as head of the negara adat, then, that the king "owned" the realm. Like the gods, and as one, he ensured its prosperity—the productiveness of its land; the fertility of its women; the health of its inhabitants; its freedom from droughts, earthquakes, floods, weevils, or volcanic eruptions; its social tranquility; and even (tamed as it was into a vast, manicured park of angled paths, rectangular courtyards, and square terraces) its physical beauty. Whether in Water-Opening ceremonies at sacred lakes, first-fruits rites at mountain shrines, demon exorcisms at seashore ones, or royal celebrations at his palace, the king was represented as the prime "guardian," "custodian," or "protector," *ngurah*, of the land and its life, sheltering it as the royal parasol sheltered him and as "the vault of heaven" sheltered them both. In that capacity and in those terms, tutelary ones, not tenurial, the realm quite literally was his "property," *druwé raja*.

And the motor, again, was state ceremony. The prodigal exuberance of such ceremony, the pervasive sense of material abundance we have repeatedly remarked, was both the image of the realm's prosperity and, in line with the model-and-copy view of things, its author. The ceremonial splendor imaged the king's centrality by converging on him as its focus; it imaged the powers that lodged in that centrality by depicting them in terms of assembled wealth; and it imaged the social field over which those powers ranged in terms of the populace from which the wealth was assembled. The extravagance of state rituals was not just the measure of the king's divinity, which we have already seen it to be; it was also the measure of the realm's well-being. More important, it was a demonstration that they were the same thing.

— 5 —

The king's relation to himself, as the paradoxical formulation itself suggests, is the most elusive of the social paradigms of royal authority, the most difficult to translate into modes of expression other than those in which it was embedded. It is the more difficult because of its oddly depersonalized nature, as we would see it: the seeming abandonment of individual identity and will in favor of existence as a sort of human ideogram. The ceremony that pictured the priest as the king's jewel, and the realm as the king's park, pictured the king as the king's icon: a sacred likeness of—well, kingship.

In struggling to characterize the king's role in this regard, the phrase that comes immediately to mind is T. S. Eliot's "still point of the turning world"; for, insofar as he was an actor in court ceremonies, his job was to project an enormous calm at the center of an enormous activity by becoming palpably immobile. Sitting for long hours at a stretch in a strictly formal pose, his face blank, eyes blanker, stirring when he had to with a slow formality of balletic grace, and speaking when he had to in a murmur of reticent phrases, while all about him people were laboring heavily to construct an extravaganza in his honor, the king was The Great Imperturbable, the divine silence at the center of things: "The Void-Self . . . inactive . . . devoid of form."

However, even the immobility, the impassivity, and the placidity, the materials of the icon, were themselves paradoxical: like the repose of squatting Buddhas or the poise of dancing Sivas, they issued from a strenuous athleticism of the spirit. The king's ability to project himself (or, better, his kingship) as the stationary axis of the world rested on his ability to discipline his emotions and his behavior with meticulous rigor; to train his mind on its own depths in a sustained, intense, reflective trance; and to form in those depths exact and elaborate imaginings of the gods. The long, reiterating chain of exemplary display, linking "the Supreme Brahman embodied in the primeval sound" to "the whole of the . . . country . . . helpless, bowed, stooping," crossed at the king a critical juncture between what men could conceive and what, conceiving it, they could be.

The exemplary center within the exemplary center, the icon king depicted outwardly for his subjects what he depicted inwardly to himself: the equanimous beauty of divinity. Put that way, the whole thing sounds like so much legerdemain, a Steinberg hand drawing itself. But as imagination for the Balinese was not a mode of fantasy, of notional make-believe, but a mode of perception, representation, and actualization, it did not seem so to them. To visualize was to see, to see to imitate, and to imitate to embody.

Whatever the objective validity of this conception that reality consists in an aesthetic, type-and-token hierarchy of sensuous expressions in which those lower down are not less real, just less exquisite,
less dazzling, and less potent (and who is to pronounce upon that?)
—in Bali it is rock truth. As a sign in a system of signs, an image in
a field of images, which is what in court ceremonies he strenuously
transformed himself to being, the king was distinct in that, "sitting"
at the point above which the hierarchy was incorporeal, he marked
the threshold of the sheer ideal.

But the paradox of an active passivity, a forceful sitting still, extended even further; for the king as sign conveyed not merely the
quiet gentleness of a tranquil spirit, but also the blank severity of
a just one. Impassive benevolence toward goodness was matched by
impassive violence toward evil; and war (or, less grandly, royal punishment) was, in its way, as much a ritual activity as was Water
Opening. Indeed, the chess-like mode of waging war, which we have
already seen in the fall of Mengwi and the *puputan* "endings" vis-à-
vis the Dutch, followed the same quiet-center model: the king
emerged from the palace to meet his fate only after first his pawn
kawulas, then his minor-piece perbekels, and finally his major-piece
punggawas, each in turn, in an ascending, desperate display of
status, had been routed. "His passions bridled by meditation," P. J.
Worsley writes, "[the ideal king] strives to pursue a virtuous way
of life, to rule his realm disinterestedly . . . harsh toward his enemies . . . gentle toward the loyal and the virtuous." Cruel as the
heat of the sun and equable as the glow of the moon, his mind
trained on empowering visions, the king was presented in the
grand dramas of the theatre state as a fixed figuration of authority,
an "abstract and anonymous [man] who behave[s] in a way wholly
predictable within the logic of the image in which [he has] been
formed." With holy water, hymns, lotus seats, and daggers, he was
a ritual object.

— 6 —

The king was also, however, a political actor, power among powers
as well as sign among signs. It was the king's cult that created him,
raised him from lord to icon; for, without the dramas of the theatre
state, the image of composed divinity could not even take form. Yet
the frequency, richness, and scale of those dramas, and thus the
extent of the impress they made upon the world, was in turn dependent upon the extent and, as we have seen, the diversity of the

political loyalties that could be mobilized to stage them. And, closing the circle, such mobilization of men, skills, goods, and knowledge was the prime task and primary art of statecraft, the capacity upon which, on the material side, supremacy depended. It was not enough just to sit still, even passionately still. To be the master representation of power, it was necessary also to traffic in it.

The social mechanisms through which such trafficking was mediated—descent ties, clientship, alliance, the perbekel system, rent, taxation, trade—have already been described, and their centrifugal tendency toward heterogeneity has been stressed. What was high centralization representationally was enormous dispersion institutionally, so that an intensely competitive politics, rising from the specificities of landscape, custom, and local history, took place in an idiom of static order emerging from the universalizing symbology of myth, rite, and political dream. Aside from the practical difficulties it presented for anyone desiring to make his way toward the glowing apex and center of things (that is, for just about anyone with a prayer of doing so), this situation introduced a paradox into negara politics, a paradox that neither statecraft nor its practitioners could ever quite resolve, and that became as a result the central political dynamic: the closer one moved toward imaging power, the more one tended to distance oneself from the machinery controlling it.

This was not just the "loneliness at the top" that is perhaps characteristic of all complex political systems, and certainly of all autocratic ones. For the problem here was not that officials concealed, either from fear or prudence, the truth of things from the king; as there was virtually no staff there were virtually no officials. Nor was it that royal policies had to be phrased in such general terms that the king lost contact with concrete realities; as there was virtually no administration there were virtually no policies. The problem was that the negara changed its character from its lower reaches to its higher. At the lower, it engaged the hundreds of crisscross village polities, prying from them, via a cloud of perbekels, sedahans, and subandars, the bodies and resources to stage the court operas. At the higher, progressively removed from contact with such polities and the crudenesses associated with them, it was turned toward the central business of exemplary mimesis, toward staging the operas. Functional, or, as the Balinese would say, "coarse" toward the bottom, the negara was aesthetical, "refined" toward the top—a model itself of the nature of hierarchy.

The result was that at any point in the hierarchy, but most intensely and unevadably near the top, where the "far-beaming blaze of majesty" consumed so much more fuel, the necessity to demonstrate status warred with the necessity to assemble the support to make the demonstration possible. In particular, the most immediate associates of the king, the other great punggawas—jealous kin, grudging lieutenants, near equals, and implicit rivals—were concerned to see that the king's ritual deactivation was literal as well, that he became so imprisoned in the ceremony of rule that his practical dependence upon them was maximized and their own possibilities of display were enhanced. The politics of competitive spectacle were chronically unquiet, because one lord's success was another lord's opportunity; but they were also basically stable, because that opportunity was in turn inherently self-limiting.

Now that first the colonial bureaucracy and after it the republican have locked the negara in Weber's iron cage, it is difficult to recover the character of political struggle when its energies were parochial and its ambitions cosmic; but that it was a wonderful mixture of motion and fixity seems clear. Each lord, at whatever level and on whatever scale, sought to distance himself from his nearest rivals by expanding his ceremonial activity, turning his court into a nearer Majapahit and himself into a nearer god. But as he did so he laid himself open to becoming a locked-in chess king, separated from the intricacies of power mongering by the requirements of his own pretensions: a pure sign. As a result, despite the intense and unending maneuvering, rapid movement upward in political stature, though it occurred, was rare. Like so much of the contention over prestige that marks Balinese society in virtually every aspect, the normal result was local commotion and general standoff, an overall maintenance of status relations amid a repeating and often quite vigorous effort to alter them. The sphere within which any particular lord could actually play the divine-king game was circumscribed by the points where he lost touch with his social base if he became too grand; yet the threat of falling behind in the spectacle race if he failed to stay grand enough kept him pushing against those limits. Like its plot and scenery, the cast of the theatre state was not easily changed. Though the nineteenth century was rent by virtually continuous intrigue, dispute, violence, and an enormous amount of micro-upheaval, the overall pattern of repute and precedence, the structure of regard, was largely the same at its end as at its beginning. Whatever the vastness of aspiration, there was a very great deal of running in place.

The situation we have seen in Tabanan was thus characteristic:

a paramount lord with a subparamount at his symbolic heels; sub-subparamounts at theirs; leading lords at the subsubparamounts'; minor lords at the leading lords'; and so on down through the finer distinctions of the separate houses, each aspirant trying to lessen the gap on the upward side and widen it on the downward. Because the actual control over men and resources (the political center of gravity, so to speak) sat very low in the system, and because concrete attachments were multiple, fragile, overlapping, and personal, a complex and changeful system of alliances and oppositions emerged as the lords tried to immobilize their immediate upward rivals (make them dependent) and maintain the support of their immediate downward ones (keep them deferential). And though important noises could now and then be heard, as a branch split or a house was leveled, the main sound was a hum of intrigue, constant, diffuse, and without direction.

Over larger periods of time or over larger stretches of space, major shifts in political fortune could and did, of course, take place: Majapahit gave way, Gèlgèl appeared; Gèlgèl gave way, Klungkung appeared. But for all that, the characteristic form seems to have reconstructed itself continually, as Balinese theory claims that it should; new courts modeled themselves on vanished ones, reemerging under different names and in different places as but further transcriptions of a fixed ideal. Like particular kings, particular states were mortal; but like kings, their mortality does not seem to have made much difference. The scale of things varied, and their brilliance, as well as the details of their immediate expression. But not, so far as I can see, between, say, 1343 and 1906, what they were all about.

— 7 —

Power, defined as the capacity to make decisions by which others are bound, with coercion its expression, violence its foundation, and domination its aim, is the rock to which, heir despite itself to the sixteenth century, most of modern political theory clings—the great simple that remains through all sophistications and to which all reasonings, whether of justice, liberty, virtue, or order, must eventually return. This cycle of terms, and related ones like control, command, strength, and subjection, defines the political as a domain of social action. Politics, finally, is about mastery: "Women and Horses and Power and War."

This view is hardly wrong, even for places where the horses are docile. But, as the evocation of Kipling suggests, it is a view, and, like all views, it is partial and grows out of a specific tradition of interpretation of historical experience. It is not given in the sheer nature of things (whatever that may be), a brute fact brutely apprehended, but is an extended, socially constructed gloss, a collective representation. Other traditions of interpretation, usually less self-conscious, produce other glosses, different representations. It has been the central argument of this work, displayed in the very divisions of its content and directive through the whole of its unfolding, that the life that swirled around the punggawas, perbekels, puris, and jeros of classical Bali comprised such an alternate conception of what politics is about and what power comes to. A structure of action, now bloody, now ceremonious, the negara was also, and as such, a structure of thought. To describe it is to describe a constellation of enshrined ideas.

It ought not to be necessary, since Wittgenstein, to insist explicitly that such an assertion involves no commitment to idealism, to a subjectivist conception of social reality, or to a denial of the force of ambition, might, accident, cleverness, and material interest in determining the life chances of men. But as the social sciences, for all their topical and practical modernity, live philosophically not in this century but in the last, possessed by fears of metaphysical ghosts, it unfortunately is necessary. Ideas are not, and have not been for some time, unobservable mental stuff. They are envehicled meanings, the vehicles being symbols (or in some usages, signs), a symbol being anything that denotes, describes, represents, exemplifies, labels, indicates, evokes, depicts, expresses—anything that somehow or other signifies. And anything that somehow or other signifies is intersubjective, thus public, thus accessible to overt and corrigible *plein air* explication. Arguments, melodies, formulas, maps, and pictures are not idealities to be stared at but texts to be read; so are rituals, palaces, technologies, and social formations.

The whole description of the negara developed in the foregoing pages is intended to be such a reading: that part of it devoted to irrigation or village organization or landscape or taxation equally with that devoted to myth, iconography, ceremony, or divine kingship; that part devoted to treaties as that devoted to temples; that to trade as that to priestcraft; and that part devoted to the structure alike of genealogies, clientship, courtyards, and cremations. The confinement of interpretive analysis in most of contemporary anthropology to the supposedly more "symbolic" aspect of culture is a mere prejudice, born out of the notion, also a gift of the nineteenth century, that "symbolic" opposes to "real" as fanciful to sober, figurative to literal, obscure to plain, aesthetic to practical, mystical to mundane, and decorative to substantial. To construe the expressions of the theatre state, to apprehend them as theory, this prejudice, along with the allied one that the dramaturgy of power is external to its workings, must be put aside. The real is as imagined as the imaginary.

That Balinese politics, like everyone else's, including ours, was symbolic action does not imply, therefore, that it was all in the mind or consisted entirely of dances and incense. The aspects of that politics here reviewed—exemplary ceremonial, model-and-copy hierarchy, expressive competition, and iconic kingship; organizational pluralism, particulate loyalty, dispersive authority, and confederate rule—configurated a reality as dense and immediate as the island itself. The men (and, as consorts, intrigantes, and place markers, the women) who made their way through this reality—building palaces, drafting treaties, collecting rents, leasing trade, making marriages, dispatching rivals, investing temples, erecting pyres, hosting feasts, and imaging gods—were pursuing the ends they could conceive through the means they had. The dramas of the theatre state, mimetic of themselves, were, in the end, neither illusions nor lies, neither sleight of hand nor make-believe. They were what there was.

NOTES

Each note is keyed to a page and line of the text by a pair of numbers above the note; the first number refers to a page, the second number to a line on that page. The line keying is loose in that it refers to the first line of a passage to which a note, either in part or whole, is relevant.

Within the notes themselves, cross-references to points in the text are indicated by the word *text*, followed by a page number; to points in the notes by *notes* and a page number. Again, cross-references only refer to the page on which the relevant passage begins.

4-3

For *negara*, see Gonda, 1952, pp. 61, 73, 243, 423, 432; Juynboll, 1923, p. 310; Pigeaud, n.d., pp. 303, 309. For *desa*, see Gonda, 1952, pp. 65, 81, 342; Juynboll, 1923, p. 302; Pigeaud, n.d., p. 66. In Bali, *desa* is found in inscriptions as early as the mid-tenth century, and *negara*, in the mid-eleventh (Goris, 1954, vol. 1, pp. 71, 106). Both terms appear repeatedly in classical Javanese writings, notably the *Nagarakertagama* (Pigeaud, 1960-63, vol. 5, pp. 144, 205-206).

The use of *desa* in the sense of "dependency," "a territory governed by a sultan" (Gonda, 1952, p. 81) is found in the Dyak language, where the verb *mandesa* means "to subject," "to pacify." In some areas, for example West Sumatra (Willinck, 1909) and Ambon (Cooley, 1962), the reverse of this process seems to have occurred, so that the term *negeri* is used for local, politically autonomous settlement complexes as an expression of their independence. In Bali, the term *puri* ("palace") is rather more commonly used than *negara* as such, but it has essentially the same multiple meaning (see Pigeaud, 1900-63, vol. 3, pp. 9, 13). It derives from Sanskrit, *pura*, meaning "castle," "town" (Gonda, 1952, p. 219). Though today *pura*—that is, with a terminal *a* rather than *i*—means "temple" in Bali, earlier this contrast seems not to have been made (Korn, 1932, pp. 10-11). See *notes*, p. 215.

137

In modern Indonesian, *negara* means "state," *negeri*, "country" or "land," though the two are sometimes also interchanged. On the use of the term *desa* in Bali, see *notes*, p. 156.

4-15

The denomination of the "classical period" in Indonesian history has been a continual source of difficulty. Most scholars have used "Hindu" or "Hindu-Javanese," merely noting that the term "Hindu" is intended to cover forms both of Buddhism and Brahmanism (e.g., Coedès, 1948; Krom, 1931). Harrison (1954) has used "Indianized" in an attempt to avoid this problem (cf. the translation of Coedès, 1948: Coedès, 1968); but, as this term suggests a rather broader and deeper impact of India on Indonesia than seems to have taken place, I have chosen "Indic" (and "Indicized") to stress the predominantly religio-aesthetic rather than social, economic, or political nature of Indian influence.

4-19

Much depends, of course, on what one regards as a proper state and on one's view of the nature of classical political organization. Thus Krom (1931), with his highly integral, "Roman Empire," view of traditional state structure, can reduce the number of "kingdoms" in precolonial Java to a few dozen at most, whereas Schrieke (1957, pp. 152-217), with a sociologically more realistic approach, can list well over 200 "realms" of various sorts, descriptions, and degrees of autonomy. For the archipelago as a whole, Purnadi (1961) reports that at the beginning of the twentieth century there were still no less than 350 independent or semi-independent principalities in existence, by that time virtually all of them outside Java.

4-21

For the oldest inscriptions, see Krom, 1931, pp. 71-80; de Casparis, 1956. Chinese reports of Indicized states in the archipelago appear somewhat earlier, but are not altogether certain (Krom, 1931, p. 62). That the process of state formation was well begun by the time Indicization began is, however, by now beyond much doubt (van Leur, 1955, pp. 92ff.). For a general review of Indonesian historiographical problems, see Soedjatmoko et al., 1965.

4-30

For a similar characterization, see Stutterheim, 1932, pp. 31-33; Wertheim, 1965. The "Oriental despotism" reference is to the "hydraulic state" theories of Wittfogel (1957; for his Bali references, see pp. 53-54).

5-12

For a methodological explication and New World application of the "developmental" or "structural" approach, see Phillips and Willey, 1953, and Willey and Phillips, 1955. For a coercive argument for the (prospective) usefulness of such an approach in Southeast Asia, together with a multitude of suggestions as to problems it might begin by attacking, see Benda, 1962. By far the most restrained, useful, and readable of the annalistic syntheses of Indic-period history is Coedès, 1948 (English translation, Coedès, 1968), and for Indonesia alone, Krom, 1931. Hall, 1955, contains the best English summary. When mainland Southeast Asian and Chinese sources are systematically combed, as they by and large have not been, the annalistic history of Indonesia may improve somewhat in reliability. For a review and evaluation of the few attempts to write developmental history—there called "sociological"—see Wertheim, 1965. For an attempt of my own on a recent and local scale, see C. Geertz, 1965 (cf. C. Geertz, 1956). Koentjaraningrat (1965) reviews "anthropological" approaches to the study of Indonesian history generally.

6-15

Berg, 1961b. The Krom work referred to is Krom, 1931.

6-19

Schrieke, 1955, 1957; van Leur, 1955; see also Bosch, 1961b. Both Burger (1948-50) and Wertheim (1959) take a generally developmental rather than annalistic approach to Indonesian history, but neither is more than incidentally concerned with the Indic period as such.

7-25

Raffles, 1830, vol. 2, p. cxliii. What Raffles actually said, however, was that Bali formed "a sort of commentary on the ancient condition of Java," a much more acceptable formulation. For an example of this sort of uncritical use of Balinese ethnography for a reconstruction of social and religious life in Indic Java, complete with paintings (by Walter Spies) offered as pictures of life in Majapahit (and even Shailendra) times, see the chapters on "De Maatschappij" and "De Godsdienst" in Stutterheim, 1932.

8-37

For general summaries of Balinese history, see Swellengrebel, 1960; Hanna, 1976. Van Eck (1878-80) gives an excellent schematic review of the course of events up to about 1840, and Shastri (1963) gives an annalistic account of the pre-Majapahit period based mainly on Balinese sources and traditions. For an excellent history of the writing of Balinese history, see Boon, 1977, pt. 1.

Direct Dutch rule in the south-Balinese heartland began only in the first decade of this century. (North Bali was reduced in 1846-49, direct administration beginning in 1882. The Balinese areas of Lombok—for the history of which, see van der Kraan, 1973—were brought under administrative control in 1894.) Of course, "official" Dutch "sovereignty" over the Netherlands East Indies as a whole, and Dutch control over inter-island relations, had a marked effect on Bali long before then. Significant Dutch interference in Balinese internal affairs dates from the end of the eighteenth century in connection with the slave trade, and in 1839 various south-Balinese kings and princes signed the first contracts giving the Dutch nominal sovereignty (van Eck, 1878-80). For a description of the military side of Dutch activity in Bali in the nineteenth century, see Nypels, 1897, and van Vlijman, 1875; for a Balinese view, see Geria, 1957; for Lombok, see Cool, 1896. Brief summaries of the Dutch takeover in Bali can be found in Tate, 1971, pp. 307-311, and Hanna, 1971. But for all this, compared to its impact on Java at least, Dutch rule had but marginal effect on the internal life of Bali prior to this century.

10-1

The use of the term "Indic" in this work implies no more than that the states involved were prominently marked with some ideas, practices, symbols, and institutions whose provenance is India; its use does not assume any judgment about the relative importance of Indian, Oceanian (most especially Polynesian), and Chinese influences, either in the states' formation or in their nineteenth-century forms. In particular it is not an "Indian-colony" view, and as such it is equivalent to "classical" and used interchangeably with it.

11-1

Balinese tradition places the founding of Mengwi in 1728 (Simpen, 1958a). For earlier wars between Mengwi and its neighbors, see Friederich, 1959, pp. 131-132. For a military doctor's brief description of Mengwi and its rulers in 1881, see Jacobs, 1883, pp. 198ff; cf. van den Broek, 1834, pp. 178-180, who made a one-day visit there around 1820. The 1891 war is briefly described from the Tabanan point of view in Tabanan, n.d., pp. 104-106.

11-15

In addition, there were two other important kingdoms, Bulèlèng in the north and Jembrana in the west; but these were by then under direct Dutch control.

11-18

The king himself was, again, borne on the shoulders of his retainers. The suicide marches (*puputan*, literally "ending") are described in Covarrubias, 1956, pp. 32-37; Hanna, 1976, pp. 74-75. Baum (1937, pp. 337-417) has a fictionalized but generally convincing account of them, and Nieuwenkamp (1906-10, pp. 169-176, 201-203) has brief eye-witness accounts; van Geuns (1906) describes how Badung and Tabanan looked just after them. For Balinese views, see Simpen, 1958b; Mishra, 1973, 1976; Tabanan, n.d., pp. 114-126.

There were, in fact, two separate puputans in Badung, for there was more than one "king"; and yet a third ruler seems to have been murdered by his chief priest as the Dutch advanced. Mishra (1973) estimates from Balinese manuscript sources that "no less than" 3,600 Balinese died in the Badung puputans. Dutch casualties (their army consisted of upwards of 5,000 men) are unknown, but were very slight at best. The puputan is an old tradition in Bali: Friederich (1959, p. 24) reports one in the Balinese part of Lombok dur-

ing the first part of the nineteenth century in which the king and all
but two members of a royal family committed suicide upon defeat
by a rival Bali-Lombok state (Mataram). Cf. Worsley, 1972, p. 231,
for a Bulèlèng example.

13-3

Aside from the literature quoted, the following description and
analysis is based on an extended series of interviews, mainly with
older men, conducted in Bali during 1957-58. The three most important informants were I Wayan Gusti Purna of Tabanan, Ida
Bagus Putu Maron of Ubud, and Cakorda Gdé Oka Ijeg [Iyeg]- of
Klungkung. Gusti Purna, a Wesia, born about 1880, was a lower
official (*perbekel*) in the Tabanan state at the turn of the century,
succeeding his father who had fought in the Mengwi wars. After
the Dutch conquest in 1906 he was appointed "official village chief"
(*bendesa*) of the town of Tabanan, a novel administrative unit, a
position he held until his retirement in 1937. Ida Bagus Maron, a
Brahmana, was born in 1885 in Mengwi, where his father was a
court priest. At the conquest of Mengwi by Badung and Tabanan,
his family fled to Pliatan, where his father again became attached
to the court, Ida Bagus Maron himself becoming a tax collector and
irrigation inspector (*sedahan gdé*) during the Dutch period. He
was one of V. E. Korn's "adat law" informants in the nineteen-
twenties and thirties (see C. J. Grader, n.d., pp. 29ff.). Cakorda Gdé
Ijeg, a Satria, was born in 1895. A ranking member of the royal
family of Klungkung, he participated in the puputan of 1908, being first wounded by gunfire and then, when he failed to die,
stabbed by his mother. Recovering nonetheless, he was exiled by the
Dutch to Lombok for twenty-two years, after which time he was
brought back to head the public works department, a job he still
held in 1958. In addition to these men, about thirty other people
provided information of greater or less extent, and of course material from my fieldwork in general has been brought in where relevant in the description. This too is probably the appropriate place
to acknowledge that a good deal of the material upon which this
study is based was gathered by my wife and coworker, Hildred
Geertz, and some by an Indonesian assistant, E. Rukasah.

13-24

The quotation is from von Heine-Geldern, 1942.

13-36

The quotation is from Swellengrebel, 1960. For more on this theme, see C. Geertz, 1968, 1973c, 1973g, 1977a.

14-4

The 1343 date is from the Javanese side—that is, the *Negarakerta-gama* (Pigeaud, 1960-63, vol. 3, p. 54)—and in fact this source suggests not one, but several opposing Balinese kings (Pigeaud, 1960-63, vol. 4, p. 143). The Balinese tradition puts the conquest a little earlier and recounts two expeditions (Swellengrebel, 1960, p. 22).

Contrary to what has sometimes been asserted, not only the ruling classes, but almost the entire population claims to be *wong Maja-pahit*, a fact van Eck noted already in the mid-nineteenth century (cited in Korn, 1932, p. 160). Those few (by now, probably less than one percent) who do not are referred to as *Bali Aga*, a generally derisive term meaning "indigenous Balinese" (Goris, 1960c). Some commoner Balinese see themselves as descendants of "pioneer" immigrants from Java who arrived in Bali prior to the Majapahit invasion (Sugriwa, 1957b).

14-14

The quotation is from Swellengrebel, 1960, p. 23. Scholars know little more. The first dated inscription, about setting up a monastery and royal resthouse in a mountain village, comes from the end of the ninth century (Goris, 1954, vol. 1, p. 6; vol. 2, pp. 119-120; on Balinese inscriptions, see also van Stein Callenfels, 1925; Stutterheim, 1929; Damais, 1951-69; de Casparis, 1956); and the oldest written sources of any sort are not older than A.D. 600 (Goris, n.d., p. 25). At the beginning of the eleventh century the first named king appears, and the language of the edicts shifts from old Balinese to old Javanese (Goris, 1954, vol. 2, pp. 129-130). Historical relations with Java are known from the eleventh century, and Javanese expeditions against Bali are reported from the thirteenth (Swellengrebel, 1960, p. 20; Pigeaud, 1960-63, vol. 3, p. 48). But from all this, little of real substance emerges except that Bali was Indicized before intensive Javanese contact began and that some still-present customs—three-day cycling markets, irrigation societies, ritual corvée—are very old. For a largely arbitrary, five-stage periodization of Balinese history (prehistoric, old indigenous, old Hindu-Balinese, late Hindu-Balinese, modern), see Goris, n.d. For some (unpersuasive) speculations on pre-Majapahit Bali, see Quaritch-Wales, 1974, pp. 105-115.

14-17

Not only virtually all (male) nobles and priests can recount the following legend, but perhaps a majority of commoners as well. As with all legends, details of the story vary significantly with respect to the social position of the narrator, who is concerned to justify or undercut one or another present arrangement. In Bali, the main versions are by region, and the version given here follows that of my Klungkung informants. For a written version (in Indonesian), designed to be taught in the primary schools, see Njoka, 1957; for a Balinese-language version, Regeg, n.d. (a); for a Dutch summary, Kersten, 1947, pp. 99-101; for a modern historical account, Berg, 1927, pp. 93-167; for a classical Balinese text on Gèlgèl, Berg, 1929; for primary texts from other regions, Worsley, 1972; Tabanan, n.d.; Berg, 1922.

15-6

For the view that Indic-period literary materials are more useful for a comprehension of Indonesian religio-political concepts than as reliable historical records, see Berg, 1927, 1939, 1951a, 1961a. Despite this insight, Berg has nevertheless attempted (1950, 1951b, 1965) to "reinterpret" such materials, despite their surface unreliability, so as to yield a hitherto concealed annalistic history, a somewhat cryptographic effort in which I am disinclined to follow. For criticisms of some of Berg's more substantive historical arguments and conclusions, see Bosch, 1956; de Casparis, 1961; and Zoetmulder, 1965.

15-34

Bali is pictured at this time as a unitary state involved in nearly perpetual combat with Blambangan to the west and Lombok to the east, and beyond them, less continually, with Pasuruan, Makassar, and Sumbawa. After the dissolution of Gèlgèl—about the same time that Dutch power was becoming solidly established in the archipelago—the legend concentrates entirely on intra-Bali conflicts between lord and lord, region and region.

16-38

The extraordinarily complex and highly irregular Balinese system of prestige stratification has yet to be adequately described, though Korn (1932, pp. 136ff.) gives a great deal of useful, if unorganized and unanalyzed, data. As I am concerned here only with the relation of stratificatory concepts to political thought, I make no attempt to outline the system as such. For some comments on stratification, or hierarchy, at the village level which suggest, but do not develop, my general views as to its nature, see C. Geertz, 1959, 1963b, 1964; Geertz and Geertz, 1975. Cf. Boon, 1977, pp. 145-185; Boon, 1973, pp. 173-246; Kersten, 1947, 99ff. For some Balinese views, see Bagus, 1969b.

17-1

Thus, as each region in Bali has a legend to account for the spatial branching and subbranching of royal power from an original, unitary center, so (virtually) each title group in Bali has such a legend to account (in genealogical, sinking status terms) for their present rank. For some published examples, see Sugriwa, 1957b, 1958; Regeg, n.d. (b), n.d. (c); Berg, 1922. "Royal" examples, where the "geographical" and "genealogical" myths of course converge, include Regeg, n.d. (a) and especially Worsley, 1972. A number of other examples (e.g., Tabanan, n.d.) exist in manuscript form.

17-7

The doctrine of reincarnation is known in Bali in a vague, general, and rather idiosyncratic way, but it is of relatively small importance; and the entire dharma-karma-samsara doctrine, as an effective social belief, is absent. Cf. C. J. Grader, n.d., pp. 66-69.

17-12

The application of the Indian varna system to the Balinese title hierarchy is, and seems always to have been, a very loose and irregular matter upon which the Balinese themselves do not always agree. Though the varna—in Bali, *warna*—concept has its uses, both for the Balinese and for scholars, in giving a highly general picture of the stratificatory situation, a circumstantial understanding of Balinese prestige ranking can only be had by thinking of the ranking of the literally scores of actual titles, a matter concerning which most of the detailed research remains to be done. For a full outline of the warna pattern of thought among Balinese intellectuals, complete with "high," "medium," and "low" subcategories within each category, see Korn, 1932, p. 146ff. Korn himself regards all this as "somewhat artificial" and argues that the Dutch desire to preserve the caste system as the (so they thought) "fundamental basis of Balinese society," and to use it for administrative and legal purposes, led to a much greater systematization of it than ever existed among the Balinese (pp. 175-176).

On the deification by the Balinese of their Majapahit "ancestors" (*Batara Maospait*), see Worsley, 1972, pp. 54-55, 96. On recent changes in the operation of the title-warna system, see Boon, 1977, pt. 2; Boon, 1973, chap. 4; Bagus, 1969b.

18-4

For the Mahayuga system as such, see Basham, 1952, pp. 321-322. The higher levels of the system, the four-thousand-million-year *kalpa* cycle or the three-million-year *manvantara* one, seem to have no importance in Bali at all. For Balinese time reckoning, see Covarrubias, 1956, pp. 313-316; Goris, 1960b; C. Geertz, 1973h.

18-18

Bateson, 1937. Cf. Worsley, 1972, pp. 75-82.

19-35

Karengasem, somewhat separated by a dry and hilly area from the central core region, forms a pocket slightly off to one side; but the distance from the wet rice line to the coast is about the same as in Klungkung. For the distribution of wet rice growing in Bali, see Raka, 1955, p. 29.

20-4

The population figures are from the Indonesian Bureau of the Census. The percentage of the total population of Bali living in the south is virtually unchanged between the 1920, 1930, 1960, and 1970 censuses. The admittedly very approximate and unreliable estimates of Raffles at the beginning of the nineteenth century give about the same proportions for a population put at less than half the present one (Raffles, 1830, vol. 2, p. cxxxii). (For 1900, van Eerde [1910] estimates the Balinese population at about 750,000, with another 20,000 in the Balinese-settled parts of Lombok.)

The longtime centering of Balinese civilization in the south is also indicated by the fact that virtually all the early inscriptions (Goris, 1954) are from south Bali (a number are from the central mountain region, but were erected by southern lords), as well as by the traditional name of the north-Bali kingdom of Bulèlèng, Den Bukit, which means literally "on the other side of the mountain(s)."

20-29

Liefrinck, 1877.

22-3

The one possible exception is Bangli. But the prominence of Bangli was only a temporary phenomenon, a reflex of the Dutch presence in Bulèlèng. In fact, its role, never really very crucial in an all-Bali setting, was more that of the most powerful upland court than of the least powerful lowland one. For a few years during the mid-nineteenth century, however (Liefrinck, 1877; *text*, p. 89), it does form something of a marginal case.

22-41

For examples, see Korn, 1932, p. 401; Friederich, 1959, p. 123.

23-2

For an overly sharp, somewhat misinterpreted division between "appanage-areas" (i.e., lord-influenced regions) and "old Balinese areas," see Korn, 1932, passim. Korn's theories are summarized and applied to some contemporary examples in Lansing, 1977, chap. 1. For a critical view, see C. Geertz, 1961.

23-6

For some examples, see Gunning and van der Heijden, 1926.

24-3

The references to "despotism," and so on, are again directed against Wittfogel (1957) and work derivative from him (e.g., Hunt and Hunt, 1976). On the problem of frontiers in Indicized states, see Leach, 1960, from whom the "MacMahon line" quote comes. His work is on Burma, but, in this regard, fits the Balinese case precisely. On Balinese "neutral zones" (*kewalonan*), see Korn, 1932, p. 437; de Kat Angelino, 1921a. For a slight exception to the generalization that borders were not matters of "interstate" political concern, see Korn, 1922, p. 63. Worsley (1975, p. 112) argues, on the basis of the *Babad Bulèlèng*, for defined boundaries for Den Bukit, but this seems a literary optical illusion.

24-33

Korn, 1932, p. 440. A description of the main "princely families" in south Bali around the middle of the nineteenth century can be found in Friederich, 1959, pp. 119-136.

26-20

Van Eerde (1910, p. 5) says that in the Balinese areas of Lombok 6,000, of a population of around 20,000, were triwangsa. This is thirty percent, which is much higher than the seven to ten percent usually cited, largely without evidence, for Bali proper, and may be closer to the truth, though still a bit high. (Gerdin [1977] estimates a twenty percent figure for contemporary Lombok.) Of the 6,000 triwangsa, 2,000 were Brahmanas (of whom 175 were priests—*pedanda*); 4,000 were Satrias and Wesias, with (at an even more general guess) about 200 of them politically significant.

27-4

For a case history of a powerful Sudra house, see Boon, 1973, chap. 2; Boon, 1977, chap. 4.

27-25

For a discussion of this point and a full description of the Balinese kinship system, see Geertz and Geertz, 1975. Cf. Boon, 1973, 1976, 1977; Gerdin, 1977; Belo, 1936.

28-8

Dadia is actually the commoner term for these groups in the Klung-kung region, and it is employed here merely for simplicity. In fact, terms vary widely (Geertz and Geertz, 1975; Gerdin, 1977; Lansing, 1977). Perhaps the most common term for gentry dadia is *batur*. Commoner and gentry dadia differ somewhat in structure and mode of functioning (Geertz and Geertz, 1975), and assertions in the text are designed to apply to gentry dadia.

30-22

Primogenitural succession was not in fact universal, but it was strongly preferred. When circumstances forced a deviation, the inconsistency was always quickly rationalized in an attempt to avoid the legitimacy conflicts which tended to follow it, and very commonly a return to the original core line occurred in the succeeding generation (sometimes the disfranchised elder brother was simply "remembered" as a younger brother by succeeding generations and depicted as such in genealogies). Genealogical manipulation was made easier by the fact that in the genealogies themselves individuals appeared not under personal names, but general titles. On all this, see Geertz and Geertz, 1975.

31-11

As a sub-dadia always remained a subpart of the dadia, it could sink only so low, no matter how far back its core-line origins. One does not find the descent to mere commonality reported in some other Southeast Asian systems—the Thai, for example (Jones, 1971). The meanest sub-dadia still partook of whatever status the dadia as a whole achieved within the larger political system, and in fact sub-dadias which had drifted quite far from the core tended to be lumped together so far as rank was concerned; the nicety of discrimination tended to diminish as groups moved further from the center.

35-25

The size of "harems" in nineteenth-century Bali (then as now Bali had a virilocal residence rule) is difficult to determine with any precision. Covarrubias (1956, p. 157) speaks of "old records" mentioning kings with as many as 200 wives, but neglects to give a reference. Korn (1932, p. 469) speaks of "the king" having 80 to 100 or more wives at the beginning of this century and remarks that "the time of princes with 500 wives lies far behind us." It may, in fact, lie as far back as "once upon a time."

The presence of different-status wives in the lord's harem led to severe complications of the succession pattern outlined above. These are too intricate to go into here, save to say that in theory at least only the children by endogamous wives (*padmi, parameswari*) had full succession rights; those by hypergamous wives (*penawing*) were graded according to their mothers' origins. See Geertz and Geertz, 1975; Boon, 1977.

35-38

For a discussion of a similar pattern with similar implications in Burma, see Leach, 1954, pp. 215-219. The wargi relation was not exclusive. One lower dadia could have such ties with several higher ones. The term *wargi* was not used for affinal or matrilateral ties between status equals, and though the term literally means relative through the mother (and *perwargian*, the whole group of such relatives) it was thus never used for such relatives when one's mother came from within one's own dadia.

37-11

For the lawbook reference, see Korn, 1960.

37-20

For a list of bagawantas in the various regions of early nineteenth-century Bali, as well as a brief description of their functions, see Friederich, 1959, pp. 106-107. No Brahmana priest could enter the all-Bali state temple at Besakih (*text*, p. 40) except in the company of a lord to whom he was bagawanta.

On the siwa-sisia relation generally (where the latter, "disciple," term is more carefully glossed as "one desirous of obtaining holy water" or as "one who feels constantly in a giving-receiving relationship with a [Brahmana priestly house, a *griya*]"), see Hooykaas, 1964b. Brahmana priests are also sometimes called *patirtaan* (from *tirta*, "holy water") by their sisia (Swellengrebel, 1947), or else called *surya*, from the (Sanskrit-borrowed) word for "sun" (Hooykaas, n.d.).

37-39

A fuller description of commercial life in the negara is given below, *text*, p. 87, where the appropriate documentary references will also be found.

39-27

The quoted phrases are from a treaty between Gianyar and Badung (plus Tabanan) concluded not so very long before these two became once again mortal enemies. See Korn, 1922, p. 99.

40-18

At this level, political marriage was rarer than at the intraregional level; and, when it did occur, it was more symmetrically balanced so as to maintain at least the semblance of status equality. (It was not called *wargi*.) In fact, the delicacy of the adjustments and the combustibility of the sentiments involved was such that the negotiation of interregional marriages probably led at least as often to conflict as it did to solidarity.

40-21

On the Sad Kahyangan see C. J. Grader, 1960b, and n.d., pp. 20-28; see also Goris, 1960a. Sad Kahyangan lists, either from informants or in the literature, do not always consist of precisely six temples, but sometimes eight or nine. *Kahyangan*, "place of the gods" (*hyang* —"god," "spirit"), is an elevated word for *pura*, "temple." *Sad* is "six."

40-34

The congruence between relative political importance and relative scale of expression in Besakih was far from exact. Some very powerful negaras (Gianyar, Badung) had but limited representation, whereas by the nineteenth century some less consequential ones (Kaba Kaba, Sukawati, Blahbatuh) had whole temple sections associated with them. But this seems to have been a mere result of more rapidly changing political fortunes outrunning more slowly moving ceremonial forms. Klungkung's preeminent symbolic position was, however, quite clearly expressed in her "possession" on the centermost courtyard. For a circumstantial account of Besakih as a spiritual paradigm of all-Bali political relations, see Goris, 1937; cf. Hooykaas, 1964a, pp. 172-187; C. J. Grader, n.d., pp. 17, 26-27, 46-51.

41-1

For examples of such treaties, some dating back to the beginning of the eighteenth century, see Korn, 1922; Liefrinck, 1915, and 1921, pp. 370-461. Cf. Utrecht, 1962.

41-12

Korn, 1922, pp. 95-101. Whether all treaties were concluded in such a ceremonial manner is not clear, for the bulk of the treaties do not indicate the immediate context in which they were signed.

42-24

The catch phrases of the treaties, which were used to refer to these "certified negaras," speak alternately of the "seven" (*pitung*), "eight" (*akutus*), or even—when only the eastern regions plus Lombok are in view—"four" (*petang*) negaras, though the actual states listed under these rubrics are not always precisely the same (Korn, 1922, p. 105).

43-16

Korn, 1922, pp. 67-71, 79, 83. Again, one needs to remember the minuscule size of many of these political entities if one is to get the feel of the thing.

43-27

van Eck, 1878-80.

44-8

van Eck, 1878-80. For a detailed description of the very complex series of struggles which took place in the Bangli-Klungkung-Karengasem-Gianyar area in the second half of the ninetenth century, see Gunning and van der Heijden, 1926; de Kat Angelino, 1921a. Friederich (1959, pp. 119-136) gives a general review of the "quarrels without end" among lords in the first half of the century.

45-11

Dorpsrepubliek means, simply, "village republic." The classic summary statement of this view of the Balinese village, "That the village forms a closed, self-contained unit—a republic, as Korn has appropriately called it—may be assumed to be generally known," is Goris's very influential paper on "The Religious Character of the Village Community" (1960a); but the theme is found in virtually all the colonial-period work on Balinese life. See especially Korn, 1933 and 1932, pp. 75ff. For an alternative view of Balinese village organization, see C. Geertz, 1959 and 1964, and *text*, p. 45.

45-16

The "patriarchal communism" phrase is from Covarrubias, 1956, p. 57. ("The feudalism of the Hindu aristocracy was curiously only superimposed on the Balinese patriarchal communism, and centuries of feudal rule have failed to do away with the closed independence of the village communities.") His is perhaps the baldest statement of the dorpsrepubliek theory. For a vivid, novelistic treatment, based on Dutch scholarly sources, of desa-negara relations in these terms, see Baum, 1937. For a "non-hydraulic," "conquest" (but not much more persuasive), despotism view of (Lombok) Balinese state organization, see van der Kraan, 1973.

46-3

The main, and quite partial, exception to this was Singaraja in north Bali. But there the urban development was a reflex of the development of the Java Sea trade economy and was mainly staffed by non-Balinese: Bugis, Chinese, Arabs, Javanese, Malays, and others (*text*, p. 88).

47-2

The main architect of this theory is, once more, Korn (e.g., 1932, pp. 78, 93—of which my brief summary is a paraphrase). Goris (1960a), again, also employs it freely (and, again, much less subtly), as though it were an established fact rather than a highly speculative and, so far as I can see, not very well-supported hypothesis; and it is presented with the same air of just-so certainty, and the same lack of supporting evidence, in Swellengrebel's summary of Balinese

culture (1960, p. 32). For a particularly vivid example of a desperate
attempt to square the known, or somewhat known, facts of political
structure in eighteenth- and nineteenth-century Bali with the dorpsrepubliek notion by invoking Javanese imperialism as the recon-
structive force—much as Krom (1931) once invoked Hindu imperialism for Java—see van Stein Callenfels, 1947-48. It is not only
the Balinese who subscribe to the "myth of Majapahit." This "appanage" conception of rural social organization in "lowland" regions is also summarized in Lansing, 1977, chap. 2.

48-6

In C. Geertz, 1963b, pp. 85-90. The need for schematic description
here makes it impossible to do even approximate justice to the details of Balinese village organization, particularly to their variation.
For more extended descriptions and analyses, see C. Geertz, 1959,
1962, 1963b, 1964; H. Geertz, 1959; Geertz and Geertz, 1975; Hobart,
1975. Again, terms vary widely; again, I have used those current in
Klungkung.

48-11

Unlike the negara system, which direct Dutch incursion after 1906
altered rather radically (see *notes*, p. 254), the desa system of today
is not vastly changed—at least with regard to the aspects of it discussed here—from that of the nineteenth century. Thus, the use of
the past tense should not be taken (as by and large it can be taken
in my descriptions of "the Balinese state") as indicating that the
phenomena mentioned have either disappeared or been considerably transformed.

49-23

A similar use of *krama* seems to appear in the old Javanese text,
Kidung Sunda, in the form of *balakrama* (*bala*, "army"), meaning,
evidently, "soldiers" or "guards" (Gonda, 1952, p. 305). Modern
Javanese villagers also often use the word in this sense, and "Pak
Krama" is perhaps the most common "John Doe" term for a Java-
nese peasant.

50-3

The subak is extensively discussed below (*text*, chap. 3, under "The

Politics of Irrigation"), where the appropriate references are also provided.

51-11

The terms applied to the temple congregation were, and are, more various than those applied to the hamlet and the irrigation society. In some cases, *pemaksan* indicates a voluntary worship group of some sort, rather than the obligatory one discussed here. However, among the many terms used for the nonvoluntary "three-temple" congregation we are concerned with here, *pemaksan* is perhaps the most common, and it is widely used for "worship group" pure and simple. For this definition, see Kusuma, 1956a. Though *paksa*, the root from which pemaksan derives, means "coercion," "force," or even "violence" or "punishment," as well as "obligation," "task," and "necessity," in modern Balinese it apparently in turn derives from a Sanskrit root meaning "faction," "party," "group of adherents," "opinion" (Gonda, 1973, pp. 234, 546, 556).

51-19

There have been some attempts (e.g., Goris, 1960a) to use *agama* ("religious text") as the functional equivalent in Bali of *hukum* (i.e., "Muslim law") or even of canon law in medieval Europe. But such a view has no place in Balinese thought, where a*gama* simply means the more directly religious, that is, sacred, aspects of adat (cf. C. Geertz, 1973e). Actually, the hukum-adat contrast does not hold universally in the rest of the archipelago, especially in Java, which, though Muslim, contains great blocs of people whose concept of the nature and place of adat is rather more like the Indic Balinese than the properly Islamic notion from which it stems. See, in this connection, C. Geertz, 1960, esp. pt. 1. For Indic law in Southeast Asia generally, see Hooker, 1978.

51-26

The number of these variations is virtually infinite, and a good deal of Balinese ethnography has consisted merely in recording them. See especially Korn, 1932—a sprawling, disordered, but magnificently detailed and carefully researched seven-hundred-page tome largely devoted to their compilation.

For some examples of the matters mentioned in the text: In some hamlet councils all married men sit, in others only those with children; in some, men retire from participation when their sons enter, in others they remain until their wife dies, in yet others until they themselves die. Some hamlet officers are elected, others are chosen in rotation, others appointed by outgoing officers, others succeed by inheritance; and both modes of recompense and periods of office vary widely. In some hamlets fines are heavy to the point of onerousness, in some light to the point of ineffectiveness; and virtually all stages in between are also found. How long after their death persons are to be buried, how long members of the pemaksan are ritually polluted (*sebel*) following a death (and the implications of such pollution for social activities), and how many days of work hamlet members must contribute when one of them holds a cremation show the same wide variation from pemaksan to pemaksan. (In some pemaksan, there is even a *sebel* period after marriage—Korn, 1932, p. 180.) In some villages triwangsas must go to temple festivals, in others they are forbidden to do so; in some they sit on hamlet councils, on others they do not; in some they are liable to public-works obligations, in others not; and recognition of various sumptuary rights—to build certain styles of gateways, to be buried in a separate cemetery, and so on—is accorded them in some places, refused them in others. In some villages pots may not be made, in others bluing is forbidden, in others rice wine may not be made; opium smoking is considered pemaksan-polluting in some, and goats may not be bred in at least one village (Korn, 1932, pp. 81-82). As for "ritual technicalities," they are endless, running from divergent practices following the birth of twins (Belo, 1970b; H. Geertz, 1959), through the form and length of temple festivals (Belo, 1953), to the mere prohibition of certain rituals altogether. (In one hamlet I studied, the famous Rangda-Barong dance drama [Belo, 1949] was even forbidden as "unlucky"; and, reputedly, in some hamlets even gamelan orchestras may not play.) The main point, however, is that although every pemaksan differs in some adat matter from every other one, or at least every other nearby one, within a single pemaksan, no matter how large or how bounded, there is complete consensus.

For examples of written desa adat constitutions (*awig-awig desa adat*), the first an actual one, the second a modern composite, see Geertz and Geertz, 1975, pp. 182-196, and Sudhana, 1972.

52-9

Actually, there are various more indigenous terms used as equivalents of *desa adat,* all indicating, in one way or another, the notion of sanctified space: *perbumian, wewengkan desa, bumi, gumi pelasan, payar, kuhum* (Korn, 1932, p. 81; see also Korn, 1933, p. 26). As noted earlier, the term *desa* itself, unqualified, is reserved for the whole complex of local groupings and is, in fact, both rather vaguely and quite variously applied. On this problem, see C. Geertz, 1959. Reading present arrangements into the past, even the fairly recent past, is a tricky business; but I see no reason to believe that the basic outlines of the village system were different in the nineteenth century from those in the mid-twentieth, and what fragmentary evidence on village organization in the nineteenth century we do have (e.g., van Stein Callenfels, 1947-48; van Bloemen Waanders, 1859) supports this view.

52-11

The quotation—a standard Balinese formula—is from Liefrinck, 1927, p. 230. "Belongs" is not the best translation here, for it is really not a "property" concept in the Western sense that is involved (*text,* p. 127).

52-16

There is usually also an official head of the whole unit. This man, most often called the *bendesa adat,* is not a "village chief" in any recognizable sense, but the ranking expert on matters of adat, the person to whom questions of proper procedure are referred when there is doubt. Further, each of the three temples has attached to it a priest (*pemangku*) of its own who is responsible for conducting the ceremonial activities prescribed for it. This temple priest, who is never a Brahmana and usually a Sudra, must not be confused with the Brahmana high priest (*padanda, pandita*) referred to earlier.

52-34

For the negara as an adat "custom community," see *text,* p. 128.

53-4

In cases (more frequent than has sometimes been represented) where the three temple congregations do not wholly coincide, it is the Pura Balai Agung pemaksan which is taken as defining the desa adat boundaries. Balinese often refer to the desa adat as "one Balai Agung." For a general, somewhat overregularized, outline of the Balinese temple system, see Goris, 1938. For a brief but perceptive discussion of the desa adat and its relation to the banjar, see Hunger, 1932.

53-8

For a full description of such a ceremony (called an *odalan*), see Belo, 1953; cf. Hooykaas-van Leeuwen Boomkamp, 1961; Hooykaas, 1977.

Typically, each temple holds a three-day ceremony every 210 days (or, in the case of the Pura Balai Agung, which follows the solar-lunar calendar, every 355 days). This means that nearly one day in twenty is devoted to ritual alone. Further, at least a week of preparation is necessary for each ceremony; so the Balinese are concerned, in some measure or another, with Kahyangan Tiga matters nearly one day out of every seven, though of course the division of labor within the pemaksan considerably reduces the burden on any one individual or family. For some sense of the immense amount of "work" (*karya*) involved in temple festivals, see again Belo, 1953; Hooykaas-van Leeuwen Boomkamp, 1961; C. Grader, 1939.

53-20

For a concrete example of this partial dispersion and partial coincidence of membership among co-present corporate groups, sekas, in one Balinese "desa," see C. Geertz, 1964. However, even in so deviant a village as Korn's Tnganan (Korn, 1933), the locus classicus of dorpsrepubliek theorizing, it can be seen. On the "seka principle" (literally, *seka* means "to be as one"), "the equality of members in the context of the group of which they are members, the irrelevance of that membership with respect to other groups to which they may belong; and the legal precedence of originative groups over derivative ones," see Geertz and Geertz, 1975, pp. 165-166; cf. pp. 30-31, 115-116.

54-29

Tabanan (n.d.) is, in a sense, actually something of a written version of this "constitution." Completed in its present form sometime after the Dutch intrusion into Tabanan in 1906, it is not clear whether it is the work of a single author drawing on earlier palm-leaf manuscripts and summarizing and reworking them or the accumulation of a series of such manuscripts unreworked (for the former view, see Worsley, 1972, p. 85, n. 241). It consists of a discursively presented dynastic genealogy, in the broad sense of a family history, for the Tabanan ruling dadia (or *batur*, the elevated term for dadia) and certain allied and client dadias, plus the record of various events connected with various points in the genealogy. The general, but far from systematic, ordering is by the reigns of core-line kings; the various events and affiliated lines are joined to them where appropriate.

The earliest sections trace the origins of the first Tabanan core-line king back to Java—that is, to Airlangga, King of Daha in 1037. The field generals of the 1334 Majapahit invasion of Bali, the so-called "Arya," are in turn traced back to him, the invasion is described, and the allotting of the various parts of Bali to them (though they themselves remain resident as "interior ministers" at Samprangan) is recounted. Arya Kenceng, who is assigned Tabanan, is thus considered the founder of its royal line. (Sometimes, as in the Den Bantas genealogy given below, another of the field generals, Arya Damar, is regarded as having "started" Tabanan. Sometimes Damar and Kenceng are represented as being the same person. In contemporary Tabanan all three views are found; but, some Bali-wide differences in status claims aside, not much turns on this.) Various sumptuary rights, most especially those surrounding cremation, are thus established, as is the general relative status of the line in Bali.

The following sections then describe the local foundation of the line and the establishment of the Tabanan puri proper under one Raja Singasana. Various earlier rulers, usually referred to by the title *kijai*, are recounted, as well as a complexity of local differentiations, formations of new houses, etc. Some early wars, especially with Mengwi and Penebel, are described, as is the formation of the Krambitan house, first as pemadé, "second king" (*text*, p. 160), later as an independent, but allied, line.

The concluding sections then tell how the Tabanan state reached its "final" shape, including how the Kalèran house was established as the second ruling house, how the whole range of houses known to the nineteenth century was formed, and how this all happened through an assortment of intrigues, marriages, atrocities, assassinations, wars, peace ceremonies, cremations, and so on. The Dutch

incursion and the suicides of the king and crown prince in captivity
are extensively described, as is the establishment of the Dutch con-
troller's office "in front of Puri Kalèran" and—the real "end"—the
outcaste marriage in 1912 of a woman from one of the ranking
houses to a Menadonese Christian clerk, in that office, named
Kramer. After a few obviously appended notes concerning the formation of some of the most recent houses, the manuscript closes.

55-2

These maps were drawn on the basis of informants' memories: the
sketch of Tabanan around 1900 is given in Schwartz (1901), and the
very elaborate written and annotated genealogy is still in the possession of the extant house of Den Bantas (see map 3 and fig. 3). There
are some discrepancies, none of them critical, which appear when
the material from the three sources is collated: most of these seem
to turn either on the use of different names for the same houses
(most house names, especially of more peripheral ones, are place
names of one sort or another, though the houses are not necessarily
located in the places named) or on differences of opinion as to
whether certain distant houses were or were not related to the core
line. In any case, the house list is reliable for the major houses, the
main possibility of error being that two or three minor houses have
been omitted or physically mislocated. For photographs of some of
the Tabanan puris and jeros, see Moojen, 1926, plates 1, 33, 34, 38,
45, 46.

The period dates I am using for Tabanan are, of course, the
defeat of Mengwi by Tabanan and Badung as the *a quo*, and the
sack of Tabanan by the Dutch as the *ad quem*—the last flowering
of the classical state. Again, the term "lineage" is used here for
simplicity in the colloquial, but not the technical, sense. There is,
alas, no established technical term for the sort of kin groups Balinese
dadia are, though (an inside joke) I am thinking of promoting
either "lindrids" or "kineages." See Geertz and Geertz, 1975.

55-4

On the question of whether Hario (Arya) Damar or Hario Kenceng is to be regarded as the apical ancestor, see *notes*, p. 159. As *Batara* means "God" (it is applied to the first five kings of Tabanan), the
issue is fairly notional anyway.

55-8

With the suicide of these two men (Cakorda Gusti Ngurah Rai Perang and Gusti Ngurah Gdé), the wrecking of their palace, and the exile of all their close relatives to Lombok (i.e., all the people of the Gdé, Dangin, Mecutan, Den Pasar, and Taman houses; see fig. 3), the lord of Kalèran, the "second king" of Tabanan, who, for internal political reasons, had been more cooperative, was made the ranking indigenous official (*punggawa gdé*) of the area. On the recent history of the Tabanan gentry in general, see *notes*, p. 254 and C. Geertz, 1963b.

55-20

There are (at least) two origin legends current in Tabanan concerning the origins of Krambitan. In one, the founders of Badung, Tabanan, and Krambitan were half brothers; the last was highest in status, but he went off to settle in Krambitan because he liked the scenery. In the other, the Krambitan founder was a son of the king of Tabanan by a high-status wife, but he was passed over for succession in favor of a son by a low-status wife as a result of an oath sworn by the king (cf. Geertz and Geertz, 1975, pp. 132-133). Korn (1932, p. 303) reports that a nineteenth-century Javanese writer on Bali, Raden Sastrowidjojo, claimed that the mother of Tabanan's crown prince had to be from Krambitan; but I have never heard anyone say this, nor does the genealogy support it. Schwartz (1901) says that the legend places Hario Damar's palace in Krambitan; but I have never heard that asserted either, nor indeed that he had a local palace at all, a view the genealogy again supports by placing the foundation of the Tabanan puri with the sixth core-line king and the separation of the Krambitan house with the seventh. In all such matters, it must be remembered that stories, genealogies, and the like are always and inevitably claims to status in this system, and so naturally they vary from source to source, depending upon particular interest. Scholarly searches for "the real truth," or arguments over it, are thus largely bootless and anyway misplaced. What is sociologically critical is the structure of the system, not which particular entities appear in which particular places within it. This is yet another point at which attempts to write unwritable annalistic history (or fix unfixable details) can only generate illusions.

55-39

I have also ignored, both on maps 1 and 2, and in my total of thirty-three royal and noble houses, the secondary and tertiary houses—jero gdés and jeros—in the Krambitan, Kaba-Kaba, and, except for Marga and Blayu, Perean dadias. (Krambitan alone, where there were three puris, had about twenty associated jeros of various status.) Nor have very peripheral houses and minor independent lines in the countryside been listed or mapped, a complete census of them being impossible to reconstruct. Were all these included, the number of triwangsa houses in the Tabanan area having some political significance toward the close of the last century would rise to about a hundred.

58-1

In order to keep the structural outlines of what is in any case a very complicated system reasonably clear, I have reduced the details of kinship organization among the gentry to a minimum. Some of these details can be found in chapter 4, "Kinship in the Public Domain: The Gentry Dadia," in Geertz and Geertz, 1975, pp. 117-152; and the reader interested in what might be called the "micro-anatomy" of traditional Balinese politics is advised to look there. The genealogy of figure 3 was obtained, along with an annotated key to it, from Jero Den Bantas, and it was further annotated with the help of various royal-house informants. Some minor errors (in fig. 15, p. 126 of Geertz and Geertz, 1975), discovered in reworking the original material, have been corrected.

It needs to be stressed, one more time, that such genealogies are less historical records than documents explaining and justifying current status relationships. Though the general order of rank within the Tabanan royal house seems to have been largely consensual during the period under discussion, minor differences as to who "came out" exactly when, and thus who outranked whom, can easily be found. Over longer time spans, altering rank order by rearranging genealogies was common; and, in fact, in my material from Gianyar, which was rather less internally stable than Tabanan in the late-nineteenth century, such tinkering with pedigrees is quite obvious.

The simplification mainly consists in the elimination of cadet houses no longer extant in the 1891-1906 period, about thirty of them, and of all the women, fifty or so, the vast majority of whom married somewhere within the royal dadia (or did not marry at all, a common fate for very high-status women).

Finally, because of the anomalous situation created by the suicides of the last two core-line descendants, my discussion takes the point of view of the seventeenth king, the one who acceded in 1868; this is in line with the practice of the Tabananers themselves, for whom he was the last "real king."

58-21

The structure of the royal house can also be represented in terms of the differentiating-kinship pattern discussed above, in which case it appears as a set of royal sub-dadias, ranked in terms of their order of crystallization, and expressed in the pervasive inside/outside (*jero/jaba*) imagery of Balinese hierarchic symbology (*text*, p. 107). Thus, anyone to the right of you in this series is "jero" (and thus superior in status) to you; anyone to the left is "jaba" (and thus inferior in status); and no two houses are, or in the nature of the case can be, equal to one another—a principle thoroughly general to Balinese social structure. Though the microrankings within the sub-dadias are as my main informants represented them, they are even less consensual than the macro-ones, and they surely would often be disputed by one or another member of the houses concerned. (Each house has, of course, a core and periphery, an "inside" and "outside" genealogy of its own tracing the steps of *its* replication since *its* founding. For a partial example, taken from Beng, see Geertz and Geertz, 1975, p. 150).

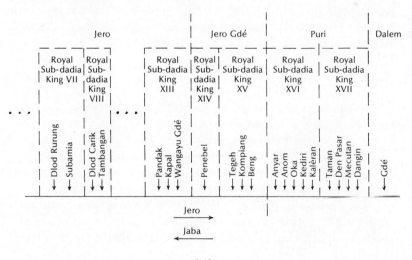

Puri Gdé (also sometimes called Puri Agung, *agung* being an honorific [*halus*] form of *gdé* with the same meaning, much as *dalem*—a Javanese loanword—is of *jero*) is left outside of all sub-dadias because it was, of course, the central member of each, at each stage. The symbolic representation of the core house, and the king, as an essentially unchanging, or replicating, entity is further discussed below (*text*, chap. 4), and the same principle also again applies, mutatis mutandis, within each of the houses themselves.

58-24

As with the term *dadia*, the proper term for its royal-line equivalent, *batur dalem*, is also used to refer to the group's ancestral temple, located in the northeast corner of its core house (see map 2). The right (and obligation) to participate in the once-in-210-day ceremonies, here dedicated to the deified ascendants of the line, was the mark of membership, however peripheral, in the ruling house.

The terms "line," "house," and so on, which in English I find myself forced to use, are indeed rather awkward, because they may refer to anything from the whole Tabanan dynasty to a differentiated subset of it, of narrower or broader scope, to a single core or cadet group. In my experience, "line" is not used by Balinese, who just talk about "Tabanan," "Klungkung," "Kalèran," "Penebel," or whatever. And, as the text has made clear, I trust, there is no generic, "status-neutral" term for "house" as such, but just *dalem*, *puri*, *jero*, *griya*, *umah*, and *pekarangan*, for example (*umah* was applied to prominent Sudra houses, *pekarangan* to ordinary ones). For the "origin point," "way station," and "title" idiom in which Balinese in fact talk about what we conceptualize as "descent" matters, see Geertz and Geertz, 1975; cf. Boon, 1977.

60-18

The same sort of game went on with the titles borne by the members of the various houses. For a man from, say, Subamia, everyone in the whole grand family was *cakorda* together; for the king, only he was *cakorda*, and everyone else was *gusti ngurah* or, even less elevated, *gusti*, the *ngurah* ("ruling") being reserved for his sons, or perhaps even for the crown prince alone. Some people went so far as to distinguish between *cakorda déwa* (*déwa*, "god"), the paramount lord proper; *cakorda ratu* (*ratu*, "king"), members of the royal sub-dadia; *ratu*, members of the Kalèran-Kediri-Oka level; and *gusti ngurah,* everyone else in the dadia. Female titles, kinship-reference terms, forms of politesse, dining customs (for a good, brief review of this, though for Lombok, see Gerdin, 1977), and sumptuary privileges, similarly developed and similarly graded, also were caught up in this endless scuffle for status. No one, however, seems to have disputed either relative position or the overall rank order as such, at least over the fifteen years here covered: Beng never claimed to outrank Kalèran, nor Kediri to outrank Mecutan. The pattern was rather to try to represent oneself and one's house as being as close to the center as possible—to minimize the differences between oneself and the paramount lord. By the same token, one tried to represent everyone lower in rank as being as far away from the center as possible—to maximize the differences between oneself and those more peripheral.

60-23

For this *dubblebestuur* system in Bali generally, see Korn, 1932, pp. 287-292. (However, Korn's venture in speculative history—the theory that the system had its origins in the making of existing "Hindu-Balinese" lords into "younger brother" lords of the "Hindu-Javanese" Majapahit conquerors—ought not to be taken seriously. And his statement that there was a clear division of territory between the senior and junior lines is certainly incorrect, so far as Tabanan is concerned, and generally incorrect, so far as I can see.) Raffles (1830, Appendix K) mentions dual kings in Bulèlèng in the early nineteenth century, and their existence can be inferred from Friederich's account of Badung a few decades later (1959, pp. 123-136).

60-27

Van Eck (1878-80) reports this Gdé-Kalèran division as existing in 1857. Schwartz (1901) confirms it for around the turn of the century, remarking that the senior king from Puri Gdé, though nearing eighty (my informants say a hundred and twenty-five!), was very vigorous, did not smoke opium, appeared every day in the forecourt of his palace to meet anyone who wished to see him, and went out into the countryside himself to attend to any more serious problems, while the junior king from Kalèran was fat, liked women, and was addicted to cockfights.

60-37

At least one of the reasons for the power of Kalèran, Kediri, and Anom after 1891 seems to be that these houses gained the lion's share of the rice lands detached from Mengwi in the Tabanan-Badung-Mengwi war. See de Kat Angelino, 1921a. Subamia's strength came mainly from its influence in the northwestern part of the realm, where the main, Chinese-exploited export coffee lands were concentrated (*notes*, p. 94).

61-19

For the political "history"—a cacaphony of abductions, assassinations, executions, litigations, marriages, and adoptions, plus a certain amount of arson, sorcery, and queen-mother intrigue—of one Tabanan house, Jero Gdé Beng, written (in 1946) by one of its members, see Geertz and Geertz, 1975, pp. 173-181. Cf., for the line as a whole, Tabanan, n.d.

Once more: figure 3 is but Balinese theory, and disputable Balinese theory, about genealogical connections. The fact that Friederich (1959, p. 126) reports Kediri as a very powerful Tabanan house in the eighteen-forties makes it most unlikely, for example, that it was formed as late as 1844, when the sixteenth cakorda seems to have ascended the throne (van Eck, 1878-80).

61-24

For a history and description of this house (there called "Marketside East," which is what *dangin peken* means), see Boon, 1977, pp. 70-86; 1973, pp. 19-102. Like the two-king system, the central role of large Sudra houses was general in Bali (Korn, 1932, p. 288). For a particularly vivid example, see van Eerde, 1921.

61-35

Among the more important of such houses (they can be found on map 3), several may be mentioned. Malkangin, a Sudra house about two miles up the spur from the capital, had the same sort of *penyarikan*, "secretary," relationship to Kalèran as Dangin Peken had to Gdé. Kebayan Wangayu Gdé (not to be confused with the Tabanan jero there) was a Sudra house whose members were responsible for the Sad Kahyangan all-Bali temple on the slopes of

Mount Batu Kau, and thus for some important regional rituals (Peddlemars, 1932). Jero Samsam was a Satria house, supposedly originating from the Klungkung royal house, that had settled out in the thinly populated western part of the region, where, though loosely allied to Tabanan (which, in formal terms, it outranked), it had a certain degree of independent local power. And Pupuan was a highland Sudra house, strategically located between the spheres of influence of Tabanan and Badung (as Samsam was between those of Tabanan and Jembrana), which, although supposedly subservient to Jero Subamia (which had been originally located there before it moved, at Gdé's request, to Tabanan), seems to have been in almost perpetual dissidence.

61-39

The factional alignment of Negara Tabanan toward the end of the nineteenth century can thus be summarized as follows:

Cakorda	Pemadé
Gdé	Kalèran
Patih	*Patih*
Subamia	Beng
Punggawa	*Punggawa*
Dangin	Kediri
Mecutan	Kompiang
Den Pasar	Tegeh
Taman	
Oka	
Anom	
Anyar	
Penyarikan	*Penyarikan*
Dangin Peken	Malkangin
Bagawanta	*Bagawanta*
Griya Pasekan	Griya Jambé

(Penebel was "neutral," or at least tried to be.)

The other fourteen houses were attached to one of the punggawas (patihs, pemadé, or cakorda) as perbekels. But which was exactly attached to which, especially as attachments could be multiple, and as there were many other perbekels, is impossible to reconstruct with confidence.

It would be quite wrong to take this structure as in any sense a bureaucracy, a system of "offices," even an embryonic one. It was an often very sharp and always far from settled political factionalization, arranged, like everything else in Bali, into hierarchical (elegant, *halus*, to coarse, *kasar*) "title" categories quite unreflective of power realities, governmental responsibilities, or, the role of the bagawanta court priest slightly aside, technical specialization. (For the commercial specialization of the Chinese trademaster [*subandar*], Singkeh Cong, see below, *text*, p. 94; for that of the state judges [*kerta gdé*] of Griya Jaksa, below, *notes*, p. 241. On the concepts of *halus* and *kasar* generally, see Geertz, 1960, pp. 231-234— a Javanese reference but essentially applicable here.)

Finally, it should be remarked that the terms *punggawa* and *perbekel* applied both to houses as a whole and to individual adult males within them; so there could be, for example, several "punggawas" in a large house like Kediri or Subamia. The lack of obligatory linguistic marking for number in Balinese simply adds to the ambiguity brought about by the flexibility and relativity of such terms of reference (as well as by the Balinese penchant for using them metonymically).

62-1

Estimating the size of Tabanan's population in the nineteenth century is obviously a speculative business. Van den Broek's 1834 estimate of about 180,000 for ca. 1820 (p. 180), however, is surely far too high.

63-7

As always, there was a multiplicity of names for these various states of political condition, some of them denoting slightly different forms or subtypes. Along with *parekan*, one finds such terms as *pekandelan, roban, abdi*; along with *kawula* (which comes from a Sanskrit word for "family," "descent group," "house"—Gonda, 1973, pp. 122, 150, 430), such terms as *panjak druwé* or *pengayah*; along with *perbekel, mantri*; along with *punggawa, manca* or *gusti*. Also, as always, the terms were rather flexibly used, even though the underlying categories were in themselves quite sharply demarcated. Thus, lower lords were sometimes said to be parekans of the major ones; or only the really prominent lords (from Kalèran, Kediri, Beng, or Anom) were called punggawa, the others being merely mancas.

There is no possibility of putting any simple terminological order into the system, or any strictness of application, even though the four categories were distinct whatever they were called, whatever secondary subcategories were conceived to exist within them, and whatever their placement within the general system of title stratification. For the high degree of subdifferentiation within the general parekan category, see de Kat Angelino, 1921b; within the kawula category, de Kat Angelino, 1921a (Hooker's [1978] rendering of it, in a medieval Javanese law text, as "king's share," seems to be a result of taking a metaphor for a literal description); within the perbekel and punggawa categories, Korn, 1932, pp. 286-306.

63-15

Just what is to be counted as a "slave" in traditional Indonesia is not an altogether settled problem. I am, myself, in some doubt that there were ever very many slaves, in the Western sense of the term, in Bali itself, as opposed to Balinese transported by Europeans and others to Batavia and elsewhere in the islands. Schrieke (1955, p. 81) says that in the late sixteenth century the army of the Javanese north-coast kingdom of Demak consisted "of purchased Balinese, Buginese, and Macassarese slaves." Wertheim (1959, p. 239) claims that in the later years of East India Company rule "more than half the population [of Batavia] consisted of slaves," and that house servants were "all slaves, male or female, mostly supplied from Bali, Timor, and other parts of the archipelago." Van Eck (1878-80) gives the number of Balinese slaves brought to Batavia by 1778 as 13,000 and adds that Raffles, who was governor of the East Indies during the British interregnum of 1811-16, ended the trade. Van den Broek (1834, p. 224) still reports some, however, about 1820; and Neilsen (1928, pp. 55-56) says a small amount of slave trade out of Bali, especially by Chinese, Buginese, and Macassarese, continued until about 1830. Chinese may have sometimes held true slaves in Bali; Liefrinck (1877) reports Bangli Chinese as holding about twenty, which they had bought, he says, from the lords.

Within Bali, whether you are inclined to call the more lowly and recourseless sort of parekans—such as prisoners of war, criminals, and debt peons—slaves (as are de Kat Angelino, 1921b, and Liefrinck, 1877) or not (as is Korn, 1932, p. 173) is of secondary importance. What is of primary importance is to understand the relations between political status categories in classical Bali—the various kinds of parekans, kawulas, perbekels, and punggawas—in their own terms, an effort in which such European categories as "slave," "serf," "steward," and "baron" (or even, I must admit, "noble," "lord," and "king") are as likely to prove misleading as helpful. In any case, slavery, in the sense of complete personal unfreedom, seems to have disappeared in Bali by the nineteenth century, if ever it existed as a domestic institution, and never to have been of central importance (Korn, 1932, pp. 172-173). Another thing the Balinese negara was not is a "slave state."

63-37

Just how many more they held is impossible to determine. Whatever quantitative or quasi-quantitative statements about parekans, kawulas, perbekels, and punggawas are made in the sequel must be understood to be very vague estimates by my informants, who, the simple problem of memory apart, could not have ever known very exactly, as we shall see, how many people any particular lord controlled (even he was usually not altogether certain).

However, in order to give a general idea of the overall dimensions of the system, I would guess (on the basis of what fragmentary data I do have and a good deal of *ceteris paribus* reasoning) that there were about 50 punggawas (all the adult male members of the first fourteen houses of the royal lineage of the three major Krambitan houses and of the three houses in the Perean-Blayu-Marga dadia); perhaps 150-200 perbekels (including, again, some Sudras), whose loyalty was unevenly distributed among these punggawas; and about 75,000 to 85,000 kawulas (or ten to twelve thousand houseyards), even more unequally distributed among the perbekels. As for the parekans, perhaps 2,000 for all the houses, half of them for Gdé alone, is as reasonable a guess as any.

64-9

Actually, this accounting is incomplete, for my informant could no longer remember all his holdings, though he said the remainder, perhaps another thirty houseyards or so, were equally scattered, some of them in "parcels" of one houseyard in a hamlet. As mentioned, the holdings of perbekels varied in quantity, the general range being between twenty and four hundred houseyards (only two perbekels, one from Dangin Peken and one from Malkangin, held the latter number), though the "ideal" number was two hundred;

and at least one perbekel is remembered to have held exactly one houseyard, and several others only a half dozen or so.

Also it should be noted that one house, whether a peripheral jero or a client house, could have several perbekels in it, depending upon how many adult men it contained; and these perbekels could be attached to different punggawas. For example, one Tabanan peripheral house, Dlod Rurung, had perbekel attachments at once to the punggawas in Anyar, Kaleran, and Gdé, while an unrelated client house had attachments to Gdé, Subamia, and Anom. It is simply impossible to untangle, at this late date, the full network of dispersive ties, either between kawulas and perbekels or between perbekels and punggawas.

64-31

For a contemporary confirmation of the people-not-territory pattern of rule in Tabanan (and, for that matter, in south Bali generally), see Schwartz, 1901. There were, however, a few exceptions, especially near the permeable edges of the "kingdom"—the "political ecotones," as I called them earlier (chap. 1)—where security sometimes dictated the control over an entire hamlet, or at least most of it, by one perbekel. My informant's holding of forty houseyards near the Jembrana border—the bulk (though not the whole) of the hamlet's population—was an example of this. But such cases were uncommon, were considered abnormal and, apparently, were not very enduring. Contrariwise, at the center, Tabanan proper (considered as a village) was perhaps the most highly divided: every punggawa had some kawulas in every one of the fifteen hamlets comprising Tabanan, and none was clearly dominant in any. In general, the rule, "the closer geographically to the court the greater the dispersion of ties," holds; but, contrary to what has sometimes been implied by "adat law" theorists concerned to develop a sharp contrast between so-called appanage and non-appanage areas in Indicized Indonesia (see van Vollenhoven, 1918-33), dispersion was the rule throughout the realm, not merely in the immediate environs of the court.

64-40

A Balinese houseyard (pekarangan) almost always consists either of a nuclear family or of a group of agnatically connected nuclear

171

families; but it is only rarely that the members of a lineage or a dadia will all live in a single houseyard (Geertz and Geertz, 1975). Thus, the custom of allotting loyalties to lords by houseyard frequently split fairly close relatives into different bekelans, as can be seen from the still-continuing distribution of *sisias* of Brahmana priests by houseyard, where full brothers often have different allegiances.

There were, again, some exceptions to this dispersive pattern, having to do in this case with certain craft groups (most notably smiths; see de Kat Angelino, 1921c) and with foreigners (Chinese, Buginese). Moreover, priestly lineages were sometimes allotted as a group to one perbekel (frequently chosen from among themselves), and through him to one punggawa. But these arrangements were also uncommon and seen as special. The various bekelans in a hamlet were usually headed by one of their number called a *juru arah* ("herald," a term applied to a number of other kinds of "town crier" offices as well). His function was to transmit messages from the perbekel and to organize the local bekelan members with respect to their negara duties, but he had virtually no independent power.

65-5

Korn, 1932. Korn says the whole 700 were allotted to the "head lord" in Tabanan, but my evidence does not support this. In general, Balinese tend to speak of everything "belonging" to the king, as they speak of everything "belonging" to the gods. But the first usage is as figurative as the second, and in fact identical in meaning with it, and must not be taken as an attempt to describe political (or economic) reality, but metaphysical. I shall return to this point, one of the more fertile sources of scholarly misinterpretation of the nature of the classical Indonesian polities, in the Conclusion.

65-18

Perhaps the most striking index of this fact is the virtually complete lack of structural significance in the desa system of the houseyard, the unit according to which supralocal political (and religious) loyalties were allocated. Hamlet, irrigation-society, and temple-group membership went not by houseyards, but by nuclear family; and, insofar as descent groups played a role in the local political system, it was only to the degree that they grew beyond the houseyard scale, and in any case their elemental units were also nuclear families, not houseyards (see C. Geertz, 1959; Geertz and Geertz, 1975). In the desa system, the houseyard was at most a merely residential unit with but a few quite marginal economic and ritual functions (Korn's encyclopedic survey [1932], focused so sharply as it is on village organization, scarcely finds it necessary to speak of the houseyard at all); in the negara system, on the other hand, the houseyard was the main, in fact the only, local membership unit. However, even then it was not a corporate unit. Though kawulas were allocated by houseyard, the duties involved fell on the individuals within it. If there were five men in the houseyard, they all had to fight in their lord's wars; if there were six women, they all had to cook at their lord's festivals. (Even children had their tasks: running errands, carrying water, etc.) The houseyard was the mode of penetration of the negara not into the desa *polity*, from which it was kept rather carefully at arm's length, but into the desa *population*.

66-17

Lords acquired land through agnatic inheritance, purchase, the military reduction of other lords, political gifts, the dowries (called *tatadan*) that normally went along with wargi-type "tribute" marriages (above, *text*, p. 35), and the preemption of lands of the heirless dead and of criminals; but a lord had no legal claims whatsoever upon his kawula's property. (Preempted land went to the ruling lineage as a whole, not to the lord of the property holder involved; it was then distributed among the punggawas according to kinship-cum-political principles. In fact, preemption does not seem to have been an important source of noble landholding.) Lords could also alienate land, not only to one another, but also to commoners—by sale; by gift for some special, usually personal service (wet nursing the lord's child, acting as his go-between in a marriage with a Sudra girl, etc.); as a reward for a treachery or as insurance against it; and so on.

Uncultivated land was another matter, however, governed by other principles. The lords laid formal claims to such "waste" land if it lay outside the boundaries of any desa adat (*text*, p. 127), and their holdings of such land could be, on occasion, both extensive and continuous. In 1860, a European rented about 6,000 acres of such land from a Jembrana lord and planted it with cotton, cacao, coconuts, and tobacco—one of the few examples (apparently not very successful) of plantation exploitation in Bali (Korn, 1932, p. 547). Jembrana was thinly populated, however, and other Balinese lords' access to such unworked but workable lands was much more limited. With the important exception of coffee-land grants to Chinese toward the latter part of the nineteenth century (*text*, p. 94), they were not a significant source of income for the Tabanan lords.

66-35

Admittedly it is speculative and rather drastically after the fact, but the general consensus of my informants concerning the relative landed wealth and the relative military power of the six major royal houses of south Bali at about the turn of the century is suggestive in this connection—if not of the actual state of affairs, at least of what it seemed to be to some of those who were directly involved in it. At least in *their* minds, the correlation was quite weak:

Military Power	Landed Wealth
1. Gianyar	1. Badung
2. Karengasem	2. Tabanan
3. Klungkung	3. Gianyar
4. Badung	4. Bangli
5. Tabanan	5. Klungkung
6. Bangli	6. Karengasem

Jembrana is omitted from this tabulation because, neither wealthy nor powerful, and incorporated well before 1900 under direct Netherlands East Indies rule, it no longer played a very important role in indigenous Balinese politics; and my informants knew virtually nothing circumstantial about it. Bulèlèng, under formal Dutch administration from 1882, and informal from 1850, was of course even more of a special case.

67-23

In fact, tenancy arrangements were much more elaborate and variable than these summary statements suggest. For a full review, see Liefrinck, 1886-87. References to Tabanan practices may be found in Hunger, 1933; Peddlemars, 1933; and Raka, 1955. Scheltema (1931) puts Balinese practices in the context of Indonesian land-tenure and tenancy patterns generally. It is worth remarking that none of these scholars finds it necessary to make any reference to negara political structure or, in fact, to political organization at all. Nor were tenants denominated by political terms, but by terms indicating their share of the harvest: *nandu* ("half"), *nelon* ("a third"), and so on.

Tenancy, once given, tended to be subject to local customary-law rules, not to the whim of the lord. Any attempt by a lord at arbitrary displacement or other misuse of a tenant could bring him trouble: destruction of his crops, subtle reduction of water supplied by the locally controlled irrigation society, or increased theft. In fact, in more than a few cases, lords' tenants seem to have been chosen not by the lords or their agents, but by the local population (usually the hamlet, occasionally the irrigation society); and, in any case, local sentiment had always to be considered in such matters, for the lord was essentially powerless against agricultural sabotage by hostile peasants. An indication of the real state of affairs is given by the fact that, in Tabanan, the tenant's share on lord-owned land was almost always half; on peasant-owned land, usually a third.

67-28

The argument here is not that the system of tenure or the modes of tenancy had no political significance. That would be absurd. The argument is that their significance did not arise out of an institutional fusion between them and the authoritative organization of political domination. That organization was very much more complex and irregular, and was not easily predictable from the surface features of land ownership, field labor, and agricultural technique—the so-called oriental mode of production.

The fact that land tenants were in short supply reduced the lords' political leverage, which is inherent in tenancy, as did the great strength of local institutional structure, the manifold desa polity. In some cases, the lords did attempt to consolidate the two sources of power—landed wealth and political authority—and to institute a genuinely patrimonial regime by putting parekans (who were, of course, outside the desa system) on some of their land as servant workers. But, in part because parekans were usually not very proficient farmers, in part because the number of parekans was never very great, and especially because the local communities intensely resented and actively resisted such efforts, this pattern never developed very far anywhere in Bali (see de Kat Angelino, 1921b).

A few of the larger states—Badung and Gianyar especially—also sought to establish bureaucratic administrative control over some agricultural matters, particularly toward the very end of the nineteenth century, as the Dutch threat loomed ever larger, and mostly in the areas of land taxation and irrigation; but these were all extremely short-lived (Happé, 1919, but very much exaggerated; for a sharp critique, see Korn, 1932, pp. 272ff.).

Finally, so far as "feudalism" is concerned, some lords (including some of those of Tabanan) did give the right to work plots of their land to peasants, or sometimes organized groups of them in return for certain specialized services: smithing, weaving, artistic performances, rifle bearing, certain ritual duties, message running, and so on. But this, too, did not loom large anywhere.

However, in connection with this last point, something must be said of the so-called *pecatu* system (from *catu*—"victuals," "a ration of food or drink," also used to designate a rice-field offering altar), about which a small, rather peculiar literature grew up, in Dutch, as the newly established Netherlands East Indies civil administration sought to legitimize itself in south Bali by delegitimizing its predecessors (see Gunning and van der Heijden, 1926; de Kat Angelino, 1921a; Korn, 1932, pp. 227-228, 331, 538, 585; for a critique, Boon, 1977, pp. 54-58). In some parts of Bali—most especially Gianyar, Bangli, and Mengwi, and to some extent Klungkung—certain lands, *pecatu*, were viewed as designating their holders as obligated for royal service, *pengayah dalem*; others, *bukti*, as designating them for "village" (i.e., desa adat) service, *pengayah desa*; and others, *laba*, as designating them for temple service, *pengayah pura*. Without engaging all the attempts to interpret this division in feudal-service terms, most of them inconsistent with one another, and all of them tendentious, I would argue that it was a method of classifying the sorts of labor obligations to which villagers were subject (to a lord, to a village, to a temple), not a system of land law. Pecatu lands were not royal lands "owned" and leased for service to commoners, nor were they "owned by the village collectivity and distributed to village members in return for fulfilling the village's collective obligations to the lord." (For the first view, see de Kat Angelino, 1921a; for the second, Gunning and van der Heijden, 1926; for both, Korn, 1932, p. 575. Covarrubias's notion [1956, p. 59] that *pecatu* refers to "wild," that is, uncultivated village land, is a confusion.) Pecatu lands were "owned" by those who worked them, or who contracted tenants to work them; and their yield was regarded as the productive support that made the "owners'" fulfillment of their political, or, more accurately, politico-religious, duties possible. (The whole question of "ownership" in classical Bali is a vexed one, as already remarked, and as further discussed below, *text*, p. 127; but it is not clarified by confusing imperative, ritual, proprietary, and usufruct claims, or by assuming that the Balinese confuse them.) The Dutch suppression of the perbekel sort of tie after the 1906-8 conquest led to the levying of the remaining negara duties directly through the land-tenure system, and thus to the creation of a sort of "pseudofeudalism," which, not entirely without policy motivations, Dutch scholars then read anachronistically back into the classical past. One result of all this is that the exact character of the pecatu system—whose general importance has been greatly exaggerated in any case—is more easily seen in earlier writings on Bali (e.g., Liefrinck, 1877; 1886-87; but see also Boekian, 1936, for a supporting Balinese view) than in those of the nineteen-twenties and thirties. On the post-Dutch development of the Balinese negara, see C. Geertz, 1963b, and *notes*, p. 254.

67-32

Only rice was subject to rent payments. In the nineteenth century, whatever small amount of dry crops could be grown on the rented land between rice plantings was left to the tenant, though he usually would make small gifts of such food to the lord. According to Korn (1932, p. 301), Tabanan sharecroppers had to give the lord, besides the half-yield rent, enough cooked rice for ten people, two times a year—an economically trivial payment. None of my informants even mentioned this practice, and I am uncertain as to how scrupulously it was actually followed.

67-40

The sedahan gdé also was in charge of the lord's gardens, dispensed food to servants, budgeted the large ceremonies, and kept track of gifts. A prevalent source for sedahans, as for judges, was Brahmana houses, whose members were systematically excluded from perbekel roles, at least vis-à-vis non-Brahmanas. The sedahans of a lord (they received a percentage of their collections as salary) were often grouped into sections called, according to the location of their resorts with respect to the palace, "north," "south," "east," and "west," with the sedahan gdé considered as occupying the direction-neutral center. On directional symbolism in Bali, *text*, p. 105, and *notes*, p. 218. Sedahans were often referred to as *pangluran*; roughly, "protectors" (*notes*, p. 246).

68-15

Pajeg is, in fact, the general term for a tax of any sort, and there was a variety of levies (see *notes*, p. 184). The agricultural tax was usually specified as *pajeg padi* (*padi*, "rice"), though, again, other terms could be found. A brief inventory of land-taxation practices in Bali, in which a concern for minutiae rather impedes an understanding of the fiscal principles which the practices express, can be found in Korn, 1932, pp. 293-300.

68-19

In a few cases, especially toward the coast, where irrigation societies tended to be larger, one irrigation society was sometimes distributed, nonterritorially, between two tax areas (and thus between two lords); or, especially toward the mountains, where they tended to be smaller, two or three were sometimes lumped into one tax area. By and large, however, tax-area and irrigation-society boundaries coincided—proving, perhaps, that the Balinese were not physically incapable of rationalizing institutions, just temperamentally disinclined.

Though collected in kind (with some exceptions), the tax was calculated and assessed in terms of Chinese hole-in-the-middle lead coins called *kèpèng* (*text*, p. 91; *notes*, p. 208). Ten thousand kèpèng equaled one *timbang*, or "weight." If a man's tax was, say, two timbang, he had to pay enough husked rice to balance 20,000 kèpèng on a simple set of scales. In place of the coins themselves, the sedahans used standard stones, also called timbang (or half, or one-and-a-half timbang, etc.), previously calibrated with kèpèng and kept in the possession of the irrigation society. In Tabanan, one timbang equaled 28 *cattys* (van Bloemen Waanders, 1859); that is, weighed about 38 lbs. A timbang was not, however, the same weight all over Bali. In Bulèlèng (Liefrinck, 1886-87), for example, it was twice as much, 55 *cattys*, or about 75 lbs. A timbang there evidently —though Liefrinck doesn't say so—equaled not 10,000 but 20,000 kèpèng.

Water was distributed to the fields through a fixed grid of irrigation canals and water dividers (*text*, p. 70, and fig. 5); so the tax was reckoned according to the breadth of the irrigating stream— that is, according to the width of the water gate through which it flowed into any particular terrace or complex of terraces. Or, put another way, it was reckoned according to the share of all the water coming into the irrigation society as a whole, whatever that might be, that was diverted into any particular terrace or terrace cluster, the various determinations again being made in terms of stream breadth as measured by water-gate size.

The complexities of all this, which are considerable, can mostly be passed over here. The essential points are: first, the fiscal (but not necessarily the proprietary) unit within the irrigation society was the terrace or terraces irrigated from a single, terminal water canal; and second, since the irrigation grids were fixed in their basic outline, once constructed, so also were these fiscal units, and therefore, *but only within any one irrigation society,* so also was the relative tax burden laid upon each unit. Just how the *overall* tax burden was determined for an irrigation society (i.e., for the basic fiscal unit, or tax area, so far as the negara was concerned, since it had nothing to say about how water was distributed within the irrigation society), and thus how, derivatively, the *absolute* burden of each fiscal unit within the subak was determined, is not clear to me. Nor was it clear to any of my informants, who said that it was merely a matter of *adat,* "custom," and that in principle—but, as even they recognized, surely not in fact—it never changed, though it varied, often very widely indeed, from irrigation society to irrigation society. (Tax obligations were recorded, fiscal unit by fiscal unit, in quasi-sacred, periodically recopied palm-leaf manuscripts called *pipil*—the tax on one side, the location of the property and the owner's, or owners', name[s] and hamlet[s] on the other. Copies were held by the sedahan, by the head of the irrigation society, and by the owner[s], a practice which surely must have inhibited changes.)

Schwartz (1901) says, on the basis of what he heard from the then sedahan gdé of Puri Gdé Tabanan, that the tax amounted to about ten percent of the total harvest from any taxed field; so estimates of the actual productivity of irrigation-society lands were perhaps at least partly involved in establishing rates, despite the theory that the tax was levied on water, not on land or rice. But, given the nature of wet rice agriculture (C. Geertz, 1963a), productivity once assessed would not, in the normal case, change much either, or only very slowly. (Newly built irrigation societies, which, given the labor involved in constructing them, appeared very infrequently, were not taxed at all for the first three years of their operations, though one or another lord was sometimes awarded a plot of land in them.) In the short term, variations in tax assessments, both over time and from place to place at the same time, almost certainly were more a reflex of variations in the relative power of the taxing lords, and of the taxed irrigation societies, than they were of the extremely stable, elaborately organized ecological system upon which they were laid. The details of the specific processes involved—that is, the annalistic history—are again largely unrecoverable. But what fragmentary data I was able to gather, more from Gianyar than from Tabanan, indicate quite clearly that taxation policy was no less explosive a political issue in classical Bali than it has been elsewhere in the world.

68-30

Not, usually, on the same lands however, for lords normally did not tax one another's fields. However, land transferred from a commoner to a lord usually remained taxed (and land transferred in the other direction usually remained exempt); so even this could on occasion occur. In general practice, there were a great many exceptions to taxation (in case of crop failure, taxes were not collected; land belonging to temples, priests, various sorts of artisans, affinal relatives of the lord, and so on, was usually not taxed); and just how pervasive the whole system was, and how efficiently operated, is difficult to determine.

Schwartz (1901) says that he was told, again by the sedahan gdé of Puri Gdé Tabanan, who can be expected to have grossly understated royal income to a visiting Dutch official, that only about a quarter of the wet rice land was taxed. One of my informants, who was a sedahan to Jero Subamia, annually collected 90 timbang in taxes from three scattered irrigation societies, from which his commission was 15 timbang (other informants said the one-sixth share for sedahans was standard). He also estimated, I am sure very broadly, that Puri Gdé drew in 2,000 timbang annually (or about twenty times the one-million-kèpèng estimate given to Schwartz by the same non-disinterested Sedahan of Puri Gdé), and Krambitan 5,000. Even within the royal lineage, Gdé's tax income was not the largest. Some of the other houses, especially Kalèran, also apparently approached 4,000 or 5,000 timbang; and in any case tax income, like kawula holdings and land ownership, varied widely among lords. By means of a series of inferences, assumptions, and outright guesses, which I will not relate for the simple reason that they cannot bear too much inspection, my own estimate of the share of *total* wet rice output taken as tax by the Tabanan lords around 1900 would run between three and five percent.

68-33

Korn, 1932, p. 307.

69-16

For the first view, see Happé, 1919; for the second, as well as for a definitive demolition of Happé's argument (which Korn calls a just-so story—*gephantaseerde wordingsgeschiedenis*), see Korn, 1932, pp. 270-273.

The following description of the subak and of the relations among subaks within drainage areas is, being generalized, necessarily simplified and regularized, but I think not misleadingly so. As in the case of the "village" discussion above, the use of the past tense in this description should not be interpreted as implying that the phenomena mentioned no longer exists; the overwhelming majority of them do. Terminology is, again, extremely varied; and I have, again, rather arbitrarily standardized it by using only what I take to have been the commonest terms in Tabanan. The literature on the subak is scattered, fragmentary, and very uneven in quality, but useful data can be found, often thoroughly intermixed with useless, in Liefrinck, 1886-87, and 1921; van Eck and Liefrinck, 1876; Happé, 1919; Korn, 1923, 1927, and 1932, pp. 102-128; Wirz, 1927; Fraser, 1910; van der Heijden, 1924-25; Grader, 1960a; C. Geertz, 1959, 1964, and 1972a; Stingl, 1970; Birkelbach, 1973.

The subak is a very old institution in Bali. The first reference to it by name occurs in an inscription dated at 1022, but as early as 896 tunnel builders are mentioned (Goris, 1954, vol. 1, p. 23; Swellengrebel, 1960, pp. 10-11; see also Korn, 1932, pp. 9-10, and the references cited there). Insofar as the subak has changed, in its technical practices and in its organization, it has certainly done so extremely slowly indeed. The brief description Korn gives (1932, pp. 9-10) of a subak mentioned in an undated inscription, ca. 1050, shows no critical differences in its organization from subak organization as we know it to have been in the earlier part of the present century, and in fact as it still is in most places today. In his description of Bangli in 1876, Liefrinck (1877) remarks that no new wet rice terraces (by which he surely means subaks, not individual terraces) have been created "for many years"; and I was not able, in 1957-58, to find anyone in Bali who had any idea when his subak had been founded. By 1891-1906, the subak system was essentially completed everywhere in Bali, in its traditional form; and though marginal additions and subtractions of terraces surely went on all the time, as well as changes in existing terrace boundaries, the system as a whole was extremely stable. After 1906, and especially after 1915, Dutch modernization of waterworks, mainly in the larger subaks of the lowland regions, expanded the system somewhat.

69-34

The existence of land owned by lords and worked by local share-tenants does not contradict this generalization; for in such cases it was the tenant, not the lord, who was, de facto if not de jure (and in some cases actually de jure), the subak member. The internal quotation is one of the rhetorical chapter headings (along with "A State Stronger than Society," "Despotic Power—Total and non-Benevolent," etc.) in Wittfogel, 1957.

70-7

The group of subaks with traditionally established water rights in one dam did not form a super-subak irrigation society. Routine maintenance work at the dam was performed by parties from the separate subaks working alternately (and *never* on one another's canals) under customarily fixed schedules. In the occasional case where larger labor input became necessary—such as when a dam washed out—work was organized by the heads of the several subaks on an ad hoc, but again custom-guided, basis. There was some consultation, cooperation, and now and then conflict involved in these matters; but they took place entirely on a subak-to-subak basis.

70-34

Some of the items on the diagram—the temples, bypasses, and so on—will be explained below. For simplicity, I have diagramed a case in which only one subak is served by the main dam. I estimate (again on the basis of calculations too complex, detailed, and speculative to be worth describing here) that, ca. 1900, there were approximately 450 subaks in Tabanan, covering about 15,000 hectares. Of these subaks, about eighty percent, accounting for some forty percent of the land, were under 50 hectares, and about ninety-eight percent, accounting for some eighty-five percent of the land, were under 150 hectares. The mean subak size was thus somewhere around

35 hectares, the modal around 15, in a range running from 1 or 2 hectares up to nearly 300. The size of a subak and its topography tend to be very highly correlated: higher and (thus) less flat subaks tend to be small; lower and flatter ones are larger (see figs. 6-10).

72-1

Because the tenah is a standard unit within any one subak (though it varies from subak to subak), it is not only a water measure, but a land, a seed, and a rice measure as well. One tenah of land is that irrigated by one tenah of water. (Balinese landowners still tend to express the quantity of the land they hold in tenahs, which are relative, rather than hectares, which are absolute.) One tenah of seed is enough to plant one tenah of land. One tenah of rice is the produce of one tenah of land seeded with one tenah of seed and irrigated with one tenah of water. Intra-subak ecological variations do of course exist, water control is far from being fully precise, and real grids are not as regular as their conceptual representation. All this induces variation in tenah size—in its water, land, seed, or grain aspects, as well as incongruence among the aspects—and various sorts of ad hoc methods are used to correct for them. Also, the terrace-tenah relation is, on the ground, extremely variable, even within one kecoran. On occasion, one tenah of water may irrigate one terrace (*tebih*). But more often it will irrigate several, which may or may not belong to a single owner. In the latter cases, some local, person-to-person adjustments are necessary. All these complexities are, however, matters of the microstructure of the subak. Though, for realism's sake, they should be kept in mind, they had no bearing on state organization and need not further concern us here.

72-7

The diagram, which is a rather larger than average subak, has been simplified by showing the full grid for only one kecoran, *Aa*. The others would show the same general pattern; but, their topography and the history of their development being different, the precise sequence of divisions leading to the ultimate tenah would differ markedly.

72-36

So-called dry crops (maize, tubers, vegetables) were sometimes grown in the terraces during part of the year, though to nowhere near the extent they are today. As most of these also demand some irrigation, the subak organization became involved with them, to a limited extent. See Liefrinck, 1886-87.

74-16

It should be noted that the degree to which subaks were subdivided varied widely. In small subaks, for the most part upland ones, kecoran and tèmpèk division sometimes did not exist, in which case the "water team" would essentially consist of the subak membership as a whole, rather than a subgroup within it. Such delegation of work, from the membership as a whole to a portion of it, has increased in recent times, with the advance of monetization, overpopulation, land partitioning, tenancy, and absentee ownership. Yet that the seka yèh pattern has been the predominant one for a rather long time is clear from the literature: Korn, 1932, p. 252; Liefrinck, 1886-87; Happé, 1919.

74-24

The bulk of this work consisted of cleaning out the smaller canals, opening and closing the water gates to rechannel the water, keeping up dikes and paths, and making minor repairs on all of these—continuous, onerous, but not mass-labor sorts of jobs. Indeed, the typical arrangement (or one typical arrangement) was for two men in any given tèmpèk to be on duty, in rotation, for a twelve-hour period, and for them to do all the necessary work. Once a Balinese month, the entire team would assemble to accomplish whatever slightly larger-scale jobs—cleaning the main canal, repairing the river dam —might be necessary.

The usual term for a water-team member was *pekasih*. However, this term varied in meaning across Bali. In some areas it denoted the head of the water team—what was more often called the *klian seka yèh*—rather than its members. In others, it denoted the head of the whole subak—the *klian subak*—or even a supra-subak official, a sedahan. Water-team members were also sometimes called *Sinoman* or *pengayah subak*.

74-32

Like state taxation (*notes*, p. 178), subak taxation was both complicated and diverse in organization, and the literature on it is even more confusing and contradictory than usual. Discussions of it can be found in Korn, 1932, pp. 293-300; van Bloemen Waanders, 1859; Schwartz, 1901; Liefrinck, 1886-87; and van Eck, 1878-80.

In general, two major sorts of taxes, both levied according to the percentage of the subak's water a man used (and thus according to the relative amount of land he owned, seed he planted, and rice he harvested), were distinguished: those which were essentially secular and those which were essentially religious. It must be remembered, though, that "secular" is a very relative term so far as Bali is concerned; there, virtually nothing is completely uncolored by religious significance. The former kind of tax, usually called, as a general class, *pajeg*, went in part, as already explained (*text*, p. 68), to the lord in whose "tax area" the subak lay, another part being retained by the subak to defray its operating expenses. Though the klian subak was also responsible for the collection of the lord's share of the pajeg, and for its delivery to the sedahan, it was only the subak's share over which the subak members had actual control, in both magnitude and expenditure. The second sort of tax, usually called *suwinih* or *upeti toya*, went to support the complex, multilevel ritual system connected with wet rice agriculture discussed below (*text*, p. 75).

Fines were set out in the subak constitution (*awig-awig subak, kertasima*) and were assessed for everything from failing to attend a subak meeting to stealing water. Like the subak's share of the pajeg, they became part of the general subak treasury.

Disputes concerned boundaries, water rights, and so on, and were commonly settled "out of court." But in serious or stubborn cases, the krama subak adjudicated directly; and its decisions were binding, on threat of withholding of water—that is, exile from the subak.

"Land transfers" refers, of course, only to terraces in the subak. The transactions themselves were private. The subak's corporate role was limited to a collective witnessing, and in the case of disputes, to a collective "memory" function. For "foreign relations," see below.

75-4

Klian subaks were commonly elected, but sometimes they were co-opted by their predecessors; in some cases the office seems to have been at least semihereditary, and in a few scattered instances—none, so far as I know, in Tabanan—the lords appointed them from among candidates submitted by the subak membership. Klians were sometimes paid out of the subak treasury, sometimes by being given subak-owned land to work (often purchased by funds from that treasury), sometimes by both, and sometimes not at all. The klian usually had a staff consisting of the klians of the various tèmpèks, or even of the kecoran, plus messengers, "policemen," etc. All these men were usually appointed by him, though approved by the membership. Again, some subaks were not very differentiated internally; thus the technical and political levels of organization might coincide. But rather than being the rule, as the more stereotyped literature (Covarrubias, 1956, pp. 72ff., for example) seems to suggest, this was, in fact, the exception.

Decision making within the krama subak was by "group consensus"; theoretically, everyone had an equal voice. No differences in amount of land owned, in status ("caste"), in sex, or in any other "extrinsic" consideration affected this principle of equality. In practice, of course, such considerations did operate, as they do in any political system. But the degree to which the ideal equality was achieved seems remarkable, if we judge from present conditions; wealth and status differences among subak members are now, if anything, greater than ever, but the principle of equality of voice remains extremely forceful. For a recent study supporting this view, see Birkelbach, 1973; for an incisive modern discussion of Balinese group decision-making processes generally, see Hobart, 1975.

75-13

For a general review of the Balinese "rice cult" (itself but a modification, elaboration, and Indicization of the pan-Indonesian "rice-mother" or "rice-wedding" pattern— (Wilken, 1912b), see Wirz, 1927. A brief description of an actual harvest ritual, complete with the famous "rice-mother" (*Dewi Sri*) doll, can be found in Covarrubias, 1956, pp. 79-81; see also Liefrinck, 1886-87.

Here, again, it is necessary to emphasize the enormous variation in detail—in ritual, in organization, in terminology—over Bali, despite, or perhaps because of, its bandbox size, and that the picture given here is somewhat regularized for the sake of clarity. For some sense of the degree to which particular subak ritual systems can vary within a general pattern, see C. J. Grader, 1960a, though he deals with twentieth-century, not nineteenth-century, materials.

75-25

The notion is that the beduguls (also often called *tugu tèmpèk* or *catu*) are places where the gods "stop" or "rest" as they journey about the countryside. The "way-station" concept is general in the Balinese temple system, and even major temples (and the altars within them) are regarded as such way stations with respect to yet more important temples. All this is part of the general exemplary-center-plus-replicas view of the Balinese, and has yet to be treated adequately in the extensive literature on Balinese religion, though it is, in my opinion, at the heart of its structure. (For the role of this concept in connection with kin temples, see Geertz and Geertz, 1975, esp. p. 160.)

It should also be remarked in this connection that in addition to other alternative terms (*Mesceti, Pura Subak*) the Pura Ulun Carik is sometimes called *Pura Bedugul* (as opposed to *"bedugul"* without the *pura*, "temple," prefix). One of the major reasons for the enormous terminological variation in Bali (other reasons include status pride, intergroup jealousy, endogamy, and what can only be called obsessive playfulness) is just this exemplary-center-plus-replicas pattern, because it is possible to use almost any term all the way up and down the scale. Any temple, kin group, official, organization, title, or whatever away from the center is a replica, a diminished image of the same thing shining more brightly at or toward the center. Thus a term like *bedugul* can be applied to anything from the smallest stone altar up to a large and important regional agricultural temple; a term like *pekasih* can be applied to everyone from a water-team member to a royal tax official. A great many of the disputes concerning the relation of the Balinese state system, the *negara*, to the Balinese village system, the *desa* (also adjustable terms), as well as some of the extreme views of that relationship ("village republic" or "oriental despotism") stem from a failure to appreciate this fact sufficiently, to penetrate the extraordinary terminological screen the Balinese have constructed to the sociological realities it denotes. There is not much point in arguing over whether pekasihs were state officials or subak officials (or irrigation laborers!) until one decides what sorts of pekasihs one is talking about. The same point obtains, across the board, in everything from ritual behavior, social stratification, or political structure to land tenure, kinship organization, or law—everything.

76-4

Not all subak members attended all ceremonies; often they merely sent offerings, leaving the priest and the water team to prepare the temple and perform the actual prayers and other rites. Unlike taxes, offerings (the famous *banten*—see Belo, 1953), were not related to land size or water use, but were the same for all subak members, reflecting again the equal legal status of all such members. These *banten* offerings were absolutely obligatory. A man might try, and successfully, to evade a tax, a work task, or a fine, but never an offering requirement.

76-12

See above, *text*, p. 52. Unlike the other temples mentioned, both for the hamlet and the subak, the Pura Balai Agung was tied not to the automatically operating "permutational calendar" (see C. Geertz, 1973h; Goris, 1960b), but to the lunar calendar, which, unlike the permutational, is correlated with the natural round of seasons. Being one of the Kahyangan Tiga (*text*, p. 52), the Pura Balai Agung was located not in the subak, but at the edge (or just beyond the edge) of a settled area nearby. One quite common arrangement was that the members of the "custom village"—that is, the *pemaksan* of the *desa adat*—performed the rituals in the Pura Balai Agung, but the offerings and other material support were provided by the members of the associated subak or subaks (as with banjars, more than one might be involved). The Pura Balai Agung is one of the most interesting but least understood of Balinese temples; for some (rather speculative) discussions, see Goris, 1938 and 1960a; Korn, 1932, pp. 83ff.

76-25

Again, terms differ. The Pura Ulun Suwi (or *Siwi*) is sometimes called *Pura Kayèhan*, "water temple," or, most simply, *Pura Ém-pelan*, "dam temple."

77-14

The diagrams (which are based on Balinese Irrigation Bureau maps) are simplified in the interests of clarity, in that subaks consisting of physically discontinuous parts have been drawn as continuous; subaks directly abutting one another have been drawn as having a small space between them; and border contours have been smoothed. As indicated, however, the diagrams are drawn to scale.

The diagrams represent, of course, the contemporary (i.e., 1957-

58) situation. As subak consolidation and expansion took place under the Dutch, contemporary subaks are about twice as large (average seventy-seven hectares vs. average about thirty-five hectares) and forty percent fewer (326 vs. about 450) than at the close of the nineteenth century. This is true for all five diagrams, but the distortion is much greater in the lowland than in the highland cases, for both consolidation and expansion had their main impact in the lowlands. The critical fact, however, is that although the contrast in subak size from lowland to highland is somewhat exaggerated in the 1957-58 picture, the general gradation—low ones being large and dense, to high ones being small and scattered—obtained in the nineteenth century (and certainly before as well), and indeed was even smoother.

77-23

See also *text*, p. 67, and *notes*, p. 177. After the Dutch arrived, the sedahan system was rationalized and the sedahans, made native civil servants, were given defined "water regions" with a single sedahan gdé for each region (Tabanan, Badung, etc.) over all of them (*notes*, p. 254).

77-32

It should be clear that I do not intend these "percentages" as real figures, but merely as a way of expressing my qualitative, and rather offhand, estimate of the general proportion of labor inputs from each level of the system. It should also be added that occasionally two or even three subaks, or more usually their water teams, did cooperate on some immediate task of joint benefit to them. This was both small-scale and infrequent, however. Insofar as they could, members of different water teams or subaks preferred to work on joint tasks in rotation, rather than collectively. In any case, all such between-subak activities were arranged on an ad hoc basis among those concerned, not coordinated from above.

80-3

Only "generally determined" because calendrical calculations, not natural observation and judgment, determined the occurrence of the stages. Of course, these calendrical calculations were so arranged as to approximate ecological cycles with sufficient closeness to make the system work (but if, for certain particular reasons, they at one time or another did not work there were ways they could be "adjusted"). In all that follows it must be remembered that the Balinese are not victims of their ritual system; they *use* it. Its very usability testifies to this fact, for it can hardly have grown up by other than a slow, trial-and-error process more than casually attentive to agricultural detail. The specific stages of its development are, of course (barring the sort of careful, fine-comb archaeological work archaeologists seem resistant to practicing on "historical" materials), beyond our recovery.

The Balinese names for the ceremonies are: (1) *Amapeg Toya;* (2) *Nyamu Ngempelin Toya;* (3) *Mubuhin;* (4) *Toya Suci;* (5) *Ngerestiti* (or, more colloquially, *Ngrahinin*); (6) *Membiyu Kukung.* Seven, eight, and nine are all included under the general term *Ngusaba* plus appropriate qualifiers and are really, thus, phases of a single stage. The main justification for the nine-stage formulation (as against a seven-stage, or, eliminating Ngerestiti as a repetitive, cycle-dependent element, a six-stage formulation) is that that is the way all my informants conceptualized it. Once stage one was carried out, in any particular case, on a calendrically determined day, the time of stages two, three, and four was automatically fixed by the permutational calendar; and stages six, seven, eight, and nine were determined by a combination of the lunar, or, more accurately, the solar-lunar calendar and the actual state of affairs in the fields. (And the actual state of affairs in the fields was at least generally determined by the timing of stage three, planting. A more elegant, but quite non-Balinese, conceptionalization of the system would need only stages one and three, so long as they were temporally fixed with respect to one another and tied to the solar year. The others are derivative from these.) Stage five was fixed independently for each Pura Ulun Tjarik, the day being that on which, once every 210-day year, the pura's *odalan* fell (see *notes,* p. 158). Stage one was, at the subak level, coordinate with the *odalan* day of the Pura Ulun Suwi; stages seven, eight, nine, with the solar-lunar-determined annual celebration of the relevant Pura Balai Agung.

To make clear how all this worked in detail would necessitate an extended digression into Balinese time-reckoning systems, of which, on the calendrical level, there are, as already indicated, two: one is independent of natural seasons and permutational; the other is anchored in the natural seasons, but still basically combinatorial in its application. Both worked in an involved interrelationship with each other. It would also involve an inquiry into the associated metaphysical notions of "full" and "empty" days, a discussion out of place here. See, for some of these matters, C. Geertz, 1973h; Goris, 1960b. For the similar Javanese system, see Ricklefs, 1978, pp. 223-238. Bloch's (1977) curious, Marx-réchauffé, armchair notion that Balinese time-reckoning systems are divided between "ritual" and "practical" contexts, with permutational methods and the time sense they embody confined to the former, is merely false, however, as are the inferences he draws from it. For other discussions of this topic, some of them more systematic than others, see C. Geertz, 1972a (where a comparison is made with a quite different, North African, system of water timing); C. J. Grader, 1960a; Soekawati, 1924; Wirz, 1927; van Geuns, 1906, pp. 56-59.

80-25

The "top" of the system, the highest point at which wet rice is grown in Bali, was about 3,500 feet; but by far the bulk of the *padi* land, in Tabanan as elsewhere on the island, lay below 2,000 feet (see Raka, 1955). The "bottom" of the system was, of course, sea level, or virtually so.

80-31

Particularly along a given river gorge (*text*, p. 20), the Water Openings were quite precisely calibrated. Between gorges, however, the sequences thus produced were not exactly correlated; for the circumstances (how many subaks were involved, amount of water in the stream, topography) were not identical. But there was a broad coordination such that, at any particular altitude, the subaks of the area would, at any particular time, be at about the same general stage of cultivation.

It should perhaps also be made clear that the ceremonial cycle not only fixed the times of those tasks it explicitly calibrated (flooding, planting, harvesting, etc.); but, also, the whole cultivation sequence (plowing, weeding, clearing, etc.) was at least generally geared to it in a derivative fashion.

81-15

The technical and ecological aspects of wet rice growing are much more complex than can be described here. See, for the subject in general, Grist, 1959; for the Indonesian situation in particular, C. Geertz, 1963a; for Bali, Ravenholt, 1973.

The Balinese climatic regime is monsoonal; but only in the northern, western, and eastern perimeters is there a pronounced dry season. (In the northeast and northwest the climate grows altogether too dry for wet rice.) The southern heartland has significant rainfall all year around (about 1,500-2,000 mm. in the rice areas), permitting the growth of irrigated nonrice crops (maize, peanuts, etc.), and, in favored places, a second rice crop during the dry(er) season. However, as remarked earlier, the planting of dry(er) crops is much more widespread today than it seems to have been in the nineteenth century, as indeed is dry field cultivation in general. In 1948 about eighty percent of Balinese wet rice land was in the southern heartland; therefore, because the north and west have benefited most from European techniques (not, in any case, so very widespread in Bali) in extending their irrigated land, in the nineteenth century the southern percentage must have been somewhat higher. All in all, however, the post- and precolonial distribution of wet rice land in Bali is, unlike Java (see C. Geertz, 1963a), about the same. For an excellent recent review of Balinese agriculture in general, see Raka, 1955.

On the concept of the "limiting factor," the factor that first halts the spread of an ecosystem, see Clarke, 1954. Of course, appropriate soils and especially temperature are and have been limiting factors in Bali in certain situations. But, for the most part, neither of these has been as important as water. Wet rice distribution is determined, on the gross level, by the availability of water very much more than by the quality of soil or, except at the (geographical) top of the system, by temperature. (The development by the Balinese, in contrast to most of the rest of Asia, of nonphotosensitive rice varieties that permitted planting and harvesting at all seasons of the year seems largely to have eliminated, or much reduced, even the availability of sunlight as a limiting factor—Ravenholt, 1973.) Expansion of the subak system, on the basis of what little evidence does exist (Korn, 1932, pp. 102ff.), seems to have proceeded from the highlands downward toward the sea, as this ritual system suggests. But, again, the sort of ethnohistorical work—work demanding an unusual combination of archaeological, ecological, cultural-anthropological, historical, and linguistic competences—that could actually establish or disestablish this fact simply has not been done.

81-19

Batu Kau ("coconut shell") gives its name also to the temple, which is therefore generally known as Pura Batu Kau. By "all-Bali temple" is meant one of the "six great temples," the Sad Kahyangan, already discussed (*text*, p. 40; *notes*, p. 151). Like Besakih, the greatest of the Sad Kahyangan on the slopes of Mount Agung, Bali's most sacred mountain, Pura Batu Kau is really a temple complex, consisting of a set of physically separate and symbolically different worshiping places. Within this complex, the veneration of water resources was only a part of a much broader system of regionally focused "state" ceremonies, a point to which I shall return.

In any case, like the other Sad Kahyangan, Pura Batu Kau was explicitly associated with such veneration of water resources (lakes, rivers, springs, etc.) and dedicated to securing divine blessings on irrigation water. There were altars for the gods of the most important mountain lakes in Bali in one of the subtemples, the so-called *Pura Sasah* ("seed-sowing temple"), as well as a kind of "microcosmic" lake in the form of an artificial pond. It was at this subtemple that the regional Water-Opening rites were held. The subak heads and priests, the klians and the pemangkus, each received a small container of blessed water from the ceremony. This they took back to their separate subaks, where it was then employed in similar rites at the Pura Ulun Suwi to produce similar water for each tèmpèk or kecoran head to bring, in turn, to his bedugul for similar rites and similar distribution to, finally, the terrace holders— a kind of "replication of holy water" running from remotest source to ultimate application.

The actual rites, as well as the day-to-day upkeep, of the Pura Batu Kau were performed by a quasi-priestly (but Sudra) house in a nearby village, Kebayan Wong Aya Gdé (see map 3). This house was regarded as having been assigned this task by Hario Damar himself and as performing it "on behalf of all the people of Tabanan," and, in a more vaguely conceived way, all the people of Bali. After the main Water-Opening ceremony, which the cakorda and the punggawas also might attend, especially if there had been difficulties the year before, this group of commoners carried out the other eight steps in the sequence without the sedahans' or the klian subaks' presence. In special situations (crop failure or whatever), individual peasants (occasionally even from outside the Tabanan area) would make the pilgrimage to attend one or another of these subsequent rituals, as also, when the occasion demanded, would the king, the lords, or the sedahans.

For a limited amount of rather general data on Pura Batu Kau, see C. J. Grader, 1960b, and n.d., pp. 7, 21, 26; Hooykaas, 1964a, p.

187; Peddlemars, 1932. I am particularly indebted to my Indonesian research associate, R. Rukasah, who lived for several weeks in the village adjoining Pura Batu Kau.

82-6

The system was not so neatly hierarchial as the text might suggest. At any particular stage (say, Planting), ceremonies would be held concurrently at the temple, the various altars, in the tèmpèks and kecorans, and in the terraces; and the people attending would overlap. Again, the members would get holy water from the subak temple priest, make offerings at the bedugul altars, and simultaneously set out food on the terrace dikes for the spirits. The assignment of responsibility to the klian and his staff (including the pamangkus) at the subak level, to the water team at the sub-subak levels, and to the owner at the terrace level, was merely to be sure someone, at least, performed what had to be performed, on pain of natural catastrophe (earthquakes, rat plagues, volcanic eruptions, crop diseases). For any given subak, any particular phase in the ritual cycle could as easily be looked at, and was looked at, as one big ceremony, some of it held in the subak temple, some at the sub-subak altars, and some in the terraces—as in the stratified way that I have formulated it, for analytic purposes, in the text.

82-20

There was no wider, all-Bali, or even all-south-Bali interlocking of regional cycles, doubtless because there was no practical need for it. The rituals at Besakih did include supplications for sufficient and fertile irrigation water for the whole of Bali, however—a kind of islandwide Water Opening (C. J. Grader, 1960b).

82-25

Quoted in Wheatley, 1971, p. 457.

83-6

The ceremonial system was in turn strongly reinforced by transtemporal (i.e., "religious") sanctions. It is impossible here to go into the power of what we—but not the Balinese—would call supernatural sanctions. One can only say they were, and remain, of extraordinary force in Bali, even for a so-called traditional society. The penalty for trifling with sacred necessities, as expressed for the most part in detailed, explicit, and marvelously elaborate ritual obligations, was instant, certain, and terrible. I have, myself, never known a Balinese who took ceremonial requirements, even very minor ones, lightly. Even people who, nowadays, do not seem to believe in the gods, in the sense of believing the myths about them or even crediting them with actual "existence," still do what, in the form of ritual duties, these "nonexistent" gods (and the avoidance of catastrophe) require.

The literature on Balinese religion is vast, but almost all of it is description of customs, philological analysis of texts, or speculative systematization of "Balinese cosmology." For general introductions to Balinese religion, none of them altogether satisfactory, see Swellengrebel, 1960, 1948; Covarrubias, 1956; Stöhr and Zoetmulder, 1968, pp. 346-374; Kersten, 1947, pp. 125-170; Goris, n.d.; Mershon, 1971; Hooykaas, 1964a, 1973a; Gonda, 1975, pt. 2. For a modernist, somewhat ethicized, Balinese codification, see Sugriwa, n.d. The best book for getting a genuine feel for what Balinese "religiousness" is like, unfortunately (from this point of view) focused on only one aspect of it, is Belo, 1960. I have tried, on a much more modest scale, to describe something of Balinese religious attitudes in C. Geertz, 1973c, and 1973e. For incidental, but very perceptive, insights in this area see Bateson and Mead, 1942; Bateson, 1937; Belo, 1949, 1953; Mershon, 1970. A really comprehensive work on Balinese religion from a modern anthropological, *verstehen* point of view, however, remains to be written.

83-23

For a general review of Balinese "water law," in which inter-subak and intra-subak regulations are indiscriminately scrambled together, see Korn, 1932, pp. 604-616. See also the second Liefrinck treaty collection (1921).

These rules were often embodied, like other "customary laws," in the inter-negara "alliance" treaties (*text*, p. 41); but, as explained, these treaties were not bodies of royal legislation, nor were they the results of diplomatic negotiation in the modern sense. They were public statements of long-established (here, peasant established) practices. The rules were also written down in the individual constitutions (*text*, p. 50) of the subaks involved.

It should also be noted that there were all sorts of special arrangements among locally related subaks, including, occasionally, subak unions. The unions formed a level of weakly corporate organization that was intermediate between the intensely corporate subak and the noncorporate region. Even more occasionally, there were precedence rules according to which secondary subaks had rights conceived of as derivative from those enjoyed by other subaks. And so on, almost ad infinitum. The intricacies of all this match those of both the Balinese landscape and the Balinese mind; the latter, as I have remarked elsewhere (C. Geertz, 1959) does not regard simplicity, clarity, regularity, or consistency as virtues.

84-15

Rukun is the noun, so that it means "harmony," "peace," "concord," or "unity," though it is in fact invoked to suggest the processes by which these happy states are achieved. For an incisive discussion of the rukun concept in social context, see, Koentjaraningrat, 1961. This is a Javanese study, but with respect to rukun the Balinese situation is, institutional details aside, essentially identical to the Javanese. I have also commented on Javanese rukun processes in the Appendix to C. Geertz, 1965.

84-28

As with the krama banjar (*text*, p. 49), the krama subak explicitly forbade, in their "constitutions," the interference of any other body or institution whatsoever, including the negara, and asserted their unconditional sovereignty in their own affairs in no uncertain terms. The state as such therefore had no legal rights at all within the subak, a fact which the lords not only accepted, but regarded as a natural "given" as much as did the peasants. Within the subak, a lord, no matter how exalted, was, in legal terms anyway, nothing but a member like any other; and any formal attempt to claim special consideration on the basis of his political status within the state system would be and was sharply rejected as simply irrelevant, as the odd case where such claims were made and summarily rejected demonstrates. Again, this is not to argue that political eminence, and the power that went with it, did not count in Bali as it has counted elsewhere in the world, but merely to suggest how it in fact was forced to operate. (Nonetheless, in both the subak and the banjar the degree to which such eminence and power were contained was, in comparative terms, quite striking.)

85-7

They were not, however, the only important, or even the most important of such sources of violence. Given the combustibility of Balinese state organization already described, any kind of small scale social conflict could quickly escalate into a higher-level military confrontation. For a state inscription concerning definition of subak rights, presumably growing out of disputes which had escaped the mechanisms of local control, see Goris, 1954, vol. 2, pp. 171-172.

85-13

On acephalous polities, see Middleton and Tait, 1958; Southall, 1954.

85-38

The diagram is, again, an idealization, designed to give a general picture.

There are two other aspects of the subak system which should perhaps be touched upon. One, the symbolic role of the paramount lord as "owner" of the water of the region, is addressed below, *text*, p. 127. The other is the question of how subaks were formed, and of the possible role of state direction and planning in such formation.

In fact, the state role in rice-terrace and irrigation construction seems to have been minor at best (Happé, 1919; van Stein Callenfels, 1947-48). In the first place, the growth of the subak system was almost certainly a very gradual, piecemeal process, not an all-at-once collective effort demanding authoritative coordination of huge masses of men. By the nineteenth century the system was essentially complete, but even before the nineteenth century its expansion was slow, steady, and almost imperceptible. The notion that impressive irrigation works need highly centralized states to construct them rests on ignoring this fact: such works are not built at one blow. (See Leach, 1959, concerning "Durkheimian group-mind" notions about irrigation works in Ceylon. The Ifugao system of northern Luzon—see Barton, 1922—where there is no question of a centralized state, supports the same point. On the problem of irrigation and political centralization more generally, see Wheatley, 1971, pp. 289ff.; Adams, 1966; Millon, 1962.)

In the second place, the micro-ecological demands of wet rice growing actually militate against large-scale, centrally directed operations, and most of the more impressive technical work—surveying, tunnel building, dam construction, aqueduct building, and so on—was carried out for pay by groups of peasants specialized for these tasks. The engineering knowledge and even the technical equipment (surveying instruments, etc.) of these specialists reached a rather impressive level of development. The details of Balinese "irrigation engineering," a fascinating subject, cannot be gone into here, but for some suggestive indications concerning tunnel building (some of the tunnels were three kilometers long and forty meters deep), see Korn, 1927. A thorough study of the subject from a technical point of view remains to be made, however.

In short, Balinese subaks were built just about the same way they were maintained: locally and piecemeal. Indeed, the line between the two sorts of activity is difficult to draw. I have not found a single description in the literature of a pre-Dutch construction of a subak ex nihilo, nor could any of my informants recall such an undertaking, though they remembered in some detail a number of extensions, reductions, divisions, reorganizations, and so on, of existing subaks.

87-12

The debt that this classification, and the whole line of analysis which follows, owes to the analytical framework constructed by Karl Polanyi is obvious (Polanyi, et al., 1957; Polanyi, 1977). Perhaps in part because his own tone was so often polemical, there has grown up around Polanyi's work a persistent, oddly embittered, and not terribly incisive debate between so-called substantivist and so-called formalist approaches to the analysis of "pre-modern" economies (for reviews, see Dalton, 1971; LeClair and Schneider, 1968)—a debate in which, I confess, I find it difficult to take much interest. My own view is that maximizing, minimizing, or mini-maximizing models can have enormous explanatory power where the conditions for their application obtain, that they can be powerfully misleading when applied to situations where such conditions do not obtain, and that such conditions sometimes obtain, but more often do not, in "archaic," "primitive," or whatever you want to call economies without central banks, state planning commissions, or business schools. As the little old lady wrote to Bertrand Russell concerning solipsism, I can't understand why everyone does not hold this eminently sensible position.

The market system in classical Bali was confined to very small-scale retail trade in everyday consumables such as foodstuffs, simple implements, and fuels, and staffed almost entirely by women, Sudra and triwangsa alike, who brought their produce from home to sell. Such markets (tèn-tèn) were held in the mornings and rotated on a three-day "market-week" cycle, defining, thus, a market area comprising perhaps seven or eight desa adats. To judge from inscriptions, many of which were dated according to the market-week day and frequently addressed to the desa adats of a market area as an entity, this market area unit apparently had some sort of minor political significance in the negara system; but what exactly it was remains obscure (Goris, 1954; the first reference to markets and market weeks is for the ninth century: vol. 2, pp. 119-120). The marketplaces were commonly set up in the space in front of one or another lord's house (in Tabanan, this was Puri Anom; see map 3). And, as with everything else—land, water, people, and so on—the idiom had it that the lord "owned" the market. In any case, he levied taxes on it, as he did on the cockfights, which, in the afternoon of the market day, were often held in the cockring (wantilan) near the marketplace. (On cockfights and markets, which were very intimately related in classical Bali, see Liefrinck, 1877; van Bloemen Waanders, 1859; and C. Geertz, 1973i, n. 18.) The currency of market trade, and of cockfight betting, was the lead Chinese coin, kèpèng, already mentioned in connection with agricultural taxation (notes, p. 178, and discussed further below text, p. 91). A few scattered "royal decrees" (paswara) concerning market trade can be found (e.g., Liefrinck, 1921, p. 201); but in general they are very rare, suggesting that market regulation, as opposed to the mere legitimization of their existence, as in the inscriptions, does not seem to have been a very prominent concern of the lords. For a brief description of apparently fairly sizeable markets in Badung about 1812, see van den Broek, 1834, pp. 228-229 (though he consistently much exaggerates the scale of things in Bali).

As for traditionally fixed exchange relationships, they obtained between specialized artisans (blacksmiths, weavers, roofers, musicians, dancers, actors, etc.) or various sorts of ritual specialists and ordinary villagers. Once established, usually between groups rather than individuals, such relationships tended to be permanent (many of them are still intact) and involved reciprocal exchanges of rice and other necessities for the service or craft-product involved. Further, the more prominent lords established what I earlier called (text, p. 34) "clientship relations" with some of the more accomplished craft and artistic groups, in which the latter rendered their products or skills and the former their political patronage—relieving the artisans from certain taxes, ritual services, and ward duties, and permitting them certain sumptuary privileges, titles, and so on. (Like the Brahmanas, such groups were often permitted to choose their own perbekels, rather than being under ones appointed by the puris and jeros.) There were, in Tabanan, commoner groups of weavers, blacksmiths, silver and gold workers, and musicians with such special "by-appointment-to-the-court" status as "clients" to half a dozen of the leading houses; their privileged positions are remembered and affect social relationships (e.g., marriage) to this day. For a general discussion of such groups, see de Kat Angelino, 1921c-1922; cf. Goris, 1960c; C. Geertz, 1963b, pp. 93-97; Moojen, 1920, pp. 11-16.

87-21

On "thalassocracy" in the ancient Malay world, see Wheatley, 1961; on Javanese "bazaar states," C. Geertz, 1956. On the earliest Indonesian states generally, see Coedès, 1948; Hall, 1955, chap. 3; and, for Srivijaya, Wolters, 1967 and 1970.

The classic work on early Indonesian trade in van Leur (1955), though it needs to be supplemented by Meilink-Roelofsz, 1962 (for a brief general review, see Brissenden, 1976). Schrieke (1955, pp. 3-82) gives the Javanese picture from 1300 to 1700. As for the nineteenth century, Resink's description (1968, p. 322) of "the archipelago under Conrad's eyes" demonstrates that the general pattern was not all that much altered, at least initially, by steamships and the opening of the Suez Canal.

> Only after one has been to the Batak country, the Lesser Sudra Islands, or the hinterlands of Macassar will one really begin to grasp the fact that in Conrad's years [he was in Malay waters between 1883 and 1898] an international, ephemeral, peripheral, and heterogeneous shipping and trade economy of "white and brown" obtained along the shores of Indonesian islands, giving way just a few miles inland to what were in more than one way dark, homogeneous micro-economies of Indonesian realms and lands.

On ports of trade generally, see Polanyi, 1963, 1966; for a review of the ensuing discussion, Dalton, 1978.

87-27

van Leur, 1955, p. 86. On the European, and most especially the Dutch, spice trade, see Glamann, 1958; Masselman, 1963.

87-31

The Gibbon quotation is given in van Leur, 1955, p. 85.

88-5

Perhaps the best index of the relative commercial isolation of Bali is the fact that the number of Chinese resident there has always been very small, relative to the rest of Indonesia. Even in 1920, fifteen years after the institution of direct Dutch rule expanded the opportunities of foreign traders on the island, there were only about 7,000 (or 0.4% of Bali's total population—vs. 1.65% over all Indonesia—the lowest percentage of any region of the archipelago save Tapanuli and Timor. For estimates of the Chinese population in various states of south Bali around 1900, see Schwartz, 1901. For a general review of their role in the Netherlands East Indies overall, see van Vleming, 1925.

88-13

de Graaf, 1949, pp. 245-246, 272. Blambangan, the last Javanese negara to resist both Islamization and the Dutch, was defended to the end (1777) by Balinese troops.

88-18

Schrieke, 1955, pp. 21, 29, 32, 227. See also Meilink-Roelofsz, 1962, pp. 102, 403.

88-22

Tarling, 1962, p. 70.

88-25

de Graaf, 1949, pp. 432-434.

88-28

van Bloemen Waanders, 1859 (for a partial English summary, see Hanna, 1976, pp. 64-65). How the unfavorable balance was offset is unexplained, but all these figures should not be taken too exactly in any case. Not only are they mere estimates, but a good deal of trade went on outside the official system. Even more important, as Bali's most important harbor—indeed, its only important harbor—Singaraja was, especially after the 1850s, part of a system of administered trade, lord by lord (and Chinese by Chinese), over the whole of the island; so it cannot be understood in isolation. Van Bloemen Waanders estimates that of the yearly 30,000 *picul* of the chief export, rice, nearly 20,000 came not from Bulèlèng but from south Bali; and of the 300 cases of the main import, opium, about half went on to south Bali.

Bandar is the Persian word for "emporium" or "trade center"; *su* is the Balinese rendering of *shah*, the Persian for "king" or "lord" (Purnadi, 1961). The internal organization of the *kebandaran* "trade realms" is unclear, but they do not seem to have been territorial. Differing widely in profitability, the two most valuable rented for 1,300 florins a year, the two least valuable for 120 florins; all such rents came to a total of 4,825 florins, though each rent apparently went to a different lord who, again, was said to "own" the kebandaran. In addition to "trade rents," lords also collected tolls on traffic moving to or from the south, west, and east; taxed markets, cock-fights, dancing-girls, and salt making; sold officially stamped letters; and levied fines on illegal commerce.

For a series of nineteenth-century state edicts from the Balinese section of Lombok that set forth the monopoly position of a Subandar and the regulations governing external trade, see Liefrinck, 1915, vol. 2, pp. 1-25, esp. pp. 13-19. For Bali proper (Klungkung-Karengasem), see Korn, 1922, pp. 55-56.

89-11

Liefrinck, 1877. Imports (largely via Singaraja) are said to have run around 100,000 florins, the main one being, again, opium (about 50% by value), with cotton cloth (35%), various spices (especially, in this upland region, salt), and a few of Gibbon's "splendid trifles," such as goldwork and chinaware, making up most of the rest. Exports (a bit more dispersed, but also mostly via Singaraja) totaled about 200,000 florins and included coffee (60% by value), cattle

(20%), rice (10%), and hides and maize (about 5% each). Here also the trade was handled by Chinese leasehold subandars, ten of them (the entire Chinese population in this quite interior area is said to be "about a dozen"), who rented their "trade realms" from no less than thirteen separate lords, the total rent amounting to about 4,000 florins a year, though the Chinese were, Liefrinck dryly remarks, "also pressed for other contributions from time to time." Liefrinck does not say how these 4,000 florins were apportioned among either lords or trade realms, but one assumes that, on the general pattern, this too would have been done quite unequally.

In any case, though again the figures must not be carried beyond decimals, the lords' total income from trade rents is here almost as much as it was in the very much larger coastal Singaraja seventeen years earlier, whereas the percentage of the gross trade the rents represent is up to about one and one-half percent as against about one-half percent in Singaraja—all indicating something of a rapid expansion of trade and, *pari passu*, the intensifying interest of the lords in it. Liefrinck gives some other indications to the same effect: Prices for Bangli cattle at Singaraja have doubled in ten years. There are "now" five lord-owned toll gates between Bangli and Singaraja. Opium imports have risen in a couple decades from one or two cases a year to thirty. There is, despite the monopoly system, fierce competition among Chinese coffee buyers and much smuggling of it. The multiplicity of independent Chinese subandars is of only a few years' standing, and Chinese, client to the paramount lord, monopolizing the whole, much smaller, traffic before. The Chinese traders are now almost all China-born, not, as previously, Bali-born. Even that most Balinese of economic indicators, cock-fighting, is said to have increased dramatically in scale and frequency to the point that there is a large one "almost every day in the capital commercial area."

As for what was happening at the same time in Singaraja itself, still the entrepôt of all this, Liefrinck remarks that about two thousand people emigrated there from Bangli "last year" to work as day laborers, a remarkable and unprecedented development.

89-14

Schwartz, 1901. That the driving force of Balinese trade after 1830 was opium (as before 1815, when Raffles more or less put a stop to it, slavery had been—*notes*, p. 169) is clear for these regions too. Klungkung lords were collecting 1,000 florins a month, no less, from

letting out commercial leases to sell it; Karengasem lords were collecting 2,500; and Schwartz met Chinese peddling it in some of the
most obscure villages on the island. (Just after the Dutch takeover,
van Geuns [1906, p. 28] gives Badung's consumption as "almost a
half a ton a year.") Again, the figures are doubtless estimates; and,
as the Dutch regarded the opium trade as a major social evil (for
a discussion of the impact of opium in Bali generally, see Jacobs,
1883; cf. Kol, 1913), they are possibly exaggerated. But that opium
was extraordinarily widely used is confirmed by my informants, most
of whom said that by the end of the century nearly every adult
Balinese, male and female, was an addict; and in Klungkung, a
royal informant, then but a child, remembers that the smoke grew
so dense in the palace that the lizards fell from the walls in stupor.
The effect on the economy was, however, anything but soporific.
The demand for opium seems to have been the main motive for
the expansion, indeed virtually the initiation, of commodity export: coffee, livestock, tobacco, coconut products, sugar, and so on.
With an irony appropriate to an inward people, traditional Balinese trade got its strongest stimulus from a narcotic. (Korn [1932,
p. 538] reports "May you not fall into opium peddling" as a pa-
rental blessing in 1844 Bali.)

89-23

The two main sources on Lange, and on which the following description of the Kuta port of trade relies, are: Nielsen, 1928 (a
Danish biography translated into Dutch); and, more important,
Helms, 1882, pp. 1-71, 196-200 (a vivid and detailed memoir of life
in and around the place at the height of its development, in 1847-
49, when Helms, also a Dane, was Lange's assistant there). See also
van Hoëvell, 1849-54 (he made his famous *reis* to Bali in one of
Lange's ships). A brief, popular summary of Lange's career can be
found in Hanna, 1976, pp. 50-59. Some interesting letters to and
from Lange (the correspondents are his Balinese wife; the lords of
Kesiman, a major Badung house; lords of Tabanan and Mengwi;
and various Balinese commercial contacts) can be found in van
Naerssen, Pigeaud, and Voorhoeve, 1977, pp. 147-155.

89-39

There was a small anchorage there, with about thirty Chinese and
as many "Muslim" resident traders, which Europeans occasionally

visited, as early as the eighteen-twenties. In 1840, more or less coincident with Lange's arrival, and perhaps stimulated by it, the semi-official Dutch trading company, Nederlandsche Handelmaatschappij (N.H.M.), rented exclusive trading rights there from a local lord, that at Kasiman, for 1,000 guilders. The Dutch thus regarded Lange as an interloper. But, after harassing him for awhile, the colonial government finally decided it the better part of valor simply to make him their commercial agent there, rather than the N.H.M., whose effort never really got off the ground; and so they did, in 1844, after first rendering him a Dutch citizen. That the site was no longer, by then, any 1,000-guilder proposition is evident from the price the N.E.I. government had to pay N.H.M. for relinquishing its rights: 175,000 guilders. Finally, when the Dutch, following their military successes in the north, attacked south Bali in 1848-49, losing in the process their commanding officer and a large number of men, and being decimated by illness, Lange arranged a peace treaty—entertaining, Helms says, "all the princes, with a following of nearly 40,000 [Dutch sources say, "only 20,000"] men . . . on behalf of the Badong Radjah"—which allowed the Dutch to withdraw without further damage. However, the incursion was accompanied by a blockade; and this, it seems, was so disruptive to trade that it initiated the decline of Kuta (*notes*, p. 210). By the time of Lange's death in 1856 (Helms says of a broken economic heart, others hint poison), Kuta was once again a small, only mildly active, quite peripheral "factory," run in turn first by Lange's brother and then by his nephew, who finally liquidated the enterprise and sold his rights to a Chinese (Nielsen, 1928, pp. 62-76, 149-177; Helms, 1882, pp. 66-71, 198). When Schwartz (see Schwartz, 1901; cf. van Geuns, 1906), the Dutch resident at Bulèlèng, finally got to Badung at the turn of the century, the Kuta establishment had lost most of its former importance in favor of Kasuma, which was the Klungkung lords' burgeoning port of trade to the east, and in favor of the also-burgeoning Singaraja-via-Bangli overland outlet farther north (*notes*, p. 202). Indeed, conditions had so deteriorated, he says, that "the lords" took the lease away from the Langes' Chinese successor and tried to run the place themselves, which only completed the disaster.

91-1

Helms (1882) does mention "Manchester goods" (p. 40); so cloth was probably also important, as doubtless (though, for all his description of the 1848-49 war, he does not mention them at all) were arms. Nielsen (1928), who, like Helms, represents Lange as at once a defender of Balinese freedom, a promoter of peace, and a loyal representative of Dutch interests, does mention (p. 158) that the Balinese had a thousand rifles and twenty-five cannon at this time; but he does not go into the delicate, and self-answering, question of how they might have gotten them and the ammunition to fire them save through the offices of the N.E.I.'s commercial agent for south Bali. Hanna (1976, p. 55) says, "at the peak of his career in the mid-1840s" Lange was doing a million guilders's worth of business a year with Java alone while "the trade with Singapore and China must have been even greater."

For a passing reference to Lange's gun trading, see the letter to him from the Lord of Mengwi in van Naerssen, Pigeaud, and Voorhoeve, 1977, p. 153.

91-20

The Helms, 1882, quotations are from p. 40. As he was at Kuta only two and a half years, he was hardly in a position to observe long-term price movements. But the point is that prices were deliberately set, apparently unmanipulated, and insulated, so far as possible; and this was done in terms of coins privately purchased abroad as merchandise and locally sold as such, and not in terms of a generally evaluated "state" currency—of which, of course, the negara had none, neither here nor, so far as I have been able to discover, anywhere else in Indonesia. Indeed, Schrieke (1955, p. 247) says that, in the seventeenth century, Indonesia was so great a drain on Chinese coinage that the Chinese government attempted "in vain" to combat the export of coins, "by drastic measures"; and van Leur (1955) is dotted with anguished quotations from East Indiamen about the simple, physical lack of currency—for example, this from Jan Pieterszoon Coen, the company's great pioneer governor general to the Heeren XVII, its governing board:

> The gentlemen will understand [by which he means that they will *not* understand] that no places in the Indies . . . are supplied properly without money in cash, even if they be supplied with a tenfold cargo in merchandise; what is more, there are many places which the more they are supplied with merchandise the more serious it is, if they do not have money in cash beside, for in all the Indies there cannot be more turned over than is retailed every day. . . . (quoted on p. 220)

91-30

The notion of "equivalencies" is, again, from Polanyi.

As to the market element commonly called "price," it [is] here subsumed under the category of equivalencies. The use of this general term should help avoid misunderstandings. Price suggests fluctuation, while equivalency lacks this association. The very phrase "set" or "fixed" price suggests that price before being fixed or set was apt to change. Thus language itself makes it difficult to convey the true state of affairs, namely, that "price" is originally a rigidly fixed quantity, in the absence of which trading cannot start. Changing or fluctuating prices of a competitive character are a comparatively recent development and their emergence forms one of the main interests of the economic history of antiquity. . . .

Price systems, as they develop over time, may contain layers of equivalencies that historically originated under different forms of integration. Hellenistic market prices show ample evidence of having derived from [customary] equivalencies of the cuneiform civilizations that preceded them. The thirty pieces of silver received by Judas as the price of a man for betraying Jesus was a close variant of the equivalency of a slave as set out in Hammurabi's Code some 1700 years earlier. Soviet [administrative] equivalencies, on the other hand, for a long time echoed nineteenth century world market prices. These, too, in their turn, had their predecessors. Max Weber remarked that for lack of a costing basis Western capitalism would not have been possible but for the medieval network of statuated and regulated prices, customary rents, etc., a legacy of gild and manor. Thus price systems may have an institutional history of their own in terms of the types of equivalencies that entered into their making. (Polanyi et al., 1957, pp. 266-269)

There are some overstatements here ("rigidly fixed," etc.) as well as some debatable historical facts (the Judas example seems more piquant than likely). But, stripped of polemical ardor, the perspective makes sense of Indonesian commercial history in a way that reading back of the bears-and-bulls type of price theory does not.

On the other hand, all this is not to say that prices in one port had no influence whatsoever on prices in another, even in classical times; for Meilink-Roelofsz (1962) has shown that they did. The controversy on this matter—and indeed on the whole nature of "ancient trade" in the archipelago—mainly between her and van Leur (1955), is a complex one, and far from a simple either/or question. But the Balinese material, particularly as it comes from a century when communications had vastly advanced and trade had become markedly more rationalized, seems to support van Leur's "scattered markets" emphasis better than Meilink-Roelofsz's "integrated emporium" one.

91-34

Polanyi et al., 1957, p. 268.

91-39

Though kèpèngs—referred to variously as "lead," "copper," and "bronze" Chinese coins—were extremely widespread means of payment in classical Indonesian port-of-trade economy, and seem to have been the only currency of importance at Kuta, the variety of moneys in that economy, especially earlier on, was of course enormous.

On Java, and probably in the ports on which Javanese ships traded, circulated the lead cash imported from China, thousands of which, threaded on a string through a hole in the center of them, counted for one real of eight; and alongside it there were Spanish and Portuguese money, Chinese trading money of bar silver, Persian *larrins*, small silver bars the shape of horseshoes. In Achin people reckoned in taels of gold; on the west coast of Sumatra trade took place primarily as direct barter on the basis of money calculations; the same thing was true of Banda, but on the basis of nutmeg weights; on Ambon there was money calculation and money trade; on Sumbawa gold and silver bracelets served as money; on Bima barter exchange was carried on with small stones; in Jambi light pepper served as small change; on Buton pieces of cotton were means of exchange and measures of value. (van Leur, 1955, p. 136)

As van Leur notes (1955, p. 136), a similarly wide variation in weights and measures contributed, as well, to the fragmentation of the port-of-trade economy into discontinuous, yet intensely interactive, units. (In Kuta, kèpèngs were also used as the main measure of weight, and Balinese weights—for example, of unthreshed rice—are often stated in such terms today; *notes*, p. 178). For a similar description of multiple money—now Singapore dollars, Dutch guilders, and so on—in "Conrad's archipelago" (i.e., late-nineteenth century), see Resink, 1968, p. 320. For kèpèng exchange rates with Dutch moneys at the beginning of this century, see "Muntwezen," 1934; for south Bali just after the Dutch takeover, van Geuns, 1906, pp. 7-8. Finally, it should be noted that even in Bali there was more than one sort of kèpèng in circulation.

92-14

Helms, 1892, p. 45. He means, of course, "ordinary Balinese." Not only were Helms and Lange frequently invited to royal ceremonies, but the leading lords, saronged and parasoled, turned up along with "captains of ships, merchants, savans [sic] . . . officials from Java . . . Dutch naval officers . . . men of high culture and social powers," at "Mr. Lange's hospitable table" with some frequency (p. 44). "Wonderful indeed," continues Helms, for whom life at Kuta was a continual wonder.

> . . . were the tales told round that table; but, together with the songs which usually followed at a later stage, they caused the evenings of these cosmopolitan parties to pass harmoniously and pleasantly. The singing was to me a source of infinite amusement. It was, in a manner, compulsory for everyone to give his song. Mr. Lange's head clerk, an Englishman, who took the bottom of the table, had a great talent for comic songs, and he enforced without mercy, the rule of the song upon others. And so, in half the languages of Europe [the Balinese were apparently excepted], in comic, gay and doleful strains, the song went round. A game of billiards usually terminated the evening. . . .

Helms was not exaggerating about men of high culture and social powers: the Indologist and first serious student of Balinese culture, Friederich (Friederich, 1959), the botanist Zollinger (Zollinger, 1849), and, as mentioned, Baron van Hoëvell (van Hoëvell, 1849-54, vol. 3) were Lange's guests as well (Nielsen, 1928, p. 77). Besides Helms and the English clerk, the permanent staff also included an English physician (Nielsen, 1928, p. 100) and a "red-eyed, one-armed" Baju "sea gypsy" thug who had been with Lange since Lombok (Helms, 1882, p. 13).

92-25

The quotation is from Helms, 1882, p. 70. Again, the whole passage is beautifully evocative of Lange's (and Helms's) *Kapitalistischer Abenteuer* style and suggests that he was as much a victim of the developments he assisted as were his patrons, the Balinese lords; it is worth quoting.

> The protracted blockade which [the Dutch] had maintained during their languid [1848-49] operation against the Balinese had destroyed the trade of the island and caused him losses which he never recovered. He could not adapt himself to the altered circumstances in which the Dutch expeditions had left him; and he was not the man to retrieve his position by long-continued thrift and prudence. There was more of the bold viking than the prudent trader in his nature. He delighted in tossing about in a gale in his little yacht, the *Venus*, which he loved as though it were a living thing. He knew every rope and spar in his considerable fleet, and no laggard captain would return from a needlessly protracted voyage with impunity. He delighted in overcoming all difficulties save those of commercial life. He was not a skillful rider, yet so bold a one, that I have seen him break in obstinate and vicious horses by sheer force of will.

92-39

The main exception ("though even in this, the women had more, than their share"—Helms, 1882, p. 42) was cattle dealing. The cattle trade was very large, and Balinese oxen were much sought after. Those traded at Kuta were kept, semi-wild, on the already mentioned limestone plateau south of Kuta called Bukit (see map 4), where they roamed about in great herds along with water buffaloes "which were particularly savage," making the place "a part of the country somewhat dangerous to visit" (Helms, 1882, p. 43). The land, being "wasteland"—that is, uncultivated—was under the control of the lords, who also owned the herds. Helms (1882, p. 44) expresses astonishment that, lacking brands or other marks, the lords could tell whose animals were whose. "There was a good deal of disputing on this point, but not so much as might have been expected, as in such disputes rank and power usually settled the matter."

Such commercial cattle farming was clearly quite recent, stimulated by Lange's activities. (He also had two abattoirs at Kuta, where oxen were slaughtered to provide dried beef for the Dutch troops in Java; and this, apparently, was the mainstay of the trade.) But when it began, what its exact scale was, and, most critical for my purposes, how it was organized—almost certainly through multiple, specialized ties similar to those already described for court service, taxation, land rent, and so on—I have not been able to determine. Van Bloemen Waanders (1859) also remarks on the prominence of women on the Balinese side of the suddenly expanded trade at Singaraja. There, almost every housewife seems to have tried a little trading with the Chinese subandars.

93-8

Helms, 1882, pp. 42-43; I have altered the paragraphing. Again, "attendants" is a more accurate word than "slaves" for these women's followers, who were doubtless parekans or perhaps even paid employees (*notes*, p. 169).

94-18

My Tabanan material again comes mostly from oral sources, as described in *notes*, p. 142; but, in addition to the informants mentioned there, I also discussed these matters with the son (owner of the local movie theatre) of the last, and most considerable, subandar in Tabanan—the "Singkeh Cong" described below. There are a few incidental yet valuable references to precolonial Tabanan trade in the literature, the most important being Schwartz, 1901. See also Liefrinck, 1921, pp. 7-85; Peddlemars, 1932; van den Broek, 1834 (the earliest European notation I have seen, which has Chinese trading "domestically" in rice, cloth, cotton, and—"as smugglers"— in "slaves"); and the lithic chips of fact scattered, haphazardly and unindexed, throughout Korn, 1932.

94-23

Singkeh is the term for an Indonesian Chinese born in China, as against one born in Indonesia, called a *peranakan*. *Cong* is the Balinese version of the surname usually rendered in English as "Chung." For the force of the term *jero*, see *text*, p. 26.

211

94-38

At least the rent was calculated annually. As explained below, it was paid to different lords, and in different amounts, on ceremonial occasions: thus, irregularly. Also, though the rent was calculated in kèpèngs, it was usually paid in commodities: rice, coffee, pork, opium, porcelain, jewelry. On the negara side, the bookkeeping involved in all this was performed by the Sudra clerkly houses: the Penyarikans, Dangin Peken, and Malkangin (*notes*, p. 166).

Schwartz (1901) says that, at the turn of the century, trade income was a more important element in the lords' income than land taxation; and he estimates the latter at (the rice equivalent of) a million kèpèngs, which perhaps puts a floor under the matter, though the tax figure itself can hardly be more than a wild, conceivably exaggerated, conceivably minimized, estimate.

The "trade realm," or *kebandaran* system (*notes*, p. 202), obtained here too, with the various lords "owning" trading rights in various places and leasing them to particular Chinese. As with perbekelans, however, no exact reconstruction of these units is possible. All that is clear is that they were not simple territorial units; there were not a great many of them; and the main regions in which they were important were the two coffee areas, Marga to the northeast and Pupuan to the northwest (see map 3), along with the region in and immediately around the capital. The northeastern coffee lands above Marga were largely under the aegis of the "second king" (*text*, p. 60), Pemadé Kalèran; while the northwestern ones in Pupuan were under that of Gdé through the agency of Subamia, the chief noble power there (*notes*, p. 166). Around the capital the usual crosscutting and intersecting complexity obtained.

95-40

Other imports included, most prominently, cotton cloth, Chinese porcelain, various spices, and again kèpèngs and weapons. Other exports included dried coconut meat, palm sugar, palm oil, certain kinds of metal work, and oxen, though the latter trade seems to have been far less important than at Badung, and indeed quite trivial. These goods did not have to pass through Cong's establishment, but probably the bulk of them did. On the other hand, there was a certain amount of coffee and opium smuggling. This was difficult to carry out on a very large scale, however, given the transport problems; and the penalties for it were heavy, not excluding death.

96-8

Jembrana, which is the closest Balinese port to Java, had been administered by the Dutch since the middle of the century, though the traders there were mainly Chinese, Javanese, Buginese, and in some cases Islamized Balinese.

The Balinese boats, *jukung*, were essentially fishing boats pressed into transport service. About ten feet long, locally built, and operated by not-very-skilled sailors (the Balinese dislike the sea), they could not venture more than a few thousand yards off shore. Most of them seem to have been owned by their builders, Balinese men from fishing villages along the coast; but some were Chinese-financed, and the cakorda of Gdé owned two—"the royal navy"—which he mainly used to visit Badung.

Finally, some goods were foot-carried north (horse transport was rare in Tabanan), via Baturiti and Kintamani, to Singaraja (see map 1) for export. But this route was arduous as well as extremely dangerous, under the more or less permanently unsettled political conditions (the overland route to Kuta was closed altogether until 1891 as a result of the Mengwi war, and not terribly safe thereafter); and it was much less important than the south-coast routes.

96-12

Clearly, a great deal of trade was conducted entirely inside the jero, which in addition to administering trade also served as a mart for it. But concerning this, or concerning the internal operation of the jero as such, there is no Helms to turn to; I have only the most general sorts of information.

96-26

Schwartz (1901) met two Chinese opium sellers in a place so remote as to be scarcely inhabited; and all my informants say that the Balinese opium peddlers were legion, the majority, again, being women. (Chinese sellers set up opium "dens" all over the countryside; but many people smoked at home as well.) In Pupuan, Schwartz found fifteen Chinese coffee buyers in one small village, sixteen in another. He also reports the cotton growing.

Hamlet (or kin group) specialization in crafts and in small goods for trade is of long standing in Bali. Aside from artisans' specialties like iron smithing, carving, and weaving, other hamlet specializations that informants mentioned were the making of thatch-roofs, coconut oil, palm sugar, bricks, earthenware pots, reed mats, salt, and lime (for chewing with the betel nut); and fishing. As mentioned (*notes*, p. 199), many of these specialized goods were distributed through established systems of reciprocal exchange, by bartering rice for the specialty. But toward the end of the nineteenth century, the goods came more and more to flow through the market, which consequently grew in importance as an institution. Many of these local specializations persist even today, however, and some (e.g., gamelan instrument making; see C. Geertz, 1963b) still work through the traditional exchange patterns, though with money payments rather than barter.

98-1

Helms, 1882, pp. 59-66. I have quoted this passage before, in C. Geertz, 1977b, where some general discussion of Balinese cremation may be found. Other early descriptions of cremations (*ngabèn*) cum widow burnings (*mesatia*)—one from a Dutch mission in 1663 and one from Friederich (the same Helms saw) in 1847—are quoted in Covarrubias, 1956, pp. 377-383 (cf. van Geuns, 1906, pp. 65-71). See also Anonymous, 1849. According to van Eerde (1910), a Chinese account mentions a widow burning in Java in 1416. Dutch incursion did put an end to widow burning (but not cremation, which continues to the present), though informants claim that secret ones occurred well into the nineteen-twenties. For the suttee suicides of two wives of the cakorda of Tabanan (XVI on fig. 3) at his death in 1903, an event which seems to have played a part in the Dutch decision to intervene directly in south Bali (Hanna, 1976, p. 74), see Tabanan, n.d., p. 110.

Helms's characterization of the women as "bond slaves" is surely wrong. Female parekans were occasionally sacrificed at their lord's cremation, but they were stabbed to death first before being thrown onto the pyre; only proper wives of the lord had sufficient status to leap alive into the flames, sometimes stabbing themselves at the same time. Helms's rendering of "Surya" ("the Sun") as "Indra" (who is indeed "The Lord of Heaven") is also incorrect: it should be "Siva," whom the Balinese identify with the sun. On the so-called Balinese death cult in general, see Wirz, 1928; Crucq, 1928; Covarrubias, 1956, pp. 357-388; Kersten, 1947, pp. 155-170; Lamster, 1933, pp. 52-65; Friederich, 1959, pp. 83-99; Hooykaas-van Leeuwen Boomkamp, 1956; and *text*, p. 116. For a good series of photographs of a cremation, see Goris, n.d., plates 4.80-4.93; cf. Bateson and Mead, 1942, plates 94-96. A (notional) 1620 German engraving of a Balinese cremation is reproduced as the frontispiece to Boon, 1977.

102-8

The heavy scholarly stress on the "belief" side of Balinese religion —cosmology, theology, sacred literature, spirit notions, witchcraft, and so on—has meant that careful, detailed descriptions of much Balinese ritual life, and especially of royal ceremonies, are lacking. No really adequate technical account of a royal cremation (*ngabèn*) yet exists (for a recent—1949—and rather special, nonroyal cremation, see Franken, 1960; cf. Mershon, 1971, pp. 202ff.); and of tooth filing (*metatah*), hardly even any popular accounts exist. (For a very brief account of a triwangsa tooth filing, see Vroklage, 1937; cf. Bateson and Mead, 1942, plate 86; Mershon, 1971, pp. 147 ff., and illus. at p. 149. Mershon also has an extended narrative account of a 1937 court ritual in Karengasem, a realm-purifying rite called *Baligia*, at pp. 257-368.) Swellengrebel (1947; cf. 1960, pp. 47-50) is a useful, though fragmentary, account based on a 1903 report by Schwartz of an ordination (not, as is sometimes said, a "coronation," which the Balinese did not have: what was involved was sanctifying the king, not installing him—cf. Gonda, 1952, pp. 236, 252). A textual analysis of this ritual, *Siva-ratri*, can be found in Hooykaas, 1964a, pp. 193-236; and C. J. Grader (1960b) gives some scattered information about ritual in state temples generally. The most valuable "eyewitness" accounts of Indic royal ceremonies in Indonesia, however, are still Prapanca's of the *Shrāddha* (royal memorial) and *Phālguna-Caitra* (annual court) rituals in 1362 Majapahit (Pigeaud, 1960-63, chaps. 9 and 14). For general references concerning Balinese religion, see *notes*, p. 194.

102-21

Among the more important of such ceremonial forms carrying at least somewhat different "messages" are village temple ceremonies (Bateson, 1937; Belo, 1953; Hooykaas, 1977); the famous shadow plays (McPhee, 1970; Hooykaas, 1960 and 1973c); the even more famous witch-and-dragon dances (Belo, 1949; Bateson and Mead, 1942; Mead, 1970; de Zoete and Spies, 1938; C. Geertz, 1973c; Rickner, 1972); the demon-cleansing Day of Silence (Covarrubias, 1956, pp. 272-282; Sugriwa, 1957a, pp. 42-51; Sudharsana, 1967); the high-priest's gesture-chants to lure Siva into possessing him (Korn, 1960; de Kat Angelino and de Kleen, 1923; Hooykaas, 1966; Goudriaan and Hooykaas, 1971); rites of passage (Mershon, 1971); and the work-pacing festivals of the agricultural cycle (*text*, p. 180). For more discussion of the variation in what different Balinese cultural forms "say," and thus the impossibility of summing up Balinese culture in a single theme, see C. Geertz, 1977b; cf. 1973h. The failure to appreciate the degree to which cultural institutions "state" contrasting, even conflicting, propositions about the nature of "reality," social and otherwise, seems to me to mar Dumont's (1970a) generally brilliant discussion of "the principle of hierarchy" —a discussion which has stimulated my own.

102-28

Du Bois, 1959, p. 31.

103-18

For an excellent example of "reading" state ritual (royal funerals in fifteenth- and sixteenth-century France) for political meaning, see Giesey (1960), who remarks in his preface:

Time and time again . . . I have emerged with the conviction that some crucial innovation in the ceremonial first occurred quite haphazardly . . . and later generations when re-enacting it embellished it with clear-cut symbolism. That is to say, on the level of events themselves, chance frequently reigned; but symbolic forms affected the thought about the events especially when they were consciously [i.e., deliberately] repeated at later funerals. On the one hand, therefore, I deem that much was random or accidental, but on the other hand I see the expression of a pattern of ideas closely related to intellectual convictions of the times. Those ideas were dramatized in ritual, and verbalized if at all only incidentally. Thus the "constitutional" [i.e., "political"] aspects of the royal funeral I have had to draw usually by inference from ceremonial behavior, as the historian of liturgy finds religious belief in ritual, or the historian of art discovers the artist's thought in iconography.

Were an "annalistic" history of Balinese court ceremony available, a similar picture of irregular evolution ("chance," I think, is not quite the right word), regularized by post hoc interpretation and adjustment, would doubtless emerge. Thus, the highly integrated nineteenth-century politico-religious conceptions of the Balinese state were not inherited as a fixed pattern that had drifted, untouched by historical processes, down across the ages; but rather, they were the product of a constant process of change in both the concrete forms of ritual and the meaning symbolically given them, again in great part implicitly.

On the problem of royal ritual as political statements in general (in this case, English, Javanese, and Moroccan "Progresses"), see C. Geertz, 1977a. For general discussions of the problem of cultural interpretation in the terms employed here, see C. Geertz, 1973b, 1973c, 1973d, 1973f, 1973h, 1973i, 1975, 1976a, 1976b. On hermeneutic approaches in the social sciences more generally, see Radnitsky, 1970; Giddens, 1976; Bernstein, 1976; Taylor, 1971; Ricoeur, 1970; Gadamer, 1976.

103-29

Portions of the following passage have appeared in about the same form in C. Geertz, 1976a.

104-34

For general, textual-philological investigation of these various image-ideas, to which I am indebted, see Hooykaas, 1964a. On the concept of *sekti*, see also Gonda, 1952, p. 134. For *padmasana, idem*, 1952, pp. 135-96. For *lingga, idem*, 1952, pp. 55, 196; Stutterheim, 1929; and (though with respect to Java), Bosch, 1924. For *buwana* (*bhuwana, bhuvana*) *agung/buwana alit*, Gonda, 1952, pp. 111-112; Hooykaas, 1966, pp. 29-30, 33, 73-75, and plate 27. Except in textual excerpts I have spelled Sanskrit words Balinese fashion throughout; the use of "god" in the text can as readily be "gods," given the easy Balinese alternation between monotheistic, pantheistic, and polytheistic conceptions of the divine (these being Western categorizations in any case); and the lingga is of course seen as Siva's (and so, more properly, *Siva-lingga*) rather than "god's" in general. For a list of the main Indic gods recognized in Bali, see Covarrubias, 1956, pp. 316-318; cf. Sugriwa, n.d., pp. 17-21.

105-14

On the problem of the polysemy of religious symbols generally, see Turner, 1967.

105-18   *Padmasana*

The god- (wind) direction-color (etc.) system is extremely complex
and not entirely invariant or even internally consistent. For the
simple version given in the text, and the one most Balinese temple
priests know; see Swellengrebel, 1960, p. 47; Belo, 1953, p. 27.
Another version, in some ways more important, is the "eight-petal"
version with nine gods and eight directions (N, NE, E, SE, S . . .)
around the center (Gonda, 1952, p. 132; Hooykaas, 1964a, p. 52;
Moojen, 1926, p. 28; van Eerde, 1910; and Swellengrebel, 1947—
this last is a particularly full description including correlated varieties of plants, flowers, trees, sacrificial animals, etc.). The Indic pattern of multiple names for the same god, multiple identifications of
differently named gods, and outright fusion of gods, symbolizing the
notion that god is both one and many, is carried over in full force in
Bali and complicates the surface pattern even further (see Gonda,
1952, p. 132; Hooykaas, 1964a, p. 28). But the basic image of the
highest godhead at the lotus heart with the lesser ones deployed
around it is fixed and, insofar as anything in Bali is, clear.

Like all Balinese temple altars, of which it is perhaps the most
important, the padmasana varies greatly in the elaborateness of its
carved ornamentation, according to the general importance and
elegance of the temple—royal-connected ones being, of course, the
most elaborate. At the base of the pillar is usually a representation
of the turtle upon which the cosmos rests. Around the body of the
pillar is sometimes wound one or two fantasticated serpents, symbols
of carnality, vitality, and animal violence. Above the snakes may be
mountain motifs, representing the human realm of earthly life.
Finally, the throne itself—normally about six feet above the ground,
so as to be higher than the head of a standing worshiper, but not too
high for him to reach (more elaborate versions may be higher, with
steps to gain access)—is a simple stone chair, uncovered to the Sun
and facing toward the center of the temple. Iconographically, the
whole altar is thus a representation of the cosmos, from subaquatic
turtle to Supreme God, "who is Stainless, pure . . . and inimaginable" (Hooykaas, 1964a, p. 140; cf. Covarrubias, 1956, pp. 6-7, and
Ardana, 1971, pp. 19-20). In the grander temples the world-image
symbolism may be much more detailed than here described.

A sketch of a typical temple showing the *padmasana* location
(*kaja-kangin*: the northeast corner of the temple court in south Bali,
the southwest corner in north Bali— that is, toward Mount Agung,
above which Siva/Surya presides over *swerga*, the realm of the gods)

can be found in Covarrubias, 1956, p. 265, and an artist's representation is given facing p. 266. A similar sketch, with a more reliable text, appears in Belo, 1953, p. 15; the padmasana's placement within the array of temple altars is further pursued in van der Kaaden, 1937. For a sketch of a temple in north Bali, with the padmasana to the southwest, see Lamster, 1933, p. 33. Photographs of padmasanas can be found in Goris, n.d., plate 4.28; Moojen, 1926, plates 19, 124-128, 162, 177, 185; and in Hooykaas, 1964a, figs. 7-11, one of which (fig. 9) is a good example of the elaborateness that state temples can reach, and another of which (fig. 10) shows a three-chair (for Siva, Wisnu, and Brahma) example from the all-Bali temple at Besakih. For this last, see also Moojen, 1926, plates 203, 204; he points out (p. 123) that it is "new," having been built in 1917. An even newer (ca. 1960), more spectacular padmasana, made of white coral, perhaps thirty or forty feet high, with a gold-relief image of Siva on the chairback, built by the Balinese religious reform movement Parisada (on which see C. Geertz, 1972b and 1973e; Bagus, n.d.; Astawa, 1970; Parisada, 1970), now abuts the main square of Bali's capital, Den Pasar.

A systematic description of the offerings (*banten*; a high form of Sanskrit, *bali*, meaning "tribute," "gift," "oblation"—Hooykaas, 1964a, p. 208) is not available, so for as I am aware; but some information can be found at various points in Belo, 1953, and Hooykaas-van Leeuwen Boomkamp, 1961; cf. Mershon, 1971, pp. 34ff.; Stuart-Fox, 1974. The major work on Indic iconography in Indonesia generally is Bosch, 1948 (for lotus symbolism, see pp. 35-40, 133-144, plates 13-16).

Lotus posture: For a description (originally from a sixteenth-century old-Javanese prose treatise; cf. van der Tuuk, 1897-1912, under "padmasana")—soles of feet on thighs, palms upward, back and neck straight, eyes fixed on tip of nose, teeth of upper and lower jaw separated with tip of tongue between them—see Hooykaas, 1964a, p. 98. (In India the lotus posture was apparently the broad meaning of *padmasana*; Zimmer, 1955, vol. 1, pp. 143, 371.)

The act and experience of meditation: See Hooykaas, 1964a, pp. 98-99. Another passage from the aforementioned sixteenth-century text reads:

> *Debu-teja* means being gifted with force; *dibya-cakṣu* means being gifted with extraordinary powers; *dibya-bala* means being

gifted with numerous relatives and being a refuge for people; *dibya-darśana-dúra* is the faculty of seeing near what is far off and knowing the heart of other people—that is the fruit of practicing padmasana; force is its fruit.

Though the High God is in principle inimaginable, the padmasana iconography—turtles, snakes, throne—can be visualized as an aid to yoga practices (Hooykaas, 1964a, p. 172), as can a visualization of Siva in the lotus as such:

> You (the worshiper) should imagine/visualize Him as having an extraordinary splendour and characterised by a red colour, seated on a white lotus flower; perfectly beautiful and completely provided with ornaments; He has two arms and one face and His looks are benevolent, situated in the middle of the hollow of the lotus with a radiant disk, with a sash and a red face—in that way one should visualise God Śiva—Sun.

This is a translation of a priestly mantra, given in Hooykaas, 1964a, p. 161, entitled "Ritual Destined for the Worshiper of the Sun (i.e., Sivaite)."

Coital position: Hooykaas, 1964a, p. 102. Base of lingga: idem, 1964a, p. 213. Name of the Supreme God: idem, 1964a, p. 202. (The name is, again, Siva, or the Sun; but sometimes it is Brahma or other high gods. Goris [1931] has argued, rather speculatively from supposed "cultural survivals," that the more or less complete Sivaization of Bali by the nineteenth century is an historical development out of an earlier multiple-sect pattern in which various gods—Wisnu, Buddha, and others—were taken as central by various groups.)

Image of the cosmos: See the first section of this note. *High priest's cremation bier*: Hooykaas, 1964a; Goris, n.d., p. 198, n. to plate 4.28; Covarrubias, 1956, p. 387.

Innermost reaches of the heart: Hooykaas, 1964a, p. 217; Hooykaas, 1966, p. 71.

In classical India, *padmā*, with a long *ā* Sanskrit feminine ending, is a female symbol and refers to a goddess, Lakṣmī, the wife of Viṣṇu (see Zimmer, 1955, vol. 1, pp. 158ff.). In Bali, a lord's chief wife is called, in the most elegant language, *padmi*, apparently a blending from Sanskrit *patnī*, "wife," and *padmā*, "Viṣṇu's consort"

(Gonda, 1952, p. 370). The padma also appears as a female goddess image in the figure of the rice goddess, Dewi Sri, perhaps the most popular of Balinese deities (*notes*, p. 186).

105-37   *Lingga*

The legend of Siva's lingga is quoted by Hooykaas (1964a, p. 194) from Wilson, 1892, as follows:

It was on this day [the fourteenth day of the lunar month Phálguna] that Śiva first manifested himself as the marvellous and interminable Linga, to confound the pretensions of both Brahmá and Vishnú, who were disputing which was the greater divinity. To decide the quarrel, they agreed that he should be acknowledged the greater, who should first ascertain the limits of the extraordinary object which appeared of a sudden before them. Setting off in opposite directions, Vishnú undertook to reach the base, Brahmá the summit; but after some thousand of years the gods spent in the attempt, the end seemed to be remote as ever, and both returned discomfited and humiliated, and confessed the vast superiority of Śiva.

For photographs of Balinese stone linggas, Hooykaas, 1964a, figs. 16-20. Linggas can also be represented in paintings (Hooykaas, 1964a, fig. 15) along with iconically represented gods, written mantras, and so on. On linggas in Bali, see also Stutterheim, 1929; on "lingga worship" in early Java, see Bosch, 1924.

"On earth, the ruler acts on behalf of Śiva . . ." is in Hooykaas, 1964a, p. 143, quoting Krom, 1931, p. 124. The "deep spiritual connection" could as well be put as obtaining between the divine order, the ruling dynasty, and the Brahmana priesthood. The argument was originally advanced, mainly on the basis of Cambodian material, by Bosch, 1924. For the Balinese king called the lingga of the world, Gonda, 1952, p. 196; Grader, 1960b.

On the sprinkler as lingga, Hooykaas, 1964a, pp. 143, 148-150. On the sprinkler (*lis*) and sprinkling (*melis*, that is, "purification") as such, see Hooykaas-van Leeuwen Boomkamp, 1961. The whole rite includes, first, sprinkling the altars so the gods may sit on them, then, presenting offerings to the gods after they have sat on them, as well as sprinkling the worshipers themselves, bowed hands-to-forehead in obeisance (*sembah*) before the seated gods, which bowing completes the "communion." For a brief description, see Belo, 1953, pp. 47-52; for a glancing attempt to describe something of its meaning and atmosphere, C. Geertz, 1973e. Holy water can be made by virtually anyone (or even gathered from certain sacred springs and lakes), but only that coming from high priests has enough potency to be used in royal ceremonies. For descriptions of the complex ritual by means of which the high priest, after first conducting the soul of Siva into his body and unifying his own soul with it, prepares holy water, see Hooykaas, 1966, pp. 35-42; Gonda, 1952, pp. 167-168; cf. Goris, 1926. On holy water itself as "the central mystery of Balinese Hindu religion . . . called Āgama Tīrtha, the Religion of Holy Water," see Hooykaas, 1964a; cf. Gonda, 1975. Again, the lingga-in-the-lotus symbolism is also an iconographic unification of the masculine and feminine principles. For the Indological background, where this unification appears as the *padmayoni*, see Zimmer, 1955, vol. 1, pp. 168ff (cf. Bosch, 1948, pp. 196-199).

On the kris (but with caution), Rassers, 1959b. On the priestly headdress, Gonda, 1952, p. 196; Stutterheim, 1929. On the soul to heaven, Swellengrebel, 1960. The lingga on which the soul rides to heaven is a transformation of the "huge serpent, painted in white, black, and gilt stripes" that Helms's account (*text*, p. 198) mentions as being "shot" with flower-arrows by the high priest at the cremation—see Covarrubias, 1956, p. 387. On the tip of the noble's cremation tower, Covarrubias, 1956, p. 369 (see the drawing). On the scaffold, Gonda, 1952, p. 196. Gonda (1952, p. 197) also mentions "a sort of idol, made of coins, sandal-wood, or parts of the *lontar* (a kind of palm)" as being called a lingga in Bali, and even suggests (p. 233) that volcanoes may serve as lingga-symbols (see also Covarrubias, 1956, p. 290). Lingga motifs appear in various sorts of architectural decorations and pervade the imagery of the mantras. Lingga-divine-king cults are, of course, general in Southeast Asia; perhaps the richest material comes from Cambodia. For a general review of it, see Sherman, n.d.; for a critique of the connection, based mainly on reading the evidence from Angkor in Indian terms, see Kulke, 1978.

106-18   *Sekti*

As with these other notions (Polynesian, Arabic, American Indian, Malaysian, Greek, or whatever), sekti is not a general abstract idea, a bit of primitive theory, easily summarized in some homely and colorless formula such as "spiritual electricity." Rather, like them, it is a specifically toned and delicately nuanced religious symbol drawing its meaning into itself, as all such symbols do, from the ritual world which immediately surrounds it. For a developed critique of typologizing approaches to the definition of religious concepts, see C. Geertz, 1968, chap. 2. For the general approach to the analysis of religion employed here, C. Geertz, 1968, chap. 4, and C. Geertz, 1973c. The charisma definition is from American Heritage, 1969.

On *mūrta*, Gonda, 1952, pp. 357, 134. The most common religious use of *murti* in Balinese is in *trimurti* ("having three forms or shapes"), which indicates the three-in-one Indic trinity of Brahma, Visnu and Siva, as well as the temple altar with three compartments which is dedicated to them (Gonda, 1952, p. 134). It also appears in mantras as a stage of worship which Hooykaas (1966, p. 173; cf. pp. 126, 138) renders as "apparition—taking the shape of the God." On *śakti*, Gonda, 1952, pp. 134-135; for its application in popular ritual, Mershon, 1971.

On Brahma and Visnu as sektis of Siva, see Gonda, 1952, p. 134; Goudriaan and Hooykaas, 1971, p. 607. For a popular formulation of the trinity as "Brahma Siwa (Brahma), Saida Siwa (Visnu), and Prama Siwa (Iswara)," see Covarrubias, 1956, p. 290 who goes on to remark that "even this trinity becomes, with typical Balinese miscomprehension, a deity in itself called *Sanghyang* ["the divinity," Gonda, 1952, p. 135] *Trimurti* or *Sanggah Tiga* ["three shrines"] *Sakti.*" (The "typical miscomprehension," or rather incomprehension, is, of course, in the thinking of Covarrubias, not in that of the Balinese.)

For an interesting discussion, focused on recent Indonesian politics, of the closely related Javanese concept of power, including a contrast between it and the received Western concept, see Anderson, 1972.

107-12   *Buwana agung/buwana alit*

For the "macrocosm"/"microcosm" rendering, see, for example, Korn, 1960. Macrocosm/microcosm formulations of the parallel relation between the world of men and the world of the gods are widespread, of course, in complex traditional societies—China, Babylon, Mesoamerica, ancient Israel, India. For a general review, which stresses the similarity of these various patterns somewhat at the expense of their diversity, see Wheatley, 1971, pp. 436-451.

For the "material world"/"immaterial world" gloss, see, for example, Hooykaas, 1966, pp. 29, 33.

For textual examples of the *jaba/jero* use, Hooykaas, 1966, pp. 33, 70-78. "Soul" is not the best translation of Balinese *jiwa* (which derives from Sanskrit, *jīva*, "life"); but the effort to escape all Western connotations in translating Balinese terms can easily lead to an infinite regress. If one wanted to be awkwardly careful, something like "capacity to experience" would be (a bit) better.

On noble houses, sinking status, "going out," and so on, see *text*, chap. 2 and p. 58. As explained (*text*, p. 58), as one usually gets *puri* instead of *jero* for very high-status houses; one also gets *dalem*, a Javanese loanword for "inside," instead of *jero* for very high-status, "royal," persons and sub-dadias. *Dalem* is, indeed, perhaps the most common way in which people refer to the king, to his immediate family, and to his residence. For inside/outside imagery in the traditional Javanese state where, if anything, it was even more pervasive, see Rouffaer, 1931; Moertono, 1968, p. 27; C. Geertz, 1956, pp. 47-56. For its use in Javanese religious thought (where, as *lahir* and *batin*, it has survived translation into Islamic terms), see C. Geertz, 1960, pt. 3.

On puras (where the division is often triadic, with an outside and a "middle outside"—*jaba tengah*—court opposed to an inside), see Ardana, 1971, pp. 16-18. On jeros (or puris), van der Kaaden, 1937; Moojen, 1926, pp. 71-78, and plates 23-59 (cf., for Java, Stutterheim, 1948; and Pigeaud, 1960-63, chap. 2, "The Capital"). On the lotus, Hooykaas, 1964a, p. 159. The other examples were given spontaneously by informants.

109-5

For an analysis of Balinese conceptions of personal identity in terms of the cultural typifications which define them, see C. Geertz, 1963b; 1976a.

109-10

The terms *puri*, "palace," and *pura*, "temple," both derive from the same Sanskrit word for "fortified town"; and indeed in earlier texts *puri* (Skt., *purī*) serves for both meanings (Gonda, 1952, pp. 196-197, 219; see also *notes*, p. 137). Compare the Javanese *Nawanataya* manual of good conduct for court officials: "What is called the *nagara*? All where one can go (out of his compound) without passing through paddy fields. What is the *pura*? Inside of the Red Pavilion. What is the essence of the *puri*? Inside of the . . . main courtyard of the Royal Compound (Pigeaud, 1960-63, vol. 3, p. 121).

109-23

For a thorough summary of the "cosmological" symbolism of traditional cities and palaces from Egypt and Sumeria to China and Mesoamerica, see Wheatley, 1971, esp. chap. 5. Cf. Eliade, 1954 and 1963.
For Southeast Asia generally, see von Heine-Geldern, 1930.

112-1

The plan, which in a more general form has been reproduced
before (Geertz and Geertz, 1975, p. 144), was drawn and explicated
by Cakorda Gdé Oka Ijeg (*notes*, p. 142), who lived in it for the
first thirteen years of his life. The reigning king (*Déwa Agung*) of
the time was still young—he perished in the puputan—his father
having recently died. A great deal of detail has been omitted from
the plan, and it has been somewhat regularized. For a more literal
rendering of a puri layout (that of Gianyar), see Moojen, 1926, p. 73.
For photographs of the Klungkung puri, Moojen, 1926, plates 51,
56. A brief description of Puri Gdé Tabanan is given in van Geuns,
1906, pp. 72-75.

112-34

The "royal dadia temple" (2) is the temple of the entire royal
house of Klungkung, entrusted at any particular time to the stew-
ardship of the reigning king, here the Déwa Agung. The "royal
sub-dadia temple" (10) is a temple of narrower range, which in
1905 included as its congregation all those (patrilineally) descendant from the king's great-grandfather (plus their ritually incorporated wives), including, of course, the reigning king. On all this,
see Geertz and Geertz, 1975, pp. 143-152.

113-8

On the distribution of cadet royal lines over the landscape, see
text, p. 55 and maps 2 and 3.

113-39

Of the other sacred spaces, numbers six and seven were essentially
places to please the gods, and number four was one at which to

placate demons. Eight was a symbol of Mount Meru, of which, along with the gates (3, 15, 16), more in a moment. Five was a raised, covered stone platform where the royal judges met to decide cases (*notes*, p. 241). Ten, as noted, was a sub-dadia temple, supposedly founded by the reigning king's paternal grandfather's brother when he was reigning king, while fourteen was the origin temple for the Mengwi royal line, whose end has been described (*text*, p. 11). Just why this last was where it was and what function it had in 1905 I was not able to determine.

114-3

Though only the padmasana altar is indicated on the sketch, the core-line temple contained a large number of other altars, pavilions, and so on, each with their own significance. For complete diagrams of royal temples, see van der Kaaden, 1937; Moojen, 1926, p. 72.

114-21

More precisely, the temple is the seat (expression, embodiment, locus) of the charisma/sekti of the dynasty; the ukiran is the seat (expression, etc.) of the charisma/sekti of the palace, and more broadly of the negara—dynasty-palace-capital-realm—as a whole. On the world axis (*axis mundi*) as a general religious category, see Eliade, 1963, pp. 374-379, though his formulation is not relativistic enough to fit the Balinese data, where such axes are not stratified, but competitive (*text*, p. 124).

114-26

These "weeks" and "years," again, are not weeks and years in the Western sense, but the products of the workings of a complex permutational calendar which defines qualitative categories of time in terms of the interaction of different-length cycles of named days (*notes*, p. 190 and the references cited there). For wukus and the Balinese holiday schedule, see Goris, 1960b; for the meanings of ukiran, van Eck, 1876, p. 12, under *hoekir*.

Though the discussion in the text is in terms of the royal (i.e., the paramount "core-line" lords') houses as the paradigmatic form, the pattern is the same, in reduced version, at the secondary, tertiary, and so on ("peripheral") noble levels and at the lesser branch houses (jeros) involved. In many of these there may not be an ukiran court as a separate entity, it being located within either the inner chamber or the lord's living area, or, often, on the boundary between them (see, e.g., Moojen, 1926, p. 70, fig. 13; however, he incorrectly renders it as the "residence" [*woning*] of the "chief resident" [*hoofdbewoner*]).

114-33   *Mount Meru*

On the Indic conception of the Meru (Sumeru; Mahameru)— "the quadrangular central mountain of the universe . . . which rises from the mid-point of the surface of the earth somewhat to the north of the Himālayan ranges as the vertical axis of the egg-shaped cosmos . . . ," see Zimmer, 1955, vol. 1, pp. 47-48, 245. For its Indonesian expressions (and an attempt to associate it with the lotus stem), Bosch, 1948; cf. Stutterheim, 1926; Stöhr and Zoetmulder, 1968, pp. 308-312; Gonda, 1975.

The "shadow-play figure" is the so-called *gunungan* ("mountain"), or *kayon* ("woods"), a translucent leather near-triangle, painted to resemble a highland forest, that functions as a sort of curtain in the play (see, but with caution, as usual, Rassers, 1959a, pp. 168-186). On the "commensal offerings," huge mounds of ornamental rice, see Groneman, 1896; Tirtokoesoemo, 1931.

On the significance of Mount Agung (the gods are actually conceived to dwell above rather than on it) and the directional system associated with it, see Swellengrebel, 1960; Covarrubias, 1956, pp. 4-10; Hooykaas-van Leeuwen Boomkamp, 1956. As noted earlier, *agung* means "great," "large," "chief," etc. Besides the Mount Agung altar, similar altars, representing others of Bali's mid-island volcanoes Gunung Batur or Gunung Batu Kau (*notes*, p. 192), are also often found. For drawings of these altars, small wood and stone structures with pagoda-shaped roofs, see Covarrubias, 1956, opposite p. 266. On the paramount temple, Besakih, see *text*, p. 40.

For Meru altars as such, see Moojen, 1926, pp. 85-96 (though not everything said there is to be taken uncritically), and plates 74, 79, 88, 148, 183, 184, 198, 200-202; Goris, 1938; Goris, n.d., plates 4.31, 4.34, 4.45; Covarrubias, 1956, p. 268; van Eerde, 1910. The number of Meru roofs (which is always uneven) reflects the god—and the status of the god—to whom the structure is dedicated: eleven for Siva, nine for Brahma or Wisnu, and so on (van Eerde, 1910). It also reflects the status of the temple owners—*notes*, p. 233. There may be multiple Meru altars in one temple, and the center of a Meru forms an open shaft down which the gods descend to the temple. For a painting of a Meru altar in a royal temple (Bangli), see Lamster, 1933, p. 31.

On the "nature symbol" aspect of the Meru, see Zimmer for India (1955, vol. 1, p. 48); Rassers for Java (1959a, pp. 173ff.); and Moojen (1926, pp. 90-92) and van der Hoop (cited in Goris, n.d., p. 29) for Bali. All these scholars regard the mountain motif as "pre-Indian," or even "pre-Aryan"; part of an archaic ur-symbol complex reflected also in the Egyptian pyramids, the Babylonian ziggurat, the Tower of Babel, and so on (cf. Eliade, 1954; Wheatley, 1971, pp. 414-419). But all that, aside from being extremely speculative, is of uncertain use in interpreting nineteenth-century Balinese conceptions. For an interpretation of the great Javanese monument, Borobudur, as a Meru image, see Mus, 1935, vol. 1, pp. 356ff.; cf. Bernet-Kempers, 1959; idem, 1976. On Angkor from this point of view—one which connects the whole matter back to Tantric ideas concerning the mandala—see Mus, 1936; 1937. For a Javanese myth, dating from (ca.) the fifteenth or sixteenth century, recounting the transportation of Mount Meru from India and Java to give stability to the island of Bali—that is, stop it shaking—so that men could live on it, see Pigeaud, 1924.

On the Meru iconography of Balinese gates, split or covered, see Moojen, 1926, pp. 96-103, and plates 2, 17, 18, 35, 37, 43, 45, 47, 51, 75, 76, 87, 97, 98, 109, 110, 114, 115, 118, 120, 140-142, 150, 151, 156, 158, 159, 168, 173, 174, 191, 192, 195. Cf. Covarrubias, 1956, pp. 266-267. For good photographs of the split gate at Besakih, see Goris, n.d., plates 4.19, 4.20; see also 4.21, and, for a covered gate, 4.22. Paintings of split and covered gates are reproduced in Lamster, 1933, p. 21. The relation between these two sorts of mountain-image gates has been more discussed than clarified. It has been held that the outer split gate represents the two halves of Mount Meru severed by Siva to invite passage; the inner covered gate, normally surmounted by Meru roofs in stone, has been said to represent their reunion, to signify the accomplishment of passage. It has been held that the split gate represents the separation of male and female; the covered their identity. It has been held that the split gate represents the diversity of God; the covered, His oneness. And so on. These various interpretations are not incompatible, of course, given the extreme polysemy and overdetermination of Balinese symbolism; but the issue remains confused. Nor does etymology help much. *Candi*, which derives from a name of Durga, is the old-Javanese word for a sepulchral monument, a meaning it has apparently lost in Bali, while *bentar* means "high," "highest." As for *padaraksa*, it means "guardhouse," "strong point," "guardian" (Gonda, 1952, pp. 196, 198; van Eck, 1876, pp. 40, 194). The much-needed monograph on Balinese architecture to replace Moojen's useful but not very well-informed one (1926) might well begin with an investigation into Balinese entryways—domestic, palatial, and temple alike.

115-21

On the kris and kris design—handle form, blade shape, damascenings—see Rassers, 1959b; Groneman, 1910; Jasper and Pirngadie, 1930; Meyer, 1916-17; Solyom and Solyom, 1978; Carey, 1979, n. 58. Javanese kris stories, which are about the same in general form as Balinese, can be found at various places in Pigeaud, 1938; for a Balinese example, see de Zoete and Spies, 1938, pp. 299-300; cf. Worsley, 1972, p. 21. On heirlooms in general, see (again, for Java, where they are called *pusaka*) Kalff, 1923; for Bali, see Swellengrebel, 1947; and especially Worsley, 1972, pp. 21, 52-53, 218-219, where there is a developed discussion of the role of heirlooms, krises, regalia, or whatever in royal legitimacy. Waris (or *pusaka*; another frequent Balinese term is *kaliliran*) are not restricted to weapons, of course, but include anything handed down which is considered to be of religious significance and power, including the tradition as a whole (e.g., as in Rawi, 1958).

115-35

The quotations are from Goris, 1960b. Niwatakawaca is the demon king against whom Arjuna struggles in the medieval Javanese epic known as *Arjuna Wiwaha*. On the importance of the notion of "origin" or "origin point"—*kawitan*—in Bali generally, see Geertz and Geertz, 1975.

116-2

Tumpek actually refers to a day which recurs every thirty-five days; that is, at the end of every fifth *wuku*. All tumpeks, which "close" something (and herald, thus, the "opening" of something else) are holidays, celebrating whatever it is that their wuku is identified with: dry fields, animal husbandry, the shadow play, etc. One of the tumpeks, *Tumpek Kuningan*, is among the most important popular celebrations in Bali, commemorating the return to heaven (several days earlier) of the cremated ancestors who have descended to earth during the previous week. On all this, see Goris, 1960b; Sugriwa, 1957a, pp. 29ff. As Sugriwa notes (p. 30), *Tumpek Landep*, associated with the old royal houses and their rulers, has today declined in importance, but it continues to be observed. For a Javanese equivalent of *Tumpek Landep*—called *Nyiram*, from "to wash," "bathe," "purify"—see Groneman, 1905.

116-16

The civic spaces (including the public square—also called the *bancingah*—of which these spaces were, in a sense, an extension) formed the ground on which those "outside" the palace, the kawula subjects of the realm, summoned there by the beat of the slit gong, and those "inside" the palace, the punggawa lords of the realm, came most immediately together. Again, this occurred most prominently on the occasions of the great ceremonies. But it occurred as well in assembly for war, on the audience days of the king, and in connection with deliberations of the royal tribunal.

The cameral spaces functioned both as the king's private chambers and as his business office. In them the royal corpse, or indeed that of any member of the royal family, was washed, wrapped, chanted over, and otherwise ritually prepared before being moved to the death pavilions for public display. In them the king slept, when he was not lying with one of his wives. And in them, he forged and broke the ties of alliance, clientship, and dependency already described—that is, politicked.

The residential spaces, symbolically pivoted around the family temples, were very carefully modulated by the prevailing politesse— calibrated to the complex differences in rank between different varieties of royal wives and their offspring, and also to the no less complex differences generated by the sinking status pattern.

Finally, in the impure spaces, men and demons came into contact, and here, too, ceremony pervaded. Only, in this case, its operation was reversed. Rather than seeking to draw near to the suprahuman by minimizing and even erasing the contrast between it and the human, the attempt was to keep the infrahuman and animalistic at bay by maximizing the contrast between it and the human. Indeed, the whole dynamic of Balinese hierarchy involves attempting to draw near, by imitation, to higher ranks, and to distance, by dis-imitation, the lower ones (see below, *text*, "Conclusion"). On the Balinese phobia concerning animality from this point of view, see Bateson and Mead, 1942. On Balinese demon beliefs, Mershon, 1970; Belo, 1949; Covarrubias, 1956, pp. 320-358, though this last hopelessly confuses demons and witches (cf. de Kat Angelino, 1921d).

116-36

Bateson, 1972b.

117-8

How many commoners are cremated is difficult to establish, even for the present century, to say nothing of the last. Hooykaas (n.d.) says "perhaps only one-tenth of the population of Bali is incinerated"; Swellengrebel (1960; quoting Bhadra, n.d.) says thirty percent. As cremation was required for all triwangsas—and carried out by all but a minority of them—the proportion of Sudras cremated can never have been very great, though given their population, the number would have been significant. Sudras and most triwangsas were buried, usually for an extended period of time (in some cases, twenty-five or thirty years), before being exhumed for cremation. But important lords were usually embalmed and kept, sometimes also for fair lengths of time, in the private court of their puri or jero (i.e., no. 23 in fig. 11) before being burned. Brahmana priests could not be buried and were cremated as quickly as possible, ideally within eight days; whereas at the other extreme a small percentage of the commoner population—the so-called Bali Agas— did not cremate at all (Bateson and Mead, 1942, pp. 46, 232). In general, the higher a family's status, the more incumbent cremation was and the more rapidly it ought, in theory, to be carried out, there being specific periods recommended for the various varnas (Friederich, 1959, p. 84). Time of cremation was also dependent upon calendrical considerations (of the 210 days of the Balinese year, only 12 were suitable; Kersten, 1947, p. 159) and, of course, most especially on practical ones.

117-13

Goris, n.d., p. 126. The enormous size and expense of Balinese cremations has been remarked by almost every observer. Covarrubias (1956, p. 359) calls them "mad splurge[s] of extravagance," and alludes vaguely (p. 362) to "cremations of princes that cost . . . about twenty-five thousand dollars." Bateson and Mead (1942, p.

46) speak of people "selling everything they have" to hold them. Goris (n.d., p. 128) writes of "the whole of the largest part of an inheritance of many thousand guilders" being used up. Swellen-grebel (1960; quoting Badjra, n.d.) reports a recent cremation at Tabanan costing six or seven thousand dollars. And for the 1850s, Friederich (1959, p. 99) writes:

> . . . dead bodies in [the negara of] *Den Pasar* . . . have already laid [uncremated] for fifteen or twenty years . . . [the king of] *Kassiman* [a rival house] prevents this burning for political reasons as it might deprive him of his prestige; another reason is the property of the present prince of *Den Pasar*, whose reve-nue has been very much diminished by *Kassiman*, and who will not for years be able to amass the sum required for such a grand cremation.

Just when cremation was introduced into Bali is uncertain. (The usual statement that it is post-Majapahit—e.g., Covarrubias, 1956, p. 360—is based on little more than the fact that its origins are Indic.) In any case, the institution developed to a much greater degree of elaboration in Bali than it did in India, where it re-mained, and remains, a relatively simple affair. For a brief com-parison of the Balinese and Indian rituals, see Crucq, 1928, pp. 113-121; cf. Goris, n.d., pp. 125-130.

The whole question of the relation of Balinese forms to Indian may well be much clarified when the influence of tantraism is taken into fuller consideration, as it has already begun to be with respect to the Javanese *kraton* tradition. I am indebted to Professor F. Leh-man for this point.

117-34

As with everything Balinese, there was a good deal of variation in detail, and these activities (plus a large number of associated ones not mentioned here) could be stretched out over several days, only culminating in the *Pabersihan* proper (Wirz, 1928; Covarrubias, 1956, pp. 363ff.). Lords were generally embalmed, their corpses cared for, often for months, by royal servants (parekans—*text*, p. 63) who were considered to be "dead" as a result, and thus exiled, possibly at earlier times killed and sacrificed with their lord at his cremation (Friederich, 1959, p. 85; Covarrubias, 1956, p. 386).

High priests did not normally come into proximity with the dead, except in the case of very high-status individuals; holy water was often brought by relatives from the priest's house. There was also an extremely complex system of effigies—string figures, dolls, puppets, designs, flower and vegetable constructions, wrapped-up bundles of clothes—some representing the soul, some the body, some even parts of the body, that was involved throughout the cremation ceremonies. Though critical to an understanding of Balinese concepts of death, spirits, afterlife, and so on, as well as of personality and representation, this cannot be gone into here. On the whole subject, see especially Bateson and Mead, 1942, pp. 44, 239, 248-252; Grader, n.d., pp. 30-39.

The evening of the second day, The Obeisance, signaling the end of the pollution (*sebel*) the corpse had caused, was usually marked by music, dances—normally war dances (*baris*)—shadow plays, feasts, and other celebrations, including a public reading of *Bhima Swarga*, the story of the visit of Bima, one of the Pandawas, to the land of the dead (Covarrubias, 1956, p. 375; cf. Hooykaas-van Leeuwen Boomkamp, 1956). On sebel, see Belo, 1970b; on its connection with cremations, Friederich (1959, p. 86), who remarks that not only the royal family was sebel, but the palace as such was "unclean" when there was a corpse in it and therefore it "is not occupied by the successor until after the cremation." And an obeisance ceremony is also made by the royal family at the dynasty temple (no. 2 in fig. 11) at this time as well as at the body (Covarrubias, 1956, p. 371).

118-28

The number of holy-water carriers (Friederich [1959, p. 89] saw "more than a hundred," with water brought "from the most sacred places in Bali" and "from the [high priests] who stand in especially high esteem"); the richness of the personal effects (Friederich [1959, p. 89] saw gold betel boxes and water bottles "also of precious metal," as well as the "gaily caparisoned" king's horse Helms also mentions); the repute of the waris heirlooms for sacred power; the number of orchestras; and so on—all, of course, also varied (and, as such, were indexes of prestige), as did, within the general structure, the composition of the cortege as a whole. On these matters and on the order of march generally, see Crucq, 1928, p. 64; Friederich, 1959, pp. 89-91; Covarrubias, 1956, p. 374; Lamster, 1933, pp. 55-57. Cf. Franken, 1960.

It is possible, though there is no real evidence to prove it, that the cremation of Sudra corpses was a transformation into symbolism of an earlier custom by which commoner subjects were, like widows, actually sacrificed. However that may be, the provision of a lord with a retinue of subject souls to be annihilated with him was an important custom, and probably the main way in which those commoners who did get cremated in nineteenth-century Bali achieved it. In the nineteen-thirties, Covarrubias (1956, p. 363) saw a minor lord's cremation accompanied by no less than 250 Sudra ones, and I myself attended a high priest's enormous cremation in 1957 at which there were 460 attendant bodies, sisia (text, p. 37) of the Brahmana house, grouped into twenty towers.

The symbolism of the differing numbers of Meru roofs extends as well to the altars in the family temples mentioned above (notes, p. 227). Controversy over who had a right to how many roofs in the altar of his cremation tower was a frequent cause of dispute, sometimes even of war, among the lords of classical Bali. A simplified sketch of a "nobleman" cremation tower can be found in Covarrubias, 1956, p. 369; cf. his note at pp. 326-327. For a painting of the bull version of the animal coffin, see idem, 1956, facing p. 324. Both the towers and the coffins were made of wood, the latter out of hollowed tree trunks, by craft specialists, and then were decorated with textiles, palm leaves, mirrors, china, and plates, and carried on enormous litter frames by as many as four or five hundred men.

120-10

One of the most striking things about the cremation was indeed the lack of any special, important role for the dead king's successor. The new king was not supposed to occupy the palace as king until his predecessor had been burned, but otherwise there was no really important coronation ceremony—a few minor ritual acts aside— in the negara at all. What has sometimes been called such is in fact an ordination ceremony of a lord as a special kind of priest (resi; see notes, p. 215 concerning Siva-ratri; and Friederich, 1959, pp. 81-82; Korn, 1932, p. 144). Only a minority of kings, and then usually well into their reign, undertook this in any case.

There were a number of after-ceremonies following the cremation proper (for a list, see Crucq, 1928, p. 68). The most important of them (the ngrorasin, memukur, or njekah—Crucq, 1928; Covarrubias, 1956, pp. 384-385; C. J. Grader, n.d., pp. 14, 31-35) took place twelve (sometimes forty-two) days after death. It essentially consisted of the whole thing done again on a smaller scale, with a flower (puspa) representing the deceased. It repeated the same theme, the indestructibility of rank, in even clearer form, because it gave more emphasis to the priest's activities and the royal family than to the attending crowd, which was generally smaller.

The status aspects of cremation are also reflected in Balinese notions of afterlife. Uncremated dead remain as distinct individual souls (*pirata*) and are regarded as highly dangerous, demanding frequent pacification by means of offerings placed in the graveyards where they dwell, unfreed from their corpse. Cremated dead (*pitara*, a form of the word for "god") are considered to be no longer individuals at all and, indeed, to be beneficent, generalized ancestor-gods living at some appropriate level of heaven and worshiped in the family temple (see Goris, 1960a). Indeed, the legendary kings of Bali, that is, the kings of the Gèlgèl period and shortly after, were considered to have "disappeared" after death, having ascended directly into heaven without leaving a corpse and thus without needing a cremation, a process known as *moksa*, from the Sanskrit *mokṣa*, "final deliverance or emancipation from any bodily existence" (see Gonda, 1952, pp. 157, 240-251).

As for the Sudra corpses at a royal ceremony, they were incinerated concurrently with that of the lord on smaller, separate pyres of their own, surrounding his. For photographs of the burning ground (*sema*), see Bateson and Mead, 1942, plate 96.

121-1

The internal quotations are from Shirley, Pope, and Swift, under the extensive entry for "state" in *The Oxford English Dictionary*. The same compression of meanings is, of course, involved in the term as it appears—*état, staat, stato*—in other major European languages as well. For a comprehensive discussion of the emergence of the modern Western sense of the term "state" as "a form of public power separate from both ruler and ruled, and constituting the supreme political authority within a certain defined territory," see Q. Skinner, 1978, esp. pp. 349-358 (quotation at p. 353). The degree to which the "public power" concept of the state is present in Machiavelli is not beyond debate (I follow Hexter's [1957] view that essentially it is not). Skinner sees the crucial transition, so far as political theory is concerned, in the French Humanist Guillaume Budé's *Education of the Prince*, 1547 (Q. Skinner, 1978, pp. 354-355).

122-17

Donne, quoted in *The Oxford English Dictionary* under "state."

124-32

For general discussions of "divine kingship" in Southeast Asia, see Coedès, 1968 and 1911; Mabbett, 1969; Sherman, n.d. For Bali, see Worsley, 1975. The Sanskrit-derived *raja* and its various forms is the most common generic term for king in Indic Southeast Asia (see Gonda, 1973, pp. 130, 224, 228), but there are of course many others (*prabu, patih,* etc.), the most important in Indonesia being perhaps *ratu,* from the Malayo-Polynesian *datu, datuk*—"chief." "Divine kingship" continued in but slightly revised form in the Muslim kingdoms of Indonesia as well: see, for example, Moertono, 1968; Brakel, 1975. The "two bodies" reference is, of course, to Kantorowicz's great book (1957) on Western "medieval political theology," which has been a major influence on the direction of the present work. For a study (to my mind, strained, unpersuasive, and over-Indological) by an historian of India questioning the reality or at least the nature of "divine kingship" in Southeast Asia, see Kulke, 1978 (cf., with the same reservations, Fillozat, 1966).

124-40

The degree to which kings' claims to "sovereignty" (a cumbrous term in this concept, in any case) were necessarily universal as opposed to local is perhaps debatable. Anyway, it has been debated. Briggs (1978) has even argued, against Coedès (1968, p. 99), that the "magical" ceremony of "the founder of the Khmer Empire," Jayavarman II (802-50), pronouncing him *chakravartin* ("universal monarch"—literally, "the one who possesses the turning wheel," "the one whose wheel is turning"), did not comprise a claim to sovereignty beyond "his own kingdom." But Briggs's reason for holding this—that the same ceremony was performed in Champa in 875 and in Java in 760—seems to me to support the view that, however incompatible from a Western point of view, a multiplicity of equally valid claims to universal sovereignty in Indic Southeast Asia was seen not only as not illogical, but as part of the normal order of things. For a similar "polykraton"—*kraton,* "royal palace" —concept of the nature of (Javanese) Indic states, see van Naerssen, 1976, who writes: "I remain unconvinced that, in early Hindu Java, there was only one sovereign at a time. The historical sources at our disposal enable us to conclude that there were several independent rulers, some of them enjoying the title of *mahārāja* and others without that title. It does not necessarily follow, however, that the former were supreme rulers because they were known as *mahārājas*. To ascribe supreme authority to a ruler merely because the inscriptions mention him as a *maharājā* and at the same time to deny authority to others who may possibly also have had sovereignty would be inconsistent with what is known of the social structure of the Hindu-Javanese period at this early stage of his history." What is important, of course, is not how much real "power," "sovereignty," or "authority" this or that ruler had, something extremely difficult to estimate at this late date, but what claims he made, and how—whether in titles, rituals, or whatever—he made them.

Many of the Sanskritized names taken on by kings reflected these universal claims: Wisnumurti ("who embodies Visnu"), Sakala-buwanamandalaswaranindita ("the irreproachable lord of the whole earth-circle"), Dewasinga ("god-lion"), Sareswara ("the lord of all"), Sang Amurwabumi ("who rules the earth"), Wisnuwardana ("furthering Visnu"), Narasinga ("man-lion"—a name of Visnu), Bumi-Nata ("earth-lord"), Cakranegara ("wheel of the state"), Suryadiraja ("supreme sun king"), and so on, almost without end (Gonda, 1973, pp. 331-337; I have Indonesianized the spellings). The earliest kings whose names are known in Bali (that is, from the mid-tenth century) had names ending in "-varmadeva," roughly, "armed god" (Coedès, 1968, p. 129); and even in the nineteenth century, after all the "status sinking," the king of Klungkung was known as Dewa Agung ("great god"), that of Gianyar as Dewa Manggis ("sweet god"), and so on. For a powerful, fourteenth-century Javanese statement of the divine-king/world-ruler conception of lordship, where the king, called *déwa prabhū* ("god-monarch"), is explicitly referred to as Siva materialized (*bhaṭara girinnātha sakala*, see Canto 1 of the *Negarakertagama* in Pigeaud, 1960-63, vol. 1, p. 3; vol. 3, pp. 3-4.

This is perhaps also the place to remark that, for obvious reasons, comparative materials have been introduced into this study only occasionally, as need has seemed to demand; no systematic survey of other Southeast Asian classical polities has been attempted. Studies of such polities include: Leach, 1954; Tambiah, 1976; Vella, 1957; Quaritch-Wales, 1934; Rabibhadana, 1960; Briggs, 1951; Maspero, 1928; Woodside, 1971; Gullick, 1958; Reid and Castles, 1975; Lombard, 1967; Siddique, 1977; Schrieke, 1957; Pigeaud, 1960-63; Rouffaer, 1931; Moertono, 1968; Ricklefs, 1974; Andaya, 1975; Kiefer,

1972; Hall and Whitmore, 1976. Important studies by Michael Aung Thwin on Burma and by Shelly Errington, Jan Wisseman, and Anthony Day on Indonesia are forthcoming.

125-31

The characterization of the relation of Indian kings and Brahmins given here, and indeed the whole line of thought being developed, derives from the seminal work of Dumont (1970a, pp. 72-79, 168-170, and 1970c and 1970d; cf. Hocart, 1936; Dumézil, 1948). Dumont writes as follows:

> As we live in an egalitarian society, we tend to conceive of hierarchy as a scale of commanding powers—as in an army—rather than as a gradation of statuses. One may note *en passant* that the combination of the two aspects seems to have been anything but easy in a number of societies, for there are many instances of sovereigns whose eminent dignity was coupled with idleness. The Indian case is one in which the two aspects are absolutely separated. . . .
>
> [In the Indian case] the king depends on the priests for his religious functions, he cannot be his own sacrificer, instead he "puts in front" of himself a priest . . . and *then* he looses the hierarchical preeminence in favour of the priests, retaining for himself power only. . . .
>
> Through this dissociation, the function of the king in India has been *secularized*. It is from this point that a differentiation has occurred, the separation within the religious universe of a sphere or realm opposed to the religious, and roughly corresponding to what we call the political. As opposed to the realm of values and norms it is the realm of force. As opposed to the *dharma* or universal order of the Brahman, it is the realm of interest or advantage, *artha*. (Dumont, 1960d, pp. 67-68, italics original; on dharma and artha more generally in India, see Dumont, 1960c)

For a discussion of the quite different way in which "the realm of interest or advantage" (there called *pamrih*, "aim," "design," "hidden purpose," rather than *artha*, which there just means "wealth," "property") is conceived with respect to the royal role in Java—namely, as disruptive of his inner balance, hence of his sacredness, hence of his power—see Anderson, 1972. On dharma and kingship in Bali, see Worsley, 1972, p. 43.

Whether this marked contrast between the Indian and Indo-nesian concepts of how the imperial and the priestly functions are related is due to the fact that the main "diffusion" of Indic ideas and institutions to Indonesia took place before Brahminical caste Hinduism had completely crystallized in India itself, or whether the contrast is instead due to the separate historical development of the two civilizations after this "diffusion" (or to what degree it is due to both factors) is a moot question. My notions of how social change occurs lead me into placing more weight on the second factor than on the first, but little of the necessary research has been done. Some interesting, but unevenly persuasive, speculations con-cerning the role of Brahmins and Brahminism in "the coming of Indian civilization" to Indonesia ("The course of events amount-ed essentially to a summoning to Indonesia of Brahman priests. . . . The Indian priesthood was called eastwards . . . for the magical, sacral legitimation of dynastic interest") can be found in van Leur, 1955, pp. 96-104. For the evidence supporting the view that divine kingship developed mostly in Indonesia, after intensive Indian con-tact was past, see van Naerssen, 1976. On the evolution of Indian Brahminism and its absorption of Buddhist and Jain "renouncer" values, see Dumont, 1970a, pp. 146-151.

126-10

The quotation is from Dumont, 1970d, where the distinction be-tween types of oriental kingship is also developed.

The Indic surface of Balinese political institutions has acted to inhibit a comparative reference eastward (and perhaps northward) toward the Pacific, rather that westward, toward what the Dutch revealingly referred to as *Voor-Indië*. Such investigation would shed much light on the basic conceptions of rank and authority that animated Balinese political organization; and, though it has not been explicitly evoked here, general acquaintance with the nature of such systems has strongly influenced many of my formulations. For a review of Polynesian political forms, see Goldman, 1970; on the Japanese emperor, Jansen, 1977.

126-25

The quotation (which reflects a bit the prevailing Western as-sumption that to say that something is an ornament is to say that it is mere glitter) is from Worsley, 1975, p. 111. For the relevant section

—including the "foremost jewel" passage—of the chronicle text
(the *Babad Buleleng*), see Worsley, 1972, pp. 152-157. (Worsley's
commentaries on the king-priest relation on pp. 5, 14, 42-43, 46-47,
51, 52, 73, 77, and 81 add up to the best discussion of the matter in
the literature. For other discussions, see Friederich, 1959, pp. 105-
107; Korn, 1960, p. 150; Korn, 1932, pp. 140ff., 369ff.; Swellengrebel,
1960, pp. 64-65; Covarrubias, 1956, p. 55. See also *text*, p. 36.) The
elephant was a gift from the king of Solo, the most exemplary of the
nineteenth-century Javanese courts (Worsley, 1972, p. 29). The
identification of the priest with the king's gamelan orchestra (the
king himself was also so identified) was through the sounds the instruments made—mostly they were metallophones of one sort or
another—that is, through the psychological effects of those sounds
(they caused "anguish" in the hearts of evil people, etc.), rather than
through their physical nature (Worsley, 1972, p. 31). Skill in weapon making was not a universal accomplishment among court priests,
though it seems to have been common. Knowledge of numerological
divination procedures by means of the complex Balinese calendrical
scheme (C. Geertz, 1973h; cf. Worsley, 1972, p. 81, where the priest
determines a day for war) was, however, an expected competence
of priests. The "retainers" were not *kawula,* "subjects" (*text,* p. 63),
but *sisia,* "disciples" (*text,* p. 37). Priests had no kawulas, and no
Brahmana (save, mythologically, for the very earliest Majapahit
kings before the decline to Satriahood, etc.) ever seems to have held
significant political power in his own right in Bali. Certainly none
did in the nineteenth century. For the conceptual foundations of
the king-lingga (kris)-priest identification, see *text,* p. 105, and *notes,*
p. 221. Worsley (1975, p. 111) also remarks that the king-priest relation of the *Babad Buleleng* was not an individual tie, but one
"between two clans" (i.e., dadias), and thus, as characterized above,
text, p. 34, was a form of "clientship." ("Their agreement included
their children and grandchildren," the text runs, "so that they
would continue to model themselves upon the example of their
forefathers"—Worsley, 1975, pp. 155-157.) That such relations were
indeed lasting can be seen from the fact that the court-priest "house"
in Tabanan—Griya Pasekan—was the same ca. 1847 (Friederich,
1959, p. 107) as it is today. As for titles, the king's was Ki Gusti
Ngurah Panji Sakti; the priest's, Sri Bagawanta Sakti Ngurah
(Worsley, 1972, pp. 154-156; for "Ngurah," see below, *notes,* p. 246.
As noted above, *text,* p. 37, the terms for court priest were *purohita,*
"the one placed in front" (Dumont, 1970d, p. 54); *bagawanta,* "a
venerable, holy man" (Gonda, 1973, p. 421); and *guru loka,* "teacher

of the world" (Friederich, 1959, p. 106). Finally, it should be re-marked again that there could be, and often was, more than one such court priest at a particular court.

It must also be remembered that all the references in the text are to Brahmana priests (*padanda*), even though there are various other sorts of priests, most notably non-Brahmana temple officiants (*pemangku; notes*, p. 157) in Bali. For a survey, sees Hooykaas, 1973a, pp. 11-18; cf. Hooykaas, 1960 and 1964b. Also, as only a minority of Brahmana priests are bagawantas; so only a minority of Brahmanas are priests. (Hooykaas [1964a, p. 9] estimates their present total, surely sharply down from the nineteenth-century figure, at "only a few hundred." Priests needed the king's per-mission to be consecrated, and their wives, considered, like the priests themselves, as transcending gender, served as their coadju-tors, sometimes succeeding them in the role itself.) The central ritual activity of the padanda is to prepare holy water, *tirta*, a critical element in all important ceremonies—*notes*, p. 221. For the rites (*maweda*)—which involve "purif[ying] and empt[ying] him-self to offer an abode to the God of the Sun [i.e., Siva]" (Hooykaas, 1973a, p. 14) through the use of sacred spells (*mantra*) and gestures (*mudra*), breath control, mental concentration, and so on—see Covarrubias, 1956, pp. 300-304. Cf. Korn, 1960; Hooykaas, 1966 and 1973b; Goudriaan and Hooykaas, 1971; Gonda, 1975.

Finally, there are and always have been a small minority of Buddhist—as opposed to Brahmana or Sivaite—padandas in Bali, and these sometimes played a role in court ceremonies. See Hooy-kaas, 1973b; van Eerde, 1910; Regeg, n.d. (d). For a good, brief his-torical summary of the relations between Buddhism and Sivaism in Indic Indonesia generally, see Gonda, 1975 (for Bali, see pp. 40-42).

126-39

For the various renderings of *dharma*, see Gonda (who calls the term "untranslatable"), 1973, pp. 127, 157, 304, 410, 537.

The role of the Brahmana priest in the administration of justice in the negara, a matter of some importance, is still insufficiently clarified. (For a summary of what little there is in the literature, see Korn, 1932, pp. 370-375 and the references given there, though the statement on p. 374 that Brahmanas were insignificant in the Tabanan judicial system is incorrect. Cf., but with caution, Fraser, 1910.)

In great part, the obscurity and resultant confusion derives from the fact that, once again, the system rested on a set of "elegant" to "coarse," *halus* to *kasar*, rank designations rather than on a pyramid of functional offices—a hierarchy, not a bureaucracy. Of these designations (which also, once again, varied somewhat from place to place and were applied flexibly rather than rigidly), the four most important were: *kerta, jaksa, kanca,* and *jejeneng. Kerta,* which stems from the Sanskrit for "good order," "safety," "restfulness" (Gonda, 1973, pp. 228, 515), meant, as Gonda has most carefully put it (1973, p. 280), "adviser and interpreter of ancient texts, consulted by the prince and his judges." *Jaksa,* which comes from a root meaning "superintendent" (idem, 1973, p. 387), has been variously translated "judge," "prosecutor," "lawyer," "judicial civil servant," or "court clerk," with an unsteadiness of semantic aim indicating that Western categorizations do not fit very well; the best rendering is something suitably vague such as "a person involved in the direction of judicial hearings." *Kanca,* which means, in this context, "assistant," "aide," or "spokesman" (generally, it means "friend"; colloquially, "spouse") is essentially but a more kasar term for *jaksa,* as *jaksa* is for *kerta;* and it usually indicates some sort of advocate, bailiff, or record keeper. Finally, *jejeneng,* from the root "to stand," "to be erect," completes the series and was mostly applied to figures—parekans often—concerned with actually apprehending offenders, fetching them to the tribunal (*kertagosa, rajajaksa, pejaksan*), carrying them off to punishment, etc. As dalem, puri, jero gdé, jero, umah, and pekarangan, or as cakorda, patih, punggawa, perbekel, kawula, and parekan, these terms represented a social domain ("justice dispensing") as a system of spiritual inequalities, not as one of tasks and responsibilities.

Brahmanas, and most especially Brahmana priests, operated, of course, at the higher, more *halus,* ranges of this system, and particularly as *kerta,* "advisers and interpreters of ancient texts." (On the actual texts consulted, see Friederich, 1959, pp. 29-30; Fraser, 1910, pp. 9-12; Gonda, 1973, p. 279. For an excellent general review of "Indian derived law texts" in Southeast Asia overall, including some description of their content, see Hooker, 1978—for Indonesia, pp. 210-215—cf. Lekkerkerker, 1918). In Tabanan, these came mainly from one Brahmana house, not that of the Bagawanta, who seem never to have served in this role, the Griya Jaksa of map 2. Most of the other higher-court personnel there were drawn from the two Sudra "secretary" houses, Dangin Peken for Puri Gdé, and Malkangin for Puri Kalèran (see maps 2 and 3, p. 93, and *notes,* p. 167), though a few came from local triwangsa houses not related to the royal line. Tribunals were normally held in a covered, raised-up pavilion beside the slit gong at the front of the puri. (See fig. 11, nos. 5, 21. For a photograph of such a pavilion—combined, as was quite common in smaller puris, with "the king's public seat," no. 9 in fig. 11—see Moojen, 1926, plate 40.) Sometimes, however, they were held in the open court of the puri (no. 17 in fig. 11).

Just which cases were brought to negara tribunals and which were handled by the judicial institutions of the desa—the banjar council, the subak council—is not altogether clear, though certainly the vast majority of cases, both criminal and civil, were disposed of on the local level. Crimes by punggawas or perbekels were all tried in the king's or the junior king's tribunal; those by Brahmanas in the paramount king's only. Disputes between puris or jeros were, when possible, also adjudicated there. (All the punggawa houses had tribunals, but only those of the king and junior king seem, in Tabanan at least, to have been of real importance. Condemned men sometimes fled, or tried to, from the jurisdiction of one lord's tribunal to another's, something that could itself lead to inter-jero disputes.) Major crimes by villagers were often first judged locally, and then the perpetrator was turned over to the lords for punishment. But most of the negara-level cases, at least when we judge by the ones I was able to collect from informants' memories, seem to have been political ones (rebellion, sedition, conspiracy), status/ pollution offenses (miscaste marriages, ritual profanation, sexual perversions), or property issues among triwangsas (inheritance disputes, debt claims, theft).

The procedure of the negara tribunals (see Korn, 1932, pp. 375-401; Raffles, 1830, vol. 2, pp. ccxxvi-ccxxvii; Gonda, 1973, pp. 281-289) is even more difficult to reconstruct, mainly because it seems in fact to have been diffuse—a torrent of statements of accusation and defense, oath-ordeals, forfeits, testimony taking, all unleashed before the assembled "judges" sitting collegially. (Sometimes, when subjects of different lords were involved, judges from several tribunals sat together. Perbekels usually acted as jaksa/kanca "spokesmen" for kawulas under them; in civil actions, this could lead to them "representing" both sides.) The only fixed aspect of the process was that all verdicts were given by the lord whose tribunal it was, and his decision was definitive, whatever the various kertas, jaksas, kancas, and so on might advise. Punishments in criminal cases were caste-graded—the steeper the higher the caste—and ranged, in descending order of frequency, from fines (through reduction to parekan status); various forms of corporal punishment (exposure to the sun, breaking of limbs, putting out of eyes); exile to Nusa Penida or Lombok; to death, usually by stabbing in the graveyard, though certain sorts of criminals involved in polluting crimes (*apahkrama*)—bestiality or miscaste marriages with Brahmana women, for example—were drowned in the ocean (C. J. Grader, n.d., p. 12; *notes*, p. 246). Indian derived texts were not the sole basis of decisions in negara tribunals; royal edicts, *paswara*, were also an important source of law (Fraser, 1910, pp. 12-13; Liefrinck, 1915; Utrecht, 1962, pp. 128ff.). Indeed, even the Indic texts themselves had the effect of putting not the priest but the king "at the center of the legal world."

> [Such texts] became a more immediate foundation for the justification of kingly power than was the case in India. . . . The overwhelming impression one gets from such texts is that . . . their main characteristic is concern with the nature of royal power and its acquisition. . . . Power is concentrated at the center, in the ruler [and] the ideal form of temporal power is a world-empire into which all entities are combined into a coherent whole. (Hooker, 1978).

127-6

The quotation is *portemanteau* from Worsley, 1972, pp. 51, 42. (The "ideal relationship" which that between king and priest mirrored was, of course, that between god and king.) The relevant text is at pp. 154-155.

> Now Padanda Sakti Ngurah's affection [for the king] was so great because he recalled the past when he had been on the island of Java and there had been no one else with whom he enjoyed a close friendship. So it was that there existed a close understanding between the two at the [*griya*] of Romarsana, so that in continual friendship they looked after each other in good fortune and bad, and together they endured their difficulties; the good fortune of one was the good fortune of all; the misfortune of one was the misfortune of all, so that they behaved as though they were brothers and were thus an example for all the world.

127-14

On *druwé* (or *dué*), from the Sanskrit for "property," "worthy object," "wealth," "good," see Gonda, 1973, pp. 89, 121, 296, 471; Korn, 1932, pp. 112, 227, 229, 301, 304, 564, 569. The most common use for *druwé*, especially in the phrase *druwé dalem*, was for the so-called *pecatu* lands *(notes,* p. 176) on which certain obligations to the court were laid, and to "waste" (i.e., uncultivated) lands (Liefrinck, 1886-87). But the term was used for the king's relation to irrigation water, markets and trade realms, and subjects, as well as natural features such as lakes and mountains or cultural ones such as orchestras, masks, or temples. It was also often used, independently of any reference to the king, for collective property of the hamlet, irrigation society, or custom village, as well as for lands set aside to support temples, and, of course (often in its "coarse" variant, *gelah*) for individual private property as such.

127-26

The most famous example of the domanial view, though it concerns Java, is from Raffles: "the proprietary right to the soil in Java vests universally in the government . . . [and] those individual rights of property which are created by the laws and protected by the government, are unknown" (1830, vol. 1, p. 137; cf. p. 139). A good example of its inverse is Liefrinck's: "the rights of the individual . . . were so strongly developed that the situation is scarcely distinguishable from one governed by the ideas of European property law" (quoted in Korn, 1932, p. 542, my English being a rather free rendering of part of an impossibly Dutch sentence: "der rechten der individuen hebben zich zóó sterk geprononceerd dat . . . zij evenwel in den grond der zaak slechts weinig zijn onderscheiden van de eigendomsrechten volgens Europeesche begrippen"). For "the gods own everything," see Goris, 1960a; for "the village," van der Heijden, 1924-25. For various aspects of the "ownership" debate, see Korn, 1932, pp. 530-619; Happé, 1919; Liefrinck, 1877; van Stein Callenfels, 1947-48. The differing views, and indeed the debate itself, was, like the "village republic"/"Oriental despotism" one *(text,* p. 45), very much a reflex of differing ("direct" vs. "indirect" or "liberal" vs. "conservative") views of what colonial policy should be (see Furnivall, 1944; 1948).

It must be emphasized (because there are those who will continue to think otherwise) that nothing here or in what follows is meant to argue that resources were not appropriated, often enough rudely, or that political power, and even force, played no role in the process. The final word on the issue in this form is probably given by the Javanese proverb: "In the daytime everything we have belongs to the king; in the nighttime everything we have belongs to the thieves."

128-9

On land resources, see *text*, pp. 66ff., *notes*, pp. 174ff.; on water resources, *text*, pp. 69ff., *notes*, pp. 182ff. Not much has been said here about the domestic, household/houseyard, aspects of proprietorship, for though important generally their relevance to state organization was rather to the side. See Geertz and Geertz, 1975. On the term most often used in Bali for possession in the sense of usufruct, *bukti*, see Gonda, 1973, p. 282.

128-38

For "sacred space" on the local level, see *text*, p. 51, and *notes*, p. 156. For the "land with everything that grows on it . . ." formula, *notes*, p. 157.

129-10

The term *ngurah* (which, as Hooykaas has pointed out, is rather too casually rendered as "pure" in Geertz and Geertz, 1975, p. 129) often refers to a deity whose function is to "protect the ground" (see Grader, 1939 and 1960b; Swellengrebel, 1960; Goris, 1938). Applied to a lord, it then indicates his roles as such a "guardian" or "protector" of the (material) realm as *Ngurah Gumi* (*gumi*, "earth," "world"), or more commonly, *Ngurah Adat*. For *ngurah* as "something that overshadows, shelters (*palindongan*), a parasol (*payong*) and also the vault of heaven. . . . The princes . . . nearly all bear this title; they overshadow and protect the land," see Friederich, 1959, p. 123, n. 86. (Friederich also says it is a mark of the "Wesyan race," but that is incorrect.) An eloquent example of the park image, a pervasive one in Balinese representations of the human environment as well as of its imitative model, the divine environment, or "heaven," can be found again in the Majapahit *Negarakertagama*: "the cultivated lands made happy and quiet / of the aspect of the parks (*udayāna*), then, are the forests and the mountains, all of them set foot on by Him [the king] without [anyone?] feeling anxiety" (Pigeaud, 1960-63, vol. 1, p. 4, vol. 3, p. 21).

For an excellent discussion of the king's role as ritual "guardian" of the realm in relation to natural disasters (*merana*—epidemics, crop plagues, earthquakes, volcanic eruptions, floods, hurricanes, etc.), see C. J. Grader, n.d. The materials in Grader's study, which were gathered by V. E. Korn but left unpublished at his death, are concerned with the role of the lords in a curious mock cremation of mice (*abènan bikul*) held to end or to ward off such disasters. The ultimate causes of *merana* were considered to be the widespread commission of realm-polluting "wrong actions" (*apahkrama*)— miscaste sexual liaisons, bestiality, incest, the performance of priestly functions by caste unqualified persons—and the proximate causes were considered to be the actions of spirits of uncremated dead (*pirata*, as opposed to *pitara*, the cremated, "liberated" dead; *notes*, p. 235). The spirits, unable to mount to the heavens and join the gods, hang around human settlements and harass the living. The *abènan bikul* (the last recorded in Korn's material was held in 1937, but I have heard of ones given after the 1965 political massacres— which had themselves been preceded by a great volcanic eruption) mimicked the "real" royal cremations "as close as possible," (as the palm-leaf manuscript laying out the requirements for it, the *Jamatatwa*, put it). There were two mouses' corpses (one of them preferably an albino) dressed as a king and queen, and addressed as "Jero Giling," "Lord Spinning," "Turning Around," "Disoriented," and so on. These were placed in (three-roof) cremation towers, and a large number of attendant mouses' corpses (or just their skins or tails) were placed in smaller towers. All were burned in the appropriate animal coffins; there was the usual mass procession, with Brahmana priests playing their usual roles; there was the usual series of after-ceremonies, hands-to-foreheads obeisances, and so on (see *text*, p. 117). The whole event was carried out under the aegis of the king and at his expense, through the usual wealth-mobilizing means. The liberation of the mice-souls both corrected the polluted status of the negara adat (*panes bumi*—"hot world," comparable to the *sebel* of the desa-adat level—*notes*, p. 155) and appeased the unliberated dead. As such, it was considered a prime responsibility of the king as ngurah, together with the chief punggawas of the realm and the leading padandas. (The king witnessed the event from the *Balai Tegeh* "King's Public Seat" in front of his palace—*text*, fig. 11; and his presence was essential.) Though perhaps most often held in response to mice plaques, in the context of which it must have arisen, by the nineteenth century the abènan bikul could be and was employed in response to any negara-wide calamity—Korn's fullest case has to do with an earthquake—and even in response to a threat of one, as indicated by realm-polluting omens such as the birth of triplets, or monstrous births of either humans or animals. A number of other explicitly realm-purifying rituals conducted by the king as leader of the negara adat, usually in the Pura Penataran (q.v. below, in this note) are also noted in Grader's summary, pp. 17, 25, 43, as are all-Bali ritual-purifications conducted at Besakih, pp. 46, 48, 49, 51; see *text*, p. 40, and *notes*, p. 151. While the state of pollution existed, the gods would not come down, on the appropriate occasion, to their "seats" (*linggih*) in the temples; the purpose of the ritual was thus conceived of as *pengentig linggih*, "making the seats (thus, the status hierarchy—see *text*, p. 123) secure."

For a speculative (and, in my view, altogether implausible) theory that the "land guardian" aspects of the "Hindu-Javanese" lords are a relic of the "Majapahit invasion," in which they displaced an earlier "indigenous Balinese" earth-cult ruling class, see Korn, 1932, p. 153; cf. Friederich, 1959, pp. 142-143. In the narrow sense, *druwé raja* (or *druwé dalem*) was used for lord-owned lands as such (Korn, 1932, pp. 229, 301, 564, 659), but it was as often applied to his spiritual relation to the realm as a whole; and if either usage is "metaphorical," it is the former, not the latter (*notes*, p. 244). For the king's role at water openings, see *text*, p. 81, and *notes*, p. 192; for state temples in general, *text*, p. 40.

As there was a village Pura Balai Agung dedicated to celebrating the desa adat (*text*, p. 52; *notes*, p. 157), so there was a lord-sponsored temple at the state level, the Pura Panataran, dedicated to celebrating the negara adat. ("In the *pura pěnataran* the living unity of the realm was commemorated, celebrated, maintained, and confirmed by religious means. . . . The royal *pura pěnataran* served both for the veneration of the lord of the ground and for religious meetings of state. . . ."—Goris, 1960a.) Because of the presence within it of a stone lingga commemorating the lord's ancestors, Goris regards the Pura Panataran as "contain[ing] within itself the character of both the *pura pusěh* and *pura bale agung* on the village level." But, together with the Pura Balai Agung "Great Council Temple," the Pura Panataran "Head of State Temple" is still one of the most incompletely understood Balinese shrines, mainly because the associated desa adat and negara adat conceptions are incompletely understood—indeed, generally misunderstood—in the anxiety to separate "Hindu-Javanese" and "indigenous" elements in Balinese culture.

129-29

In economic terms, court ceremonies were very largely systems of redistributive exchange in Polanyi's sense (Polanyi et al., 1957), because the goods mobilized were either consumed on the spot by the celebrants as a whole or—to a quite significant extent—taken away by them to their homes. Actual accountings of course do not exist; but, judging by recent practices and, more importantly, by the views and descriptions of former participants, we can see that economic surplus did not flow to the court through the ceremonial system on a significant scale. Indeed, it seems that the lords generally put more into them, in material terms, than they got out. Repairs on palaces or, more occasionally, construction of state temples did use politically mobilized labor and goods; but this was as much a ritual activity as tooth filing or cremation, usually centered on a dedication (*mlaspas*) ceremony. The building and maintenance of paths, roads and so on was, like that of irrigation f..cilities or village temples, a local affair.

All this is not to say that the lords did not exact material support from their subjects, nor is it to say that such exaction was not often onerous; but it is to say that they did so mainly through the taxation, sharecropping, and tenure arrangements described earlier (*text*, p. 67), and only marginally at best through the ceremonial system, whose function was to display wealth, not to appropriate it. For a model picture of the distribution pattern, see the description of the Javanese *slametan*, of which these ceremonies were but an enormously magnified and elaborated version, in C. Geertz, 1960, pp. 11-16.

130-13

The quotation is from a mantra given in Goudriaan and Hooykaas, 1971, pp. 78-79. The word translated as "self" is the Sanskrit *ātma*, as often rendered "soul" or "mind"; it is compounded here with *sūnya*, "empty" (Gonda, 1973, pp. 420, 102), as part of a complex image of the body as a composite of divinities—Visnu in the heart, Isvara in the throat—of which this, "the Supreme Brahman" in the head or fontanel, is the integrating, summary one. For the imagery of "silence at the center-apex, commotion at the bottom-periphery" in cremation ceremonies, see *text*, p. 118; in painting, see Bateson, 1972b. The "formal pose" is, of course, the *padmasana* lotus posture discussed above (*notes*, p. 218). On the interconnections of rank, politesse, and individual "anonymization" in Bali more generally, see C. Geertz, 1973h. It should also be remarked again that the general word for a ritual or ceremony is *karya*, "[a] work"; for a court ceremony, *karya gdé*, "[a] great work."

130-29

"The Supreme Brahman" quotation is from the mantra cited in the previous note; the "helpless, bowed, stooping" one from the *Negara-kertagama* (Pigeaud, 1960-63, vol. 1, p. 3; vol. 3, p. 4, the reference to "the whole of the country" is here, of course, to "Java" [*saya-wabhūmi*]; but, for reasons which by now should be clear, that is incidental). The commonest word for trance in Bali, *nadi*, means "to become," "to exist," "to perform as," "to be possessed," "to create." (See Belo, 1960, pp. 201, 254; van Eck, 1876 [under *dadi*]; Kusuma, 1956a. Cf. Pigeaud, 1960-63, vol. 5, p. 204 [under *dadi*].)

The meditative imaging of gods, associated with body parts, colors, directions, and so on, is pervasive in Balinese ritual at all levels, but reaches particular development in court rites. The typical (Sanskritic) formula is *bayū-śabda-idep*, usually translated, for want of better, as "action-word-thought" (see Hooykaas, 1964a, pp. 26ff., 158ff., 204, 213, 223; 1966, pp. 14ff.; Gonda, 1973, pp. 102, 384, 518. For the role of the formula in the Balinese shadow play, a subject in itself, though far from an unrelated one, see Hooykaas, 1973c, pp. 19, 29, 31, 33, 36, 57, 99, 125). *Bayū* originally means "wind" or "breath," in spoken Balinese "force" or "strength," and it refers to what the mediator must "do"—make *mudra* gestures, bring offerings, control his breathing. *Śabda*, spoken Balinese *suara*, originally means "sound," "tone," "voice," "speech," and "name" as well as "word," and refers to what the mediator must "say"—prayers, songs, mantras. And *idep*, the most difficult and the most important of the three words, means something like "visualize," "envision," "image" as a verb, "picture," also as a verb, and refers to what the mediator must, as we would say, "bring to his mind," "cause to appear in his consciousness"—a richness of inner sensuousness that only an example, a quite typical ritual instruction connected with the celebration of the Siva-lingga emblem of kingship (*notes*, p. 221), can evoke.

As follows is worship in its concise form. Breath control first. Next, purify your thoughts. Put God Śiva between your eyebrows, using the mantra: [omitted here, untranslatable]. Imag-

ine that God Śiva has five head/faces, three eyes in each, and ten
arms; that He is completely adorned [with] front and ear ornaments, necklaces, a cloth with design, [a] neck ornament in the
shape of a serpent, a cloth of Indian making, arm, wrist, and
ankle rings; [that He is] looking benevolently, with all his weapons, not bigger than a thumb, of a pure appearance, radiant,
illuminating the three worlds, looking eastward. Next imagine
that your person is seated on a golden lotus-throne. Use the
mantra: [omitted]. Next, imagine that Holy Anantabhoga [a
serpent god] encircles the throne with his tail; that his head,
benevolent [in] appearance, protrudes. Use the mantra: [omit-
ted]. Imagine that the lotus is blooming. Place the Holy Fourteen Syllables, to wit: [omitted]. Next, perform Brahmánga and
Sivánga [mudras] in the heart of the lotus, accompanied by
recitation of astra-mantra in all directions of the compass. Next,
perform Brahmánga and Sivánga with the fingers, followed by
[the] astra-mantra. Next, [perform] Brahmánga and Sivánga,
[while uttering] astra-mantra in all directions of the compass.
Next, place God Śiva in your lotus of the heart while making
[the] amrta-mudrā. Pronounce the Holy Exceptional Mantra:
[omitted]; that is, [the] Holy Ten-syllable-Mantra, which causes
forming in the imagination of God Śūkṣma-Śiva. It is evident
that now God Śūkṣma-Śiva resides in the lotus of your heart.
Next, perform breath control, before you perform the following
placings: [there follows a series of instructions for placing various sacred syllables on various parts of the body—hairtuft,
fontanelle, head, lips, face, tongue, neck, heart, belly, navel,
genitals, feet]. Next, maintain supreme thinking: imagine that
your body is the token of a completely purified and perfect
man. Confirm God, by means of the homage-mantra. Mutter
the mantra: [omitted]. While muttering it, unite your own self
with Him Who deserves the name Undescribable. . . . (Hooykaas, 1964a, pp. 170-171; I have altered the punctuation, which
is arbitrary anyway)

This is literally just one of a hundred examples, and far from the
most complex, that could be given. For some others, see Hooykaas,
1966, pp. 61ff., 85ff., 90ff., 125ff.; and *notes*, p. 220. The fact that
Hooykaas translates *idep* at different points as "think," "imagine,"
"envisage," "concentrate," "become mindful of," and even "believe,"
and that in spoken Balinese it means "wish," "desire," only testifies
to the difficulty of the concept. It should perhaps also be noted that

despite the male pronouns both here and in the text, the gods are often imaged as androgynous—"Imagine the united God Siva and the Goddess Uma" (Hooykaas, 1966, p. 85); "Imagine the Deity is Half Lord-Lady/Siva/Parvati" (*idem*, p. 91; cf. 1964a, pp. 140, 168 —as well as imaged, of course, as women: Uma, Sarasvati, Durga, Sri. All this further connects with the myth of the "sinking status" reproduction, which proceeds from androgynous-asexual to opposite-sex identical twins, opposite-sex siblings, parallel cousins, and so on as one moves from gods to men and beyond them to the radically polar sexuality of animals (see Belo, 1970b; Mershon, 1971, pp. 29-31; Geertz and Geertz, 1975, though the subject, critical to an understanding of Balinese culture, has been insufficiently explored); and it is expressed in court ritual by the usual accompaniment of the king by his chief spouse surrounded by his lesser wives. See Hooykaas, 1964a, pp. 138-140. On priests' wives, where the symbolism was similar, see above, *notes*, p. 239. On Siva's wives as sekti, "activations" of Him—and thus, as His copy, as the lord's wives are of the lord—*text*, p. 106. On iconographic unification of male and female in Balinese ritual, *notes*, pp. 218, 221.

131-13

The quotations are from Worsley (1972, pp. 46, 80), as is the sun-moon trope (p. 45). Good descriptions of Balinese battles, as opposed to epic-style reports of them, are virtually nonexistent, but to judge from reports of informants who participated in them, they mostly consisted of a series of brief lance and dagger skirmishes, with the bested party withdrawing after only a few casualities. A sense for the ceremonial aspects of warfare can be gathered from the chronicle literature (e.g., Worsley, 1972, pp. 156-159, 163-165, 168-173, 177-181, 228-230, 231), from warrior dance forms such as the famous *baris* (Covarrubias, 1956, pp. 226, 230-232; de Zoete and Spies, 1938, pp. 56-64, 165-174, and plates 13-22, 74-76), and of course from the shadow play (Hooykaas, 1973c), though systematic studies are lacking, and our knowledge of concrete battlefield tactics is very sketchy, coming mainly from passing impressions in Dutch military sources (e.g., Artzenius, 1874; for Balinese soldiers in nineteenth-century central Javanese wars, see Carey, 1979, n. 58). For this reason, I append here a reorganized and edited version of a long interview with a former Tabanan perbekel about warfare as he knew it.

When war occurred the king [cakorda] called everyone to battle by way of the punggawas and perbekels. Everyone gathered near the battlefield, each lined up behind his particular perbekel, the perbekels being grouped according to their punggawas. For example, all the kawulas from Jero Subamia [the informant's punggawa] were together and they fought together. Each jero [i.e., punggawa] had a man—one of its perbekels—in charge of troops called a *pecalan*. The man in this position in the royal palace, Puri Gdé, was the *pecalan gdé* and was in general charge of the troops; but he was not a general in the sense of an overall strategist.

The cakorda made general plans, set overall strategy, at least in theory; but in the informant's experience there wasn't much strategizing: the wars were so brief and came up so suddenly that they never had very much in the way of planning. The main weapons were lances [*tombak*] and daggers [*kris*]. Guns were very rare. There were no bows and arrows [though, more generally, they were sometimes employed], and horses were not used in battle. (If a punggawa rode a horse to battle, he dismounted to fight.) Each soldier carried a lance and a kris, which he owned himself, but [usually] had no shield. Fighting was disorderly, and each man fought more or less according to his own courage, the bravest going naturally to the front, the less brave lagging behind.

Most fighting was at some natural boundary, usually a river. Both sides would try to ford the river, and often the battle took place in the middle of it. Commoners and lords were dressed alike, though punggawas usually had parasols carried over them on the way to battle. Everyone wore a white sarong, like those village priests wear today, usually without a skirt. The commoners, and after them the perbekels, did most of the fighting.

The punggawas rarely had to fight, and just received news from the perbekels about who was courageous and who was not. In one case when [his house] was in battle with Mengwi all the peasants were killed or fled, and so the punggawas were forced to fight. They fought against the Mengwi peasants; caste didn't count. There were people who went ahead into the enemy country to scout out the situation, but ambushes were generally rare. The scout (*petelik*) would just find out where the enemy was deploying and how many of them there were and then report to the punggawa. The "junior king," the lord of Kalèran, also didn't go out to fight until things got very bad. In the informant's recollection, the cakorda went out only once, the time that Marga was captured by Mengwi; but he only got as far as Tunjuk [a village about half way there], and the people wouldn't let him go any farther, because they said it wasn't necessary.

There were certain specialists (*juru bedil*) who held the few guns there were, and they were placed in the very front of the fight. The people who fought in the front lines were motivated by the fact that if they didn't get killed they would be the first to get the spoils of any captured territory, and so get more gold, cattle, etc. When Badung fought Kapal they [Badung] had some Bugis as riflemen. Kapal lost, and the Bugis were the first ones into the area and took all the valuables. In Tabanan some of the riflemen were Bugis too, and they were attached directly to Puri Gdé. It was actually the kawulas who carried out (*ngayah*, the same word used for ritual contributions to puri ceremonies) the war anyway.

I asked about length of war, and he said the Mengwi-Tabanan battle he was in lasted two days, and they quit when one or two people were killed. He thought there must have been an agreement between the two kings not to fight too hard, because neither side really tried to advance on the other. He said the king of Tabanan said after it was over that the battle had been ritual sacrifice (*caru*), like that you make to demons on "the Day of Silence" (*nyepi*). Perhaps this reluctance to fight further was because both sides thought that the enemy had too many forces, and they would have too much opposition. When Marga was captured by Mengwi the war lasted a month, and at least fifty people were killed. This was the most he ever heard of. All those who fell in battle were cremated with the expenses being borne by the king, the victim's punggawa, and his per-bekel.

The double aspect, gentle and fierce, of Indic gods—Siva/Kala, Uma/Durga—is of course well known. For Bali, see Covarrubias, 1956, pp. 316-318; Hooykaas, 1964a, pp. 43-92; Belo, 1949. On the ritual aspects of court justice, see above, *notes*, p. 241.

133-14

The main immediate effect of Dutch rule, so far as the negara is concerned, was, ironically enough, to turn it into the kind of feudal (or pseudofeudal) structure it had not previously been. The removal, through forced exile, of those members of the topmost levels of the indigenous elite (the core-line senior kings and their close relatives) who managed to survive the puputans left their inveterate rivals, the members of the next-to-topmost levels (the junior kings and their close relatives—see *text*, p. 6o), as the ranking local lords. The Dutch, needing some lords of high standing through whom to govern, transformed them into the ranking local civil servants, the so-called regents. (In Tabanan, the lord of Kalèran was accorded this post. Later, in the mid-twenties, when the fevers of the conquest had cooled and those of nationalism were heating up, the Dutch brought back many of the exiled heirs—in Tabanan, a young lord from Puri Mecutan, closest survivor of the dead king and prince—and restored them as regents as a move toward what was piously called "self-government," *zelfbestuur*.) Since the Dutch dissolved the perbekel system instantly upon taking direct control, these newly bureaucratized lords found themselves in the position of continuing to expect (and to be expected by the populace) to hold the theatre-state rituals, but without the political institution by which the task had previously been accomplished. For the most part, this dilemma was resolved by levying the ritual (but not military) obligations that had formerly fallen on their kawulas (*text*, p. 65) on their sharecropper land tenants; so for the first time service and tenancy were internally connected.

Some ritual costs, especially those having to do with "realm purification" rituals (*notes*, p. 246) were imposed on the subaks through the sedahans (C. J. Grader, n.d., pp. 8-9, 15, 20, 22, 26, 57-58; see following note). The Dutch government also sometimes subsidized the lords, especially those they had appointed regents, in such activities (idem, n.d., pp. 10, 27, 41, 60). Even opium sellers (idem, n.d., p. 12) and cockfight holders (idem, n.d., p. 42) were sometimes levied for such support.

In a similar way, the sedahan gdés (*text*, p. 67) were transformed into civil-servant irrigation-taxation inspectors, one for each of the six major southern negaras, now become clearly bounded regencies (Karengasem, Klungkung, Bangli, Gianyar, Badung, Tabanan; the two northern ones, Bulèlèng and Jembrana, had been thus transformed earlier—*notes*, p. 140). The ordinary sedahans were then set under them as subregional, "district," subinspectors; the subaks were somewhat regularized, mainly through consolidations; and a few centrally planned modern works—dams, reservoirs—were installéd. Thus a (not very powerful) "hydraulic bureaucracy," presided over by (not very strong) water officials, was also produced, also for the first time.

In trade, both Chinese storekeeping and bazaar marketing expanded as port-of-trade, lease-hold commerce was interdicted; though especially after Independence, when landlordism seemed less assured as a way of supporting negara activities, a number of lords entered into commerce as semiofficial entrepreneurs of some weight (for a fuller discussion of this, see C. Geertz, 1960b).

A number of other changes induced by the final arrival of colonialism in full form—the solidification of title ranks and the growing importance of varna distinctions; the grouping of village functional groups into territorial government villages (headed by Dutch-appointed native officials, mostly Sudras, called perbekels), and those into territorial districts (headed by Dutch-appointed native officials, called punggawas, virtually all triwangsas); the setting up of secular law courts; and, of course, the complete elimination of warfare—appeared as well. As a result, by the end of the colonial period, the negara had become, in organization at least, somewhat rationalized in the Weberian sense, while maintaining a good deal of its exemplary ceremonial activity in more or less traditional form. With the Japanese invasion, Independence, and the imposition of centralized military rule, the exemplary aspect was, naturally, put under further pressure. But the Indonesian newsmagazine *Tempo*, of 3 October 1977, reports a Gianyar royal wedding lasting four days, assembling more than 15,000 people, and costing several hundred thousand dollars; and *The International Herald Tribune* (Paris), of 12 February 1979, describes a 1979 cremation of the lord of Ubud as drawing 100,000 people—3,000 of them tourists who paid twenty-five dollars apiece for "box seats"—and sporting a sixty-three-foot cremation tower. The theatre state is far from altogether vanished, even now.

133-26

On the "absence of climax" as a pervasive theme in Balinese life, see Bateson and Mead, 1942; cf. C. Geertz, 1973c and 1973h.

134-25

Doubtless, if more could be recovered of Balinese "annalistic" history the image of continuity would be somewhat less uniformitarian, and endogenous stages of development would replace the simple sense of fixity. But the argument is not that nothing ever changed, or that the changes were without their own significance, but that the sort of deep-going transformation that took place in many other parts of Southeast Asia as a result of extensive foreign contact—most especially, but not exclusively, Western—did not occur before the turn of this century in south Bali, where the cultural parameters of political life, that is, the frame of discourse within which it moved, remained generally stable. No matter how much upheaval took place within this frame, its overall form altered but little. For a good discussion in relation to Thailand (where such foreign contact was much earlier and deeper and more continuous) of the host of problems involved here, and of the dangers of an over static view of the history of the Southeast Asian "Indic" state generally, see Keyes, 1978.

The dates, which are intended emblematically, are for the Majapahit "invasion" (*text*, p. 14) and the Dutch one (*text*, p. 11).

GLOSSARY

Until 1972, Indonesian (and thus Balinese) words were spelled according to an orthography somewhat different from that now official. (Dutch scholars of the colonial period often used rather individual would-be "phonetic" orthographies.) Thus some indigenous words in this book and in the glossary, which follows the official style, appear in somewhat different form in all but the most recent literature. The most important of such differences include: *c* for *tj* (*manca* rather than *mantja*); *j* for *dj* (*banjar* rather than *bandjar*); and *y* for *j* (*pengayah* rather than *pengajah*).

ABÈN   Also *abènan, ngabèn*. Cremation, cremation ceremony.

ABÈNAN BIKUL   Mock cremation of mice to ward off natural calamities (see MERANA).

ADAT   Custom, customary, customary law (see DESA ADAT, BENDESA ADAT, NEGARA ADAT, NGURAH).

APAHKRAMA   Literally, "wrong actions"; serious delicts leading to pollution of the realm and thus to natural calamities (see PANAS BUMI, MERANA).

AWIG-AWIG   Basic laws (of custom community, hamlet, irrigation society, temple group, etc.), usually inscribed on palm-leaf manuscripts (see KERTASIMA, LONTAR, ADAT).

BADÉ   Cremation tower (see ABÈN, MERU).

BAGAWANTA   Also *purohita, guru loka*. A Brahmana priest in ritual service to a lord, especially a paramount lord (see PADANDA, SIWA, SISIA).

BANJAR   A hamlet; the basic local political community (see SUBAK, PEMAKSAN).

BANTEN   A ritual offering.

BATUR   A lord's kin-group temple (see DADIA).

BEDUGUL   Also *catu, tugu*. A small altar, usually stone, for offerings to the gods.

BEKELAN   All those subject to the direction of a single PERBEKEL.

BENDESA ADAT   The ceremonial head of a local customary-law community (see ADAT, DESA ADAT, PEMAKSAN, PURA BALAI AGUNG).

BESAKIH   The chief state temple of all-Bali, located on the slopes of the sacred volcano, Mt. Agung (see SAD KAHYANGAN, MERU.

BRAHMANA   Highest of the four "castes" of Bali, from which high priests are drawn (see TRIWANGSA, WARNA, PADANDA, GRIYA, SATRIA, WESIA, SUDRA).

BUWANA   "World."

BUWANA AGUNG   "The great world"; that is, outer reality, the material world, the macrocosm.

BUWANA ALIT   "The little world"; that is, the inner life of man, the immaterial world, the microcosm.

CAKORDA   Also *ratu, raja, prabu,* etc. Title of a paramount lord, a "king" (see PEMADÉ, PUNGGAWA).

DADIA   A preferentially endogamous patrilineal kin group; the temple at which such a group worships its divinized ancestors (see BATUR).

DALEM   Literally, "within," "inside." Often used to refer to a paramount lord or "king," his residence, his court, or his family (see JERO, JABA).

DESA   "Countryside," "village." A general term for rural settlements and their life-ways (see DESA ADAT, NEGARA).

DESA ADAT   A local community defining a sacred space and governed by one set of customary laws (see ADAT, BENDESA ADAT, PEMAKSAN, PURA BALAI AGUNG, NEGARA ADAT).

DEWA   God.

DEWI   Goddess.

DRUWÉ   Also *dué.* (Something) "owned." Used to indicate the "spiritual" or "tutelary" relation between a lord and his realm (see NGURAH, NEGARA ADAT).

GDÉ   Also, in elevated speech, *agung.* Big, great, large. Used as a status-elevating modifier, especially in state-related contexts (see PURI GDÉ, JERO GDÉ, SEDAHAN GDÉ, KARYA GDÉ).

GÈLGÈL   Fourteenth-century Balinese kingdom. The primary exemplary state of Bali, considered to have been founded by Javanese lords and priests and to have been the unitary kingdom from which the other major Balinese kingdoms broke off (see MAJAPAHIT).

GRIYA   A Brahmana priest's residence, his household (see DALEM, PURI, JERO, UMAH).

HALUS or *alus*. (Relatively) refined, civilized, polite, graceful, smooth (see KASAR).

JABA Literally, "outside." Used to indicate relatively lower status and greater distance from center of state, society, experience, reality, divinity. General term for the fourth "caste" and for the world outside Bali (see JERO, DALEM, SUDRA, TRIWANGSA).

JAKSA Non-Brahmana legal official; judge, prosecutor, advocate.

JERO Literally, "inside." Used (often as a title) to indicate relatively higher status and closeness to the center of state, society, experience, reality, divinity. General term for upper three "castes," for the world of the court, and for the residences and households of the lords (see JABA, DALEM, TRIWANGSA, JERO GDÉ).

JERO GDÉ Residence and household of a major lord; the major lord himself (see PUNGGAWA).

KAHYANGAN "Great" temple (see PURA, KAHYANGAN TIGA, SAD KAHYANGAN).

KAHYANGAN TIGA The three main "village" temples: the Origin Temple, the Death Temple, and the Great Council Temple (see PURA PUSÈH, PURA DALEM, PURA BALAI AGUNG).

KASAR (Relatively) unrefined, crude, uncivilized, impolite, ungraceful, rough (see HALUS).

KARYA Literally, "work." Used to indicate activities involved in supporting and performing a ceremony; thus, a ceremony as such.

KARYA GDÉ Literally, "great work"; a state ceremony and the activities involved in supporting and performing it (see KARYA, RAJA KARYA).

KAWULA "Subject"; someone obligated to perform ceremonial-cum-military services for a particular lord (see PUNGGAWA, PERBEKEL, PAREKAN, PENGAYAH, DALEM, KARYA GDÉ, RAJA KARYA).

KEBANDARAN Lease-held trade area (see SUBANDAR).

KÈPÈNG Small lead or bronze Chinese hole-in-the-middle coins used as an exchange medium and in weight measurement (see TIMBANG).

KERTA A Brahmana judge (see JAKSA).

KERTASIMA Also *awig-awig subak*. The basic laws of an irrigation society (see AWIG-AWIG, SUBAK).

KESEDAHAN   Also *bukti pajeg*. Water-tax area under a single state tax collector (see SEDAHAN, PAJEG).

KRAMA   Literally, "manner," "method," "way," "style." Used, severally and collectively, to mean "member" ("membership") or "citizen" ("citizenry"), as in *krama banjar*, "hamlet member, membership," and in *krama subak*, "irrigation society member, membership."

LINGGA   Phallic image; symbol of Siva, divine kingship, sacred potency, etc.

LINGGIH   Literally, "seat." Generally used to indicate rank, station, position, place, title, "caste." Also indicates the altar(s) on which a god sits when he or she descends to the temples (see ODALAN, PADMASANA).

LONTAR   Also *rontal*. A palm-leaf manuscript.

MAJAPAHIT   Fourteenth-century Javanese kingdom considered by the Balinese to be the source of their state-level political organization and culture (see GÈLGÈL, NEGARA).

MANCA   Literally, "hands" (more literally, "five"); used to refer to a major lord (see PUNGGAWA, PAREKAN).

MANTRA   Sacred formula(s) uttered in ritual (see MUDRA).

MERANA   Supernaturally caused natural calamity (see APAHKRAMA, PANAS BUMI, ABÈN BIKUL).

MERU   Hindu holy mountain and *axis mundi*; abode of the gods. Also used to refer to temple-roof and cremation-tower replicas of it, and identified in Bali with the sacred volcano, Mt. Agung (see BESAKIH, BADÉ).

METATAH   Tooth filing, tooth-filing ceremony.

MOKSA   "Disincarnation"; to ascend to the realm of the gods after death without leaving a corpse (see PITARA).

MUDRA   Sacred hand gesture(s) used in ritual (see MANTRA).

MURTI   Form, shape, materialization; used to indicate the subsistent aspects of the divine as against the dynamic ones (see SEKTI).

NEGARA   State, realm, capital, court, town. A general term for superordinate, translocal political authority and the social and cultural forms associated with it (see DESA, NEGARA ADAT).

NEGARA ADAT   A regional or supraregional community defining a sacred space and governed by one set of customary laws (see ADAT, DESA ADAT, NGURAH, SAD KAHYANGAN).

NGURAH Guardian, custodian, protector. The paramount lord considered in his role as ceremonial head of a regional customary-law community (see NEGARA ADAT, PURA PENATARAN, DESA ADAT).

ODALAN Periodic temple ceremony during which the gods descend from the heavens to receive obeisance from the temple congregation (see PURA, PEMAKSAN).

PADANDA Also *pandita*. An ordained Brahmana priest (see PEMANGKU, BAGAWANTA, SIWA).

PADMASANA Lotus seat. Used to refer to the throne of God and to iconic representations of it in temples, rituals, etc.; also, a particular altar in a temple considered as the chief seat of the gods when they descend (see ODALAN, LINGGIH).

PADMI Also *parameswari*. A caste-endogamous chief wife of a lord, especially a paramount lord (see PENAWING).

PAJEG Tax, a tax; *pajeg padi*, agricultural tax in kind (see SEDAHAN, KESEDAHAN).

PANAS BUMI Literally, "hot earth"; general pollution of the realm as a result of some wrong action on the part of human beings (see SEBEL, APAHKRAMA, MERANA).

PAREKAN A dependent servant of a lord. Also used metaphorically to describe lords in relation to their paramount lord (see KAWULA, PERBEKEL, PUNGGAWA).

PECATU Cultivable land to which service obligations are attached (see PENGAYAH).

PEKANDELAN Lord's servant's quarters (see PAREKAN).

PEKARANGAN Commoner houseyard or compound; local unit in the state system (see PERBEKEL, UMAH).

PEMADÉ A "second" or "junior" king (see CAKORDA).

PEMAKSAN A temple congregation, responsible for the temple's upkeep and for worshiping the gods when they descend; also, the membership of a given DESA ADAT (see PURA, ODALAN, PURA BALAI AGUNG, BANJAR, SUBAK).

PEMANGKU A non-Brahmana temple priest (see PADANDA).

PENAWING A lower-caste secondary wife of a lord (see WARGI, PADMI).

PENGAYAH Service, ceremonial or material, to a lord, village, irrigation society, temple, etc.

PERBEKEL The lowest-level political functionary of the state system, responsible for the ceremonial and military mobilization of the members of a certain number of houseyards attached to a given lord (see PUNGGAWA, KAWULA, PAREKAN, BEKELAN, PEKARANGAN).

PIRATA Spirits of uncremated dead (see PITARA, PURA DALEM).

PITARA Literally, "god"; cremated, "liberated" dead (see PIRATA, MOKSA).

PUNGGAWA A lord of the realm (see PERBEKEL, KAWULA, PAREKAN, MANCA, CAKORDA).

PUPUTAN Literally, "ending"; ritualized, dynasty-ending defeat by military sacrifice/suicide.

PURA Temple (see KAHYANGAN).

PURA BALAI AGUNG "Great Council Temple" (of the gods); village temple dedicated to enhancing the fertility of the land and people of a local customary-law community (see KAHYANGAN TIGA, DESA ADAT, PEMAKSAN).

PURA DALEM "Inside Temple"; village temple dedicated to appeasing the spirits of the local uncremated dead (see KAHYANGAN TIGA, PIRATA).

PURA PENATARAN "Courtyard Temple"; a state temple dedicated to enhancing the unity and prosperity of the realm as a customary-law/sacred-space community (see NEGARA ADAT, NGURAH).

PURA PUSÈH "Navel Temple"; village temple dedicated to commemorating local settlement origins and founding ancestors (see KAHYANGAN TIGA).

PURA ULUN CARIK Also *Pura Subak*. "Head of the Ricefields Temple"; irrigation-society field temple (see SUBAK).

PURI Lord's residence, palace, household (see JERO, JERO GDÉ, PURI GDÉ, DALEM, GRIYA).

PURI GDÉ The palace and household of a paramount lord (see DALEM).

RAJA KARYA Literally, "lord's work"; state-ceremony service, or material contribution to such a ceremony (see KARYA GDÉ).

RUKUN Harmony, consensual settlement of differences, social solidarity.

SAD KAHYANGAN The six Great Temples; all-Bali temples dedicated to the prosperity of the island and its people as a whole (see BESAKIH, KAHYANGAN TIGA).

SATRIA Second highest of the four "castes," from which most higher lords are drawn (see BRAHMANA, WESIA, SUDRA, TRI-WANGSA, WARNA, JERO).

SEBEL State of ritual pollution of a village, family, etc. (see PANAS BUMI).

SEDAHAN Collector of agricultural taxes and rents for a lord (see PAJEG, KESEDAHAN).

SEDAHAN GDÉ Or *sedahan agung.* "Great" or "big" SEDAHAN; head tax and rent collector for a lord, especially a paramount lord.

SEKA Any organized group with a specific social function.

SEKA YÈH Group responsible for irrigation repairs in an irrigation society (see SUBAK).

SEKTI Spiritual energy, charisma; the dynamic aspect of a deity (see MURTI).

SEMBAH Obeisance gesture to gods, lords, superiors, etc.

SINGKÈH China-born Chinese living in Indonesia (as opposed to *peranakan,* Indonesia-born Chinese).

SISIA "Disciple" of a Brahmana priest from whom he or she receives holy water (see SIWA, TIRTA, PADANDA).

SIWA Siva, most important of the Hindu gods in Bali, identified with the Sun; also used for the Brahmana priest from whom one receives holy water (see SURYA, SISIA, PADANDA, TIRTA).

SUBAK An irrigation society; the basic local cultivation unit (see BANJAR, PEMAKSAN, SEKA YÈH, TENAH, TEBIH, TÈMPÈK, PURA ULUN CARIK).

SUBANDAR Trade leaseholder (see KEBANDARAN).

SUDRA Lowest of the four "castes" of Bali (see BRAHMANA, SATRIA, WESIA, JABA, WARNA).

SURYA The Sun; identified with the god Siva (see SIWA).

TEBIH Literally, "piece," "fragment"; a rice terrace (see SUBAK).

TENAH Fundamental unit of measure (of water, land, seed, rice) within any given irrigation society (see SUBAK).

TEMPÈK A major subsection of an irrigation society (see SUBAK).

TÈN-TÈN A small morning market.

TIMBANG An absolute weight measure calibrated in KÈPÈNGS (q. v.).

TIRTA Holy water prepared by Brahman priests (see SIWA, SISIA, PADANDA).

TRIWANGSA Literally, "the three peoples"; the upper three "castes" of Bali considered as a group against the fourth (see BRAHMANA, SATRIA, WESIA, SUDRA, WARNA, JERO, JABA).

UKIRAN Literally, "place of the mountain"; an inner court of a palace representing the axis of the world where the sacred heirlooms of the dynasty are kept and periodically worshiped (see MERU, WARIS).

UMAH A commoner's residence, household (see GRIYA, DALEM, PURI, JERO).

WARGI A political relationship between two kin groups of unequal status established by the giving of a wife from the lower-status group to the higher (see PENAWING).

WARIS Also *pusaka, kaliliran.* Sacred heirlooms (see UKIRAN).

WARNA Also *wangsa.* Literally, "color"; used to refer to the four main status categories of Bali (from Sanskrit *varna*), usually called "castes" in the Western literature (see BRAHMANA, SATRIA, WESIA, SUDRA, TRIWANGSA).

WESIA Third-ranking of the "castes" of Bali (see BRAHMANA, SATRIA, SUDRA, WARNA, TRIWANGSA).

WONG Human being.

BIBLIOGRAPHY

Dutch Journal Abbreviations

TBG   *Tijdschrift voor Indische Taal-, Land- en Volkenkunde uitgegeven door het Bataviaasche Genootschap van Kunsten en Wetenschappen*

TLV   *Bijdragen tot de Taal-, Land- en Volkenkunde van de Koninklijke Instituut*

TNI   *Tijdschrift voor Nederlandsch Indië*

Adams, R. McC.
  1966   *The Evolution of Urban Society, Early Mesopotamia and Prehispanic Mexico.* Chicago.
Adatrechtbundels
  1924   *Adatrechtbundels XXIII.* The Hague.
  1931   *Adatrechtbundels XXXIV.* The Hague.
  1934   *Adatrechtbundels XXXVII.* Leiden.
American Heritage
  1969   *The American Heritage Dictionary of the English Language.* Boston and New York.
Andaya, L. Y.
  1975   *The Kingdom of Johor, 1641-1728.* Kuala Lumpur.
Anderson, B.
  1972   "The Idea of Power in Javanese Culture." In Holt, 1972, pp. 1-70.
Anonymous
  1849   "Een Feest en Gianjar op Bali." *TNI* 1:421-429.
Ardana, I Gusti Gdé
  1971   *Pengertian Pura di Bali.* Den Pasar (Bali).
Arntzenius, J.O.H.
  1874   *De Derde Balische Expeditie.* The Hague.
Astawa, T. B.
  1970   *Pokok-pokok Sedjarah Perkembangan Parisada Hindu Dharma.* Den Pasar (Bali): Sekretariat Parisada.
Bagus, I Gusti Ngurah
  n.d.   *A short note on the Modern Hindu Movements in Balinese Society.* Den Pasar (Bali): Universitas Udayana.
  1969a   (ed.) *Kedudukan Serta Perlunja Peningkatan Mutu Pewajangan Bali.* Den Pasar (Bali).

1969b   *Pertentangan Kasta Dalam Bentuk Baru Pada Masjara-kat Bali*. Den Pasar (Bali).

Banner, H. S.

1927   *Romantic Java*. London.

Barton, R. F.

1922   *Ifugao Economics*. University of California Publications in American Archaeology and Ethnography, vol. 15, no. 5. Berkeley.

Basham, A. L.

1952   *The Wonder That Was India*. London.

Basso, K., and H. Selby

1976   *Approaches to Symbolic Anthropology*. Albuquerque.

Bateson, G.

1937   "An Old Temple and a New Myth." *Djawa* 17:291-308.

1972a   *Steps to an Ecology of Mind*. New York.

1972b   "Style, Grace, and Primitive Art." In Bateson, 1972a, pp. 128-152.

Bateson, G., and M. Mead

1942   *Balinese Character: A Photographic Analysis*. Special Publications of the New York Academy of Sciences, vol. 2. New York.

Baum, V.

1937   *A Tale of Bali*. Garden City.

Belo, J.

1936   "A Study of the Balinese Family." *American Anthropologist* 38:12-31.

1949   *Bali: Rangda and Barong*. American Ethnological Society Monographs, no. 16. Locust Valley (N.Y.).

1953   *Bali: Temple Festival*. American Ethnological Society Monographs, no. 22. Locust Valley (N.Y.).

1960   *Trance in Bali*. New York.

1970a   (ed.) *Traditional Balinese Culture*. New York.

1970b   "A Study of Customs Pertaining to Twins in Bali." 1st ed. 1935. In Belo, 1970a, pp. 3-57.

1970c   "The Balinese Temper." In Belo, 1970a, pp. 85-110.

Benda, H.

1962   "The Structure of South-East Asian History." *Journal of Southeast Asian History* 3:104-138.

Ben David, J., and T. N. Clarke (eds.)

1977   *Culture and Its Creators*. Chicago.

Berg, C. C.

1922   *Babad Bla-Batuh, de Geschiedenis van een Taak der Fami-lie Jelantik.* Santpoort (Neth.).

1927   *De Middle Javaansche Historische Traditie.* Santpoort (Neth.).

1929   *Kindung Pamancañgah, de Geschiedenis van het rijk van Gèlgèl, critisch uitgeven.* Santpoort (Neth.).

1939   "Javaansche Geschiedschrijving." In Stapel, 1939, vol. 2, pp. 5-148.

1950   "Kertenegara, de Miskende Empire-Builder." *Orientatie* 34:3-32.

1951a   *De Evolutie der Javaanse Geschiedschrijving.* Verhande-lingen der Koninklijke Nederlandse Akademie van Weten-schappen, afd. Letterkunde, n.s., vol. 14, no. 2. Amsterdam.

1951b   "De Sadeng-Oorlog en de Mythe van Groot-Majapahit." *Indonesie* 5:385-422.

1961a   "Javanese Historiography—A Synopsis of Its Evolution." In Hall, 1961, pp. 12-23.

1961b   "The Work of Professor Krom." In Hall, 1961, pp. 164-171.

1965   "The Javanese Picture of the Past." In Soedjatmoko et al., 1965, pp. 87-117.

Bernet-Kempers, A. J.

1959   *Ancient Indonesian Art.* The Hague.

1976   *Ageless Borobudar.* Wassenaar (Neth.).

Bernstein, R. J.

1976   *The Restructuring of Social and Political Theory.* New York and London.

Bhadra, I. Wajan

n.d.   "Karangan Tentang Agama Hindu Bali." Mimeo. Singa-radja (Bali).

Birkelbach, A. W., Jr.

1973   "The Subak Association." *Indonesia* 16:153-169.

Bloch, M. (ed.)

1975   *Political Language and Oratory in Traditional Society.* London.

1977   "The Past and the Present in the Present." *Man* 12:278-292.

van Bloemen Waanders, P. L.

1859   "Aanteekeningen Omtrent de Zeden en Gebruiken der Balinezen, Inzonderheid die van Boeleleng." *TBG* 8:105-279.

Boekian, I. Dewa Poetoe
1936 "Kayoebii: Een Oud-Balische Bergdesa." *TBG* 76:127-176.
Boon, J. A.
1973 "Dynastic Dynamics, Caste and Kinship in Bali Now."
Ph.D. diss., Dept. of Anthropology, University of Chicago.
1976 "The Balinese Marriage Predicament: Individual, Stra-
tegical, Cultural." *American Ethnologist* 3:191-214.
1977 *The Anthropological Romance of Bali, 1597-1972*. Cambridge (U.K.), London, Melbourne, and New York.
Bosch, F.D.K.
1924 "Het Lingga-Heilegdom van Dinaja." *TBG* 64:227-286.
1948 *De Gouden Kiem, Inleiding in de Indische Symboliek*.
Amsterdam and Brussels.
1956 "C. C. Berg and Ancient Javanese History." *TLV* 92:1-24.
1961a *Selected Studies in Indonesian Archaeology*. The Hague.
1961b "The Problem of the Hindu Colonisation of Indonesia."
1st ed. 1946. In Bosch, 1961a, pp. 3-22.
Brakel, L. F.
1975 "State and Statecraft in 17th-Century Aceh." In Reid and
Castles, 1975, pp. 56-60.
Briggs, L. P.
1951 *The Ancient Khmer Empire*. Philadelphia.
1978 "The Hinduized States of Southeast Asia: A Review." *Far
Eastern Quarterly* 7:376-393.
Brissenden, R.
1976 "Patterns of Trade and Maritime Society Before the Coming of the Europeans." In McKay, 1976, pp. 65-97.
van den Broek, H. A.
1834 "Verlag Nopens het Eiland Bali." *Tijdschrift van Oost-
Indië* 1:158-236.
Burger, D. H.
1948-50 "Structuurveranderingen in de Javaanse Samenleving."
Indonesië 2:281-298, 521-537; 3:1-18, 101-123, 225-250, 381-389,
512-534.
Carey, P.
1979 *An Account of the Outbreak of the Javanese War*. Kuala
Lumpur.
de Casparis, J. G.
1956 *Selected Inscriptions from the Seventh to the Ninth Century, A.D.* Bandung (Indonesia).
1961 "Historical Writing on Indonesia (Early Period)." In Hall,
1961, pp. 121-163.

Castles, L.

1967   *Religion, Politics, and Economic Behavior in Java: The Kudus Cigarette Industry.* Yale Southeast Asia Program, Cultural Report Series, no. 15. New Haven.

Clarke, G.

1954   *Elements of Ecology.* New York.

Coedès, G.

1911   "Note sur l'apothéose au Cambodge." *Bulletin de la Commission Archéologique de L'Indochine,* pp. 38-49.

1948   *Les États Hindouises d'Indochine et d'Indonesie.* Paris.

1968   *The Indianized States of Southeast Asia* Trans. of Coedès, 1948. Honolulu.

Cool, W.

1896   *De Lombok Expeditie.* The Hague.

Cooley, F. L.

1962   *Ambonese Adat: A General Description.* Yale Southeast Asia Program, Cultural Report Series, no. 10. New Haven.

Covarrubias, M.

1956   *The Island of Bali.* New York.

Cowan, C. D., and O. W. Wolters (eds.)

1976   *Southeast Asian History and Historiography.* Ithaca (N.Y.) and London.

Crucq, K. C.

1928   *Bijdrage tot de Kennis van het Balische Doodenritueel.* Santpoort (Neth.).

Dalton, G.

1971   *Economic Anthropology of Development, Essays on Tribal and Peasant Economies.* New York.

1978   "Comments on Ports of Trade." *The Norwegian Anthropological Review,* vol. 11, no. 2.

Damais, L-C.

1951-69   *Études d'épigraphie Indonésienne, Études balinaises, javanaises, soumatranaises.* Bulletin de l'École Français de Extrême-Orient. Paris.

Du Bois, C.

1959   *Social Forces in Southeast Asia.* Cambridge (Mass.).

Dumézil, G.

1948   *Mitra-Varuna.* Paris.

Dumont, L.

1970a   *Homo Hierarchicus.* Chicago.

1970b   *Religion/Politics and History in India.* Paris and The Hague.

1970c "World Renunciation in Indian Religions." In Dumont, 1970b, pp. 33-61.

1970d "The Conception of Kingship in Ancient India." In Dumont, 1970b, pp. 62-88.

van Eck, R.

1876 *Eerste Proeve van een Balineesche-Hollandsch Woordenboek*. Utrecht (Neth.).

1878-80 "Schetsen van het eiland Bali." *TNI* 7 (pt. 2, 1878): 85-130, 165-213, 325-356, 405-430; 8 (pt. 1, 1879):36-60, 104-134, 286-305, 365-387; 9 (pt. 1):1-39, 102-132, 195-221, 401-429; (pt. 2, 1880):1-18, 81-96.

van Eck, R., and F. A. Liefrinck

1876 "Kerta-Sima, of gemeente- en waterschaps-wetten op Bali." *TBG* 23:161-257.

van Eerde, J. C.

1910 "Hindu-Javaansche en Balische Eredienst." *TLV* 65:1-39.

1921 "Dewa Manggis V." *Onze Eeuw*, pp. 31-56.

Eliade, M.

1954 *The Myth of the Eternal Return*. New York.

1963 *Patterns in Comparative Religion*. Cleveland and New York.

Encyclopaedië

1917 *Encyclopaedië van Nederlandsch Indië*. The Hague and Leiden.

Fillozat, J.

1966 "New Researches on the Relations between India and Cambodia." *Indicaa* 3:95-106.

Franken, A. J.

1960 "The Festival of Jayaprana at Kaliangĕt." In Swellengrebel et al., 1960, pp. 235-265.

Fraser, J.

1910 "De Inheemsche Rechtspraak op Bali." *De Indische Gids* (July), pp. 1-40.

Friederich, R.

1847 "De Oesana Bali." *TNI* 9:245-373.

1959 *The Civilization and Culture of Bali*. 1st ed. 1876-78. Calcutta.

Furnivall, J. S.

1944 *Netherlands India: A Study of a Plural Economy*. Cambridge (U.K.).

1948 *Colonial Policy and Practice*. Cambridge (U.K.).

Gadamer, H-G.

1976 *Philosophical Hermeneutics.* Berkeley.

Geertz, C.

1956 "The Development of the Javanese Economy: A Socio-cultural Approach." Mimeo. Center for International Studies, Massachusetts Institute of Technology. Cambridge.

1959 "Form and Variation in Balinese Village Structure." *American Anthropologist* 61:991-1012.

1960 *The Religion of Java.* Glencoe, (Ill.).

1961 Review of J. L. Swellengrebel et al., 1960. *TLV* 117:498-502.

1962 "Social Change and Economic Modernization in Two Indonesian Towns: A Case in Point." In Hagen, 1962, pp. 385-407.

1963a *Agricultural Involution: The Processes of Ecological Change in Indonesia.* Berkeley.

1963b *Peddlers and Princes: Social Development and Economic Change in Two Indonesian Towns.* Chicago.

1964 "Tihingan: A Balinese Village." *TLV* 120:1-33.

1965 *The Social History of an Indonesian Town.* Cambridge (Mass.).

1968 *Islam Observed.* New Haven.

1972a "The Wet and the Dry: Traditional Irrigation in Bali and Morocco." *Human Ecology* 1:34-39.

1972b "Religious Change and Social Order in Soeharto's Indonesia." *Asia* 27:62-84.

1973a *The Interpretation of Cultures.* New York.

1973b "Thick Description: Toward an Interpretive Theory of Culture." In C. Geertz, 1973a, pp. 3-30.

1973c "Religion As a Cultural System." In C. Geertz, 1973a, pp. 87-125.

1973d "Ethos, World View, and the Analysis of Sacred Symbols." In C. Geertz, 1973a, pp. 126-141.

1973e " 'Internal Conversion' in Contemporary Bali." In C. Geertz, 1973a, pp. 170-192.

1973f "Ideology As a Cultural System." In C. Geertz, 1973a, pp. 193-233.

1973g "Politics Past, Politics Present: Some Notes on the Uses of Anthropology in Understanding New States." In C. Geertz, 1973a, pp. 327-341.

1973h "Person, Time, and Conduct in Bali." In C. Geertz, 1973a, pp. 360-411.

1973i "Deep Play: Notes on the Balinese Cockfight." In C. Geertz, 1973a, pp. 412-453.

1975 "Common Sense as a Cultural System." *Antioch Review* 33:5-26.

1976a "'From the Native's Point of View,' On the Nature of Anthropological Understanding." In Basso and Selby, 1976, pp. 221-237.

1976b "Art as a Cultural System." *MLN* 91:1473-1499.

1977a "Centers, Kings and Charisma: Reflections on the Symbolics of Power." In Ben David and Clarke, 1977, pp. 150-171.

1977b "Found in Translation: On the Social History of the Moral Imagination." *The Georgia Review* 31:788-810.

Geertz, H.

1959 "The Balinese Village." In G. W. Skinner, 1959, pp. 24-33.

Geertz, H. and C. Geertz

1975 *Kinship in Bali.* Chicago.

Gerdin, I.

1977 *The Balinese "Sidikara": Ancestors, Kinship, and Rank.* Dept. of Social Anthropology, Working Papers, no. 15. Gothenburg (Sweden).

Geria, I. Putu

1957 *Gaguritan Rusak Buleleng.* Den Pasar (Bali).

van Geuns, M.

1906 *Door Badoeng en Tabanan, Een en Ander Over Bali en Zijne Bewoners.* Soerabaja (Neth. East Indies).

Giddens, A.

1976 *New Rules of Sociological Method: A Positive Critique of Interpretive Sociologies.* New York.

Giesey, R. E.

1960 *The Royal Funeral Ceremony in Renaissance France.* Geneva (Switz.).

Glamann, K.

1958 *Dutch-Asiatic Trade, 1620-1740.* Copenhagen and The Hague.

Goldman, I.

1970 *Ancient Polynesian Society.* Chicago.

Gonda, J.

1952 *Sanskrit in Indonesia.* Nagpur (India).

1973 *Sanskrit in Indonesia.* 2nd ed. New Delhi.

1975 "The Indian Religions in Pre-Islamic Indonesia." In *Religionen*, vol. 2, pt. 3, pp. 1-54. Leiden.

Goris, R.

n.d.   *Bali: Atlas Kebudajaan*. Djakarta.

1926   *Bijdrage tot de Kennis der Oud-Javaansche en Balineesche Theologie*. Leiden.

1931   "Secten op Bali." *Mededeelingen van de Kirtya Liefrinck-Van der Tuuk* 3:37-53.

1937   "De Poera Besakih, Bali's rijkstempel." *Djawa* 17:261-280.

1938   "Bali's Tempelwezen." *Djawa* 18:30-48.

1954   *Prasasti Bali*. 2 vols. Bandung (Indonesia).

1960a   "The Religious Character of the Village Community." 1st ed. 1935. In Swellengrebel et al., 1960, pp. 77-100.

1960b   "Holidays and Holy Days." 1st ed. 1933. In Swellengrebel et al., 1960, pp. 115-129.

1960c   "The Position of the Blacksmiths." 1st ed. 1929. In Swellengrebel et al., 1960, pp. 289-299.

Goudriaan T., and C. Hooykaas

1971   *Stuti and Stava (Bauddha, Śaiva, and Vaiṣṇava) of Balinese Brahman Priests*. Verhandelingen der Koninklijke Nederlandse Akademie van Wetenschappen, afd. Letterkunde, no. 76. Amsterdam.

de Graaf, H. J.

1949   *Geschiedenis van Indonesië*. The Hague and Bandung (Indonesia).

Grader, C.

1939   "De Poera Pemajoen van Bandjar Tegal." *Djawa* 19:330-367.

Grader, C. J.

n.d.   "Abènan Bikul." Unpublished stencil, Bijlage 27, V. E. Korn papers, Koninklijk Instituut voor Taal-, Land-, en Volkenkunde. Leiden.

1960a   "The Irrigation System in the Region of Jembrana." In Swellengrebel et al., 1960, pp. 268-288.

1960b   "The State Temples of Mengwi." In Swellengrebel et al., 1960, pp. 157-186.

Grist, D. H.

1959   *Rice*. London.

Groneman, J.

1896   "De garebegs te Ngajogyakarta." *TLV* 46:49-152.

1905   "Het Njiram, of de Jaarlijkse Reiniging van de Erfwapens en andere Poesakas in Midden-Java." *Internationale Archiv für Ethnographie* 17:81-90.

1910 "Der Kris der Javaner." *Internationale Archiv für Ethnographie* 19:155-158.

Gullick, J. M.

1958 *Indigenous Political Systems of Western Malaya.* London.

Gunning, H.C.J., and A. J. van der Heijden

1926 "Het Petjatoe en Ambstvelden Probleem in Zuid-Bali." *TBG* 66:319-394.

Hagen, E.

1962 *On the Theory of Social Change.* Homewood (Ill.).

Hall, D.G.E.

1955 *A History of South-East Asia.* London.

1961 (ed.) *Historians of South-East Asia.* London.

Hall, K. R., and J. K. Whitmore

1976 *Explorations in Early Southeast Asian History: The Origins of Southeast Asian Statecraft.* Ann Arbor.

Hanna, W. A.

1971 *Bali and the West.* American Universities Field Service, Southeast Asia Series, vol. 19, nos. 12, 14.

1976 *Bali Profile, People, Events, Circumstances, 1001-1976.* New York.

Happé, P.L.E.

1919 "Een Beschouwing over het Zuid-Balische Soebakwezen en zijn Verwording in Verband met de Voorgenomen Vorming van Waterschappen in N.I." *Indische Gids* 41:183-200.

Harrison, B.

1954 *South-East Asia, a Short History.* London.

van der Heijden, A. J.

1924-25 "Het Waterschaps wezen in het Voormalige Zuid-Balische Rijks Badoeng en Mengwi." *Koloniale Studien* 8:266-275; 9:425-438.

von Heine-Geldern, R.

1930 "Weltbild und Bauform in Südostasien." *Weiner Beitrage zur Kunst- und Kulturgeschichte Asiens* 4:28-78.

1942 "Conceptions of State and Kingship in Southeast Asia." *Far Eastern Quarterly* 2:15-30.

Helms, L. V.

1882 *Pioneering in the Far East and Journeys to California in 1849 and to the White Sea in 1848.* London.

Hexter, J.

1957 "*Il principe* and *lo stato*." *Studies in the Renaissance* 4:113-138.

Hobart, M. M.

1975 "Orators and Patrons: Two Types of Political Leader in Balinese Village Society." In Bloch, 1975, pp. 65-92.

Hocart, A. M.

1936 *Kings and Councillors.* Cairo.

van Hoëvell, W. R.

1849-54 *Reis over Java, Madura en Bali in het Midden van 1847.* 3 vols. Amsterdam.

Holt, C. (ed.)

1972 *Culture and Politics in Indonesia.* Ithaca (N.Y.).

Hooker, M. B.

1978 "Law Texts of Southeast Asia." *The Journal of Asian Studies* 37:201-219.

Hooykaas, C.

n.d. "Hinduism of Bali." *The Adyar Library Bulletin,* pp. 270-280.

1958 *The Lay of the Jaya Prana.* London.

1960 "Two Exorcist Priests in Bali." *Man* 60:231.

1964a *Āgama Tīrtha, Five Studies in Hindu-Balinese Religion.* Verhandelingen der Koninklijke Nederlandse Akademie van Wetenschappen, afd. Letterkunde, vol. 70, no. 4. Amsterdam.

1964b "Weda and Sisya, Rsi and Bhujangga in Present-Day Bali." *TLV* 120:231-244.

1966 *Surya-Sevana, The Way to God of a Balinese Siva Priest.* Verhandelingen der Koninklijke Nederlandse Akademie van Wetenschappen, afd. Letterkunde, vol. 72, no. 3. Amsterdam.

1973a *Religion in Bali.* Leiden.

1973b *Balinese Bauddha Brahmans.* Amsterdam.

1973c *Kama and Kala, Materials for the Study of the Shadow Play in Bali.* Verhandelingen der Koninklijke Nederlandse Akademie van Wetenschappen, afd. Letterkunde, vol. 79.

1977 *A Balinese Temple Festival.* The Hague.

Hooykaas [-van Leeuwen Boomkamp], J. H.

1956 "The Balinese Realm of Death." *TLV* 112:74-87.

1961 *Ritual Purification of a Balinese Temple.* Verhandelingen der Koninklijke Nederlandse Akademie van Wetenschappen, afd. Letterkunde, vol. 68, no. 4. Amsterdam.

Hunger, F.W.F.

1932 "Adatdesa's en Gouvernements-desas in Zuid-Bali." *Koloniale Studien* 6:603-616.

1933   "Balische Deelbouw Contracten Gewijzigd als Gevolg der Huidige Crisis." *Koloniale Studien* 18 (April).

Hunt, R. C., and E. Hunt

1976   "Canal Irrigation and Local Social Organization." *Current Anthropology* 17:389-411.

Jacobs, J.

1883   *Eenigen Tijd onder De Baliers*. Batavia (Neth. East Indies).

Jansen, M. B.

1977   "Monarchy and Modernization in Japan." *Journal of Asian Studies* 36:611-622.

Jasper, J. E., and Mas Pirngadie

1930   *De Indandsche Kunstnijverheid in Nederlandsch Indië*. Vol. 5. The Hague.

Jones, R. B.

1971   *Thai Titles and Ranks*. Cornell University Southeast Asia Data Paper, no. 81.

Juynboll, H. H.

1923   *Oudjavaansch-Nederlandsche Woordenlijst*. Leiden.

van der Kaaden, W. F.

1937   "Beschrijving van de Poeri Agung te Gianjar." *Djawa* 17:392-407.

Kalff, S.

1923   "Javaansche Pusaka." *Djawa*, vol. 3.

Kamus

1975   *Kamus Indonesia-Bali*. Jakarta.

Kantorowicz, E.

1957   *The King's Two Bodies: A Study in Medieval Political Theology*. Princeton.

de Kat Angelino, P.

1921a   "De Amstvelden en de Petjatoe-Pengajah in Gianjar." *Koloniaal Tijdschrift* 10:225-265.

1921b   "De Robans en Parekans op Bali." *Koloniaal Tijdschrift* 10:590-608.

1921c   "Over de Smeden en eenige andere Ambachtslieden op Bali." *TBG* 60:207-265; 61:370-424.

1921d   "De Léak op Bali." *TBG* 60:1-44.

de Kat Angelino, P., and T. de Kleen

1923   *Mudras Auf Bali; Handlungen der Priester*. Hagen im Westfalen (Ger.).

Kersten, J.

1947   *Bali*. 3rd ed. Eindhoven (Neth.).

Keyes, C.

1978 "Structure and History in the Study of the Relationships between Theravada Buddhism and Political Order." *Numen* 25:156-170.

Kiefer, T.

1972 "The Tausug Polity and the Sultanate of Sulus: A Segmentary State in the Southern Philippines." *Sulu Studies* 1:19-69.

Koentjaraningrat, R. M.

1961 *Some Social-Anthropological Observations on Gotong Rojong Practices in Two Villages of Central Java*. Cornell University Monograph Series, Modern Indonesia Project. Ithaca (N.Y.).

1965 "Use of Anthropological Methods in Indonesian Historiography." In Soedjatmoko et al., 1965, pp. 299-325.

Kol, H. H.

1913 *Weg met het Opium*. n.p.

Korn, V. E.

1922 *Balische Overeenkomsten*. The Hague.

1923 "Hoe er Nieuw Licht werd Geworpen op het Balische Soebakwezen." *Koloniaal Tijdschrift* 12:324-332.

1927 "Balische Bevloeings-tunnels." *Koloniale Studien* 11:351-382.

1932 *Het Adatrecht van Bali*. 2nd ed. The Hague.

1933 *De Dorpsrepubliek Tnganan Pagringsingan*. Santpoort (Neth.).

1960 "The Consecration of a Priest." 1st ed. 1928. In Swellengrebel et al., 1960, pp. 133-153.

van der Kraan, A.

1973 "The Nature of Balinese Rule on Lombok." In Reid and Castles, 1973, pp. 91-107.

Krom, N. J.

1931 *Hindoe-Javaansche Geschiedenis*. 2nd ed. The Hague.

Kruyt, A. C.

1906 *Het Animisme in den Indischen Archipel*. The Hague.

Kulke, H.

1978 *The Devaraja Cult*. Cornell University Southeast Asia Data Paper no. 108. Ithaca (N.Y.).

Kusuma, I Gusti Ananda

1956a *Kamus Bali-Indonesia*. Den Pasar (Bali).

1956b *Kamus Indonesia-Bali*. Den Pasar (Bali).

Lamster, J. C.
1933 *Landschap, Bevolking, Godsdienst, Gebruiken en Gewoonten, Architectuur en Kunst van het Eiland Bali.* Haarlem (Neth.).

Lansing, J. S.
1977 *"Rama's Kingdoms: Social Supportive Mechanisms for the Arts in Bali."* Ph.D. diss., Dept. of Anthropology, University of Michigan.

Leach, E. R.
1954 *Political Systems of Highland Burma.* London.
1959 "Hydraulic Society in Ceylon." *Past and Present* 15:2-25.
1960 "The Frontiers of Burma." *Comparative Studies in Society and History* 3:49-68.

LeClair, E., and H. Schneider
1968 *Economic Anthropology.* New York.

Lekkerkerker, T. C.
1918 *Hindoe Recht in Indonesië.* The Hague.

van Leur, J. C.
1955 *Indonesian Trade and Society.* The Hague and Bandung (Indonesia).

Liefrinck, F. A.
1877 "Nota Betreffende den Economische Toestand van het Rijk Bangli, Eiland Bali." *TBG* 24:180-200.
1886-87 "De Rijstcultuur op Bali." *Indische Gids,* pt. 2 (1886), pp. 1033-1059, 1213-1237, 1557-1568; pt. 1 (1887), pp. 17-30, 182-189, 364-385, 515-552.
1915 *De Landsverordeningen der Balische Vorsten van Lombok.* 2 vols. The Hague.
1921 *Nog Eenige Verordeningen en Overeenkomsten van Balische Vorsten.* The Hague.
1927 *Bali en Lombok.* Amsterdam.

Lombard, D.
1967 *Le Sultanate d'Atjeh au temps d'Iskandar Muda (1607-1636).* Paris.

Mabbett, I. W.
1969 "Devaraja." *Journal of Southeast Asian History* 10:202-223.

Maspero, G.
1928 *Le Royaume de Champa.* Paris.

Masselman, G.
1963 *The Cradle of Colonialism.* New Haven.

McKay, E. (ed.)
1976   *Studies in Indonesian History.* Carlton (Victoria, Australia).

McPhee, C.
1970   "The Balinese Wayang Kulit and Its Music." 1st ed. 1936. In Belo, 1970a, pp. 146-197.

Mead, M.
1970   "The Strolling Players in the Mountains of Bali." 1st ed. 1939. In Belo, 1970a, pp. 137-145.

Meilink-Roelofsz, M.A.P.
1962   *Asian Trade and European Influence in the Indonesian Archipelago between 1500 and about 1630.* The Hague.

Mershon, K. E.
1970   "Five Great Elementals, Panchă Mahă Bută." In Belo, 1970a, pp. 57-66.
1971   *Seven Plus Seven, Mysterious Life-Rituals in Bali.* New York.

Meyer, J. J.
1916-17   "Een Javaansch handschrift over Pamor-motieven." *Nederlandsch Indië, Oud en Nieuw,* vol. 1.

Middleton, J., and D. Tait (eds.)
1958   *Tribes Without Rulers.* London.

Millon, R.
1962   "Variations in Social Response to the Practice of Irrigation Agriculture." In Woodbury, 1962, pp. 55-58.

Mishra, R.
1973   *Lintasan Peristiwa Puputan Bandung.* Den Pasar (Bali).
1976   *Puputan Badung, Kutipan dan Terjemahan Lontar Bhuwana Winasa.* Den Pasar (Bali).

Moertono, S.
1968   *State and Statecraft in Old Java.* Cornell University Monograph Series, Southeast Asia Program. Ithaca (N.Y.).

Moojen, P.
1920   *Bali, Verslag en Voorstellen aan de Regeering van Nederlandsch Indië.* Batavia (Neth. East Indies).
1926   *Kunst op Bali, Inleidende Studie tot de Bouwkunst.* The Hague.

"Muntwezen"
1934   "Muntwezen." In Adatrechtbundels, 1934, pp. 492-496.

Mus, P.
1935   *Barabadur.* Paris and Hanoi.

1936 "Symbolism à Angkor Thom. Le 'grand miracle' du Bayon." In *Académie des Inscriptions et Belles-Lettres: Comptes rendus-des Séances*, pp. 57-68.

1937 "Angkor in the Time of Jayavarman VII." *Indian Arts and Letters* 11:65-75.

van Naerssen, F. H.

1976 "Tribute to the God and Tribute to the King." In Cowan and Wolters, 1976, pp. 285-295.

van Naerssen, F. H., Th. Pigeaud, and P. Voorhoeve

1977 *Catalogue of Indonesian Manuscripts*. Pt. 2. The Royal Library, Copenhagen.

Nielsen, A. K.

1928 *Leven en Avonturen van een Oostinjevaarder op Bali*. Amsterdam.

Nieuwenkamp, W.O.J.

1906-10 *Bali en Lombok*. n.p.

Njoka

1957 *Peladjaran Sedjarah Bali*. Den Pasar (Bali).

Nypels, G.

1897 *De Expeditien Naar Bali in 1846, 1848, 1849 en 1868*. Haarlem (Neth.).

Oxford English Dictionary

1971 *The Compact Edition of the Oxford English Dictionary*. Oxford.

Pané, S.

1956 *Sedjarah Indonesia*. 2 vols. Djakarta.

Parisada

1970 *Sambutan dan Hasil Keputusan Sabha, Kongress II, Parisada Hindu Dharma Seluruh Indonesia*. Den Pasar (Bali): Parisada Hindu Dharma, Kabupaten Badung.

Peddlemars, M.

1932 "Monographie van de Desa Wongaja Gdé." *Mededeling Gezaghebbers Binnenland Bestuur*, no. 15, pp. 25-30.

1933 "Balische Deelbouw Contracten Gewijzigd Als Gevolg der Huidige Crisis." *Koloniale Studien* 18 (December).

Phillips, P., and G. Willey

1953 "Method and Theory in American Archeology, Part I." *American Anthropologist* 55:615-633.

Pigeaud, Th.

n.d. *Javaans-Nederlands Handwordenboek*. Groningen (Neth.).

1924 *De Tantu Panggělaran*. The Hague.

1938   *Javaanse Volksvertoningen, Bijdrage tot de Beschrijving van Land en Volk.* Batavia (Neth. East Indies).

1960-63   *Java in the 14th Century.* 5 vols. The Hague.

Polanyi, K.

1963   "Ports of Trade in Early Societies." *The Journal of Economic History* 23:30-45.

1966   *Dahomey and the Slave Trade.* Seattle and London.

1977   *The Livelihood of Man.* Ed. Harry W. Pearson. New York.

Polanyi, K., et al.

1957   *Trade and Markets in Early Empires: Economies in History and Theory.* Glencoe (Ill.).

Purnadi Purbatjaraka

1961   "Shahbandars in the Archipelago." *Journal of Southeast Asian History* 2:1-9.

Quaritch-Wales, H. G.

1934   *Ancient Siamese Government and Administration.* London.

1974   *The Making of Greater India.* 3rd ed., rev. (1st ed. 1951). London.

Rabibhadana, A.

1960   *The Organization of Thai Society in the Early Bangkok Period, 1782-1873.* Ithaca (N.Y.).

Radnitsky, G.

1970   *Contemporary Schools of Metascience.* New York.

Raffles, T. S.

1830   *The History of Java.* 2 vols. London.

Raka, I Gusti Gdé

1955   *Monografi Pulau Bali.* Djakarta.

Rassers, W. H.

1959a   *Panji the Culture Hero: A Structural Study of Religion in Java.* The Hague.

1959b   "On the Javanese Kris." 1st ed. 1938. In Rassers, 1959a, pp. 217-298.

Ravenholt, A.

1973   "Man-Land-Productivity Microdynamics in Rural Bali." American Universities Field Staff, Southeast Asia Series, vol. 21, no. 4.

Rawi, I Ketut Bambang Gdé

1958   *Pusaka Agama Hindu Bali.* Den Pasar (Bali).

Regeg, Ida Anak Agung Madé

n.d.(a)   *Babad Bali Radjiya.* 2 vols. Klungkung (Bali).

n.d.(b)   *Babad Pasek Suberata.* Klungkung (Bali).

n.d.(c)   *Babad Pasek Gelgel.* Klungkung (Bali).

n.d.(d)   *Siva-Buda.* Klungkung (Bali).

Reid, A., and L. Castles (eds.)

1975   *Pre-Colonial State Systems in Southeast Asia.* Monographs of the Malayan Branch of the Royal Asiatic Society, no. 6. Kuala Lumpur.

Resink, G. J.

1968   *Indonesia's History Between the Myths.* The Hague.

Ricklefs, M. C.

1974   *Jogjakarta under Sultan Mangkubumi, 1749-1792: A History of the Division of Java.* London.

1978   *Modern Javanese Historical Tradition.* London.

Rickner, R.

1972   *"Theatre as Ritual: Artaud's Theatre of Cruelty and the Balinese Barong."* Ph.D. diss., University of Hawaii.

Ricoeur, P.

1970   *Freud and Philosophy.* New Haven.

Rouffaer, G. P.

1931   *Vorstenlanden.* In Adatrechtbundels, 1931, pp. 233-378.

Scheltema, A.M.P.A.

1931   *Deelbouw in Nederlandsch-Indië.* Wageningen (Neth.).

Schrieke, B.J.O.

1955   *Selected Writings.* The Hague and Bandung (Indonesia).

1957   *Ruler and Realm in Early Java.* The Hague and Bandung (Indonesia).

Schwartz, H.J.E.F.

1901   "Dagverhal van Eine Reis van den Resident van Bali en Lombok." *TBG* 42:108-158, 554-560.

Shastri, N. D., Pandit

1963   *Sedjarah Bali Dwipa.* Den Pasar (Bali).

Sherman, G.

n.d.   "On the Iconographic Evidence of an Ankorian Sacred Historiography." Unpublished paper. Cornell University.

Siddique, S.

1977   "Relics of the Past? A Sociological Study of the Sultanates of Cirebon, West Java." Ph.D. diss., Universität Bielefeld.

Simpen, W. I.

1958a   *Babad Mengwi.* Den Pasar (Bali).

1958b   *Sedjarah Perang Keradjaan Badung Menentang Kaum Pendjadjah Belanda.* Den Pasar (Bali).

Skinner, G. W. (ed.)
1959   Local, Ethnic, and National Loyalties in Village Indonesia: A Symposium. Yale University Cultural Report Series. New Haven.

Skinner, Q.
1978   The Foundations of Modern Political Thought. 2 vols. Cambridge (U.K.).

Soedjatmoko et al. (eds.)
1965   An Introduction to Indonesian Historiography. Ithaca (N.Y.).

Soekawati, Tjokorde Gdé Rake
1924   "Legende over der Oorsprong van de Rijst en Godsdienstige gebruiken bij den Rijstbouw onder de Baliers."

Solyom, G. and B. Solyom
1978   The World of the Javanese Kris. Honolulu.

Southall, A.
1954   Alur Society. Cambridge (U.K.).

Stapel, F. W. (ed.)
1938-40   Gescheidenis van Nederlandsche Indie. 5 vols. Amsterdam.

van Stein Callenfels, P. V.
1925   Epigriphica Balica. Verhandelen van het Bataviaasche Genootschap van Kunsten en Wetenschappen, vol. 66, no. 3.

1947-48   "De Rechten der Vorsten op Bali." Indonesië 1:193-208.
Stingl, H.
1970   "Zur Instistitution des Obersten Bewässerungsbeamten in Buleleng (Nord-Bali)." Jahrbuch des Museums für Volkerkunde zu Leipzig, vol. 27. Akademie-Verlag, Berlin.

Stöhr, W., and P. Zoetmulder
1968   Les Religions D'Indonesie. Paris.

Stuart-Fox, D. J.
1974   The Art of the Balinese Offering. Jogjakarta.

Stutterheim, W. F.
1926   "Oost-Java en de Hemelberg." Djawa 6:333-349.

1929   Oudheden van Bali. Singaradja (Bali).

1932   Het Hinduisme in den Archipel. Groningen (Neth.).

1935   Indian Influences in Old Balinese Art. London.

1948   De Kraton van Madjapahit. Den Haag.

Sudhana, I Njoman
1972   Awig-Awig Desa Adat di Bali. Den Pasar (Bali).

Sudharsana, I Gusti Bagus
  1967 *Mengapa Hari Raya Njepi Djatuh pada Bulan Kasanga.*
  Den Pasar (Bali).
Sugriwa, I Gusti Bagus
  n.d. *Smreti Sudaya, Hindu Bali.* Den Pasar (Bali).
  1957a *Hari Raya Bali Hindu.* Den Pasar (Bali).
  1957b *Babad Pasek.* Den Pasar (Bali).
  1958 *Pracasti Pandé.* Den Pasar (Bali).
Swellengrebel, J. L.
  1947 "Een Vorstenwijding op Bali." *Mededelingen van het
  Rijksmuseum voor Volkenkunde,* no. 2. Leiden.
  1948 *Kerk en Tempel op Bali.* The Hague.
  1960 "Introduction." In Swellengrebel et al., 1960, pp. 1-76.
Swellengrebel, J. L., et al.
  1960 *Bali: Life, Thought and Ritual.* The Hague and Bandung
  (Indonesia).
  1969 *Bali: Further Studies in Life, Thought and Ritual.* The
  Hague.
Tabanan
  n.d. "Babad Arya Tabanan." Typescript in Udayana University
  Library. Den Pasar (Bali).
Tambiah, S. J.
  1976 *World Conquerer and World Renouncer.* Cambridge
  (U.K.).
Tarling, N.
  1962 *Anglo-Dutch Rivalry in the Malay World, 1780-1824.* Syd-
  ney.
Tate, D.J.M.
  1971 *The Making of Modern South-East Asia.* Vol. 1. New York,
  London, and Melbourne.
Taylor, C.
  1971 "Interpretation and the Sciences of Man." *The Review of
  Metaphysics* 25:3-51.
Tirtokoesoemo, R. S.
  1931 *De Garabegs in het Sultanaat Jogjakarta.*
Tonkes, H.
  1888 *Volkskunde von Bali.* Halle-Witterberg (Ger.).
Turner, V.
  1967 *The Forest of Symbols.* Ithaca (N.Y.).
van der Tuuk, H.
  1897-1912 *Kawi-Balineesch-Nederlandsch Woordenboek.* 4 vols.
  Batavia (Neth. East Indies).

Utrecht, E.
  1962 *Sedjarah Hukum Internasional di Bali dan Lombok*. [Jakarta?].
Vella, W. F.
  1957 *Siam under Rama III, 1824-57*. Locust Valley (N.Y.).
van Vleming, J. L.
  1925 *Het Chineesche Zakenleven in Nederlandsch-Indië*. Dienst der Belasting in Nederlandsch-Indië, ser. no. 730. Batavia (Neth. East Indies).
van Vlijmen, B.R.F.
  1875 *Bali 1868*. Amsterdam.
van Vollenhoven, C.
  1918-33 *Het Adatrecht van Nederlandsch-Indië*. 3 vols. Leiden.
Vroklage, B.A.G.
  1937 "Tandvijlfeest op Bali." *De Katholieke Missien* 10: 189-192.
Wertheim, W. F.
  1959 *Indonesian Society in Transition*. The Hague and Bandung (Indonesia).
  1965 "The Sociological Approach." In Soedjatmoko et al., 1965, pp. 344-355.
Wheatley, P.
  1961 *The Golden Khersonese*. Kuala Lumpur.
  1971 *The Pivot of the Four Quarters*. Chicago.
Wilken, G. A.
  1912a *De Verspreide Geschriften van Prof. Dr. G. A. Wilken*. 4 vols. The Hague.
  1912b "Het Animisme bij de Volken van den Indischen Archipel." 1st ed. 1884-85. In Wilken, 1912a, vol. 2, pp. 1-287.
Willey, G., and P. Phillips
  1955 "Method and Theory in American Archeology, Part II." *American Anthropologist* 57:723-819.
Willinck, G. D.
  1909 *Het Rechtsleven bij de Minangkabausche Maliers*. Leiden.
Wilson, H. H.
  1892 *Works, II*. London.
Wirz, P.
  1927 "Der Reisbau und die Reisbaukulte auf Bali und Lombok." *TBG* [Batavia] 67:217-345.
  1928 *Der Totenkult auf Bali*. Stuttgart.
Wittfogel, K.
  1957 *Oriental Despotism*. New Haven.

Wolters, O. W.

1967 *Early Indonesian Commerce: A Study of the Origins of Śrivijaja.* Ithaca (N.Y.).

1970 *The Fall of Śrivijaja in Malay History.* Ithaca (N.Y.).

Woodbury, R. (ed.)

1962 *Civilizations in Desert Lands.* Dept. of Anthropology, University of Utah, Anthropology Paper no. 62. Salt Lake City.

Woodside, A.

1971 *Vietnam and the Chinese Model: A Comparative Study of Nguyen and Ch'ing Civil Government in the First Half of the Nineteenth Century.* Cambridge (Mass.).

Worsley, P. J.

1972 *Babad Buleleng, A Balinese Dynastic Genealogy.* The Hague.

1975 "Preliminary Remarks on the Concept of Kingship in the *Babad Buleleng.*" In Reid and Castles, 1975, pp. 108-113.

Zimmer, H.

1955 *The Art of Indian Asia, Its Mythology and Transformations.* 2 vols. New York.

de Zoete, B., and W. Spies

1938 *Dance and Drama in Bali.* London.

Zoetmulder, P. J.

1965 "The Significance of the Study of Culture and Religion for Indonesian Historiography." In Soedjatmoko et al., 1965, pp. 326-343.

Zollinger, H.

1849 "Reis over de eilenden Bali en Lombok, 1846." *TBG*, vol. 23.

INDEX

NOTE: Authors referred to only in citation form have not been indexed.

LIBRARY OF CONGRESS CATALOGING IN PUBLICATION DATA

Geertz, Clifford.
   Negara: the theatre state in nineteenth-century Bali.
   Bibliography: p.
   Includes index.
   1. Bali (Island)—Civilization.   2. Bali (Island)
—Politics and government.   I. Title.
DS647.B2G38   320.9598′6   80-7520
ISBN 0-691-05316-2
ISBN 0-691-00778-0 pbk.

CLIFFORD GEERTZ is Professor of Social Science at the Institute for Advanced Study, Princeton